Economic Theory and Christian Belief

Religions and Discourse

Edited by James M. M. Francis

Volume 16

PETER LANG
Oxford · Bern · Berlin · Bruxelles · Frankfurt a.M. · New York · Wien

Andrew Britton and Peter Sedgwick

Economic Theory and Christian Belief

The children of this world
are wiser in their generation
than the children of light

(Luke 16:8)

PETER LANG
Oxford · Bern · Berlin · Bruxelles · Frankfurt a.M. · New York · Wien

Bibliographic information published by Die Deutsche Bibliothek
Die Deutsche Bibliothek lists this publication in the Deutsche Nationalbibliografie; detailed bibliographic data is available on the Internet at ‹http://dnb.ddb.de›.

British Library and Library of Congress Cataloguing-in-Publication Data:
A catalogue record for this book is available from *The British Library*, Great Britain, and from *The Library of Congress*, USA

ISSN 1422-8998
ISBN 3-03910-015-7
US-ISBN 0-8204-6284-5

Hochfeldstrasse 32, Postfach 746, CH-3000 Bern 9, Switzerland
info@peterlang.com, www.peterlang.com, www.peterlang.net

Contents

Preface

The separation of religious life from the shaping forces of modern life is all too obvious; over hundreds of years, they have been increasingly 'desynchronised'. By now, those responsible on both sides have their own ways of rationalising their inattention to each other. If economics tries to understand, if not also to improve, the means by which human beings exchange 'goods' with each other, why need economists bother with such 'abstract' matters as belief in God? And if believers in God try to understand and follow the implications of God's transformative goodness for human life, why need they bother with matters as mundane as economic exchange? Add to these the fact that both theology and economics have now become so complex as to be beyond access by non-specialists, and we can perhaps understand why the two stay apart.

Yet it seems undeniable that they must – and do – intersect. If economics has become a dominant force of modern life, how can religious people avoid tracing the implications of their faith into that? If religious belief contributes significantly to the ways life is actually lived, how can economists avoid engaging with it?

Still, it is not a foregone conclusion that either party will agree that they are important to each other. That is the most basic reason why we need a book like this. A dialogue needs to be begun to show to both that the engagement is necessary. That is not as easy as it sounds, because they need 'introductions' before they can 'shake hands'. Christians – despite their suspicions about the social sciences – need to know something about neo-classical economics, and economists – despite their doubts – need to know something of the language and life of religious belief. Then, too, since their adherents contest both Christianity and economics, different kinds of Christians need to think together about their common 'language', and different kinds of economic theorists need to focus on their areas of agreement.

Throughout, whether amongst religious people and economists, or between them, humility and respect for each other is needed!

This complex set of issues lies at the heart of this book. Undaunted, the authors lead us along the difficult philosophical pathways to better understanding, concentrating not so much on the issues that might divide an ancient way (religion) from a modern one (economics) as the deeper and more timeless ones in which they intersect, yet without shying away from the very strong claims made on both sides. Along the way, they touch on a remarkable range of topics now central to human well-being in the twenty-first century.

This is a book from which it would be difficult not to benefit. It is rich in its range, the dialogue it fosters and the re-thinking it stimulates. It is well worth careful study. And one can only hope that other books on economics and Christian belief will soon follow the example set here.

Professor Daniel W. Hardy
Cambridge

Introduction

> Economics, though subject to the requirements of logic and consistency, has flourished as a form of theology – probably, in the Western world, as the most influential branch of secular theology. Eric Hobsbawm.[1]

A professional theologian, reading the quotation above, might well take it as a challenge. If another academic discipline puts forward claims to be the modern 'queen of sciences', they must be refuted. That task may not be uncongenial; if economists really do talk the language of theology, then it should be possible for theologians to engage in dialogue with them, and perhaps to prove them wrong.

But economists are not in fact theologians, even if historians like Hobsbawm have described them as such. The point is rather that economics, and in particular neo-classical economic theory, has become profoundly influential in contemporary society. It may not affect the way people think about God, but it certainly does affect the way that they think about themselves and the world in which they live. An influential book which has the subtitle 'The Theological Meaning of Economics'[2] says that it 'offers a set of principles and understandings that give meaning to, define a purpose for, and significantly frame the perception of, human existence'. This may, or may not, justify the use of the word 'theology' in relation to economic theory; in any case it makes it a proper subject for study by theologians, even if most professional economists would be much more modest than Hobsbawm in their claims for their subject.

This book arises from a paper given to the Society for the Study of Theology at a meeting to discuss alternative 'anthropologies', that is different views of human nature and behaviour. One of the anthropologies considered was 'economic man', who might also be called a 'child of this world'. This book, then, is addressed in the first instance

1 Hobsbawm, E., *Age of Extremes*, Michael Joseph, 1994.
2 Nelson, R. H., *Reaching for Heaven on Earth*, Rowan and Littlefield, 1991.

to theologians who seek to engage with neo-classical economic theory as a system of thought with implications that go well beyond the subject matter of most economics courses. They might see it as an embodiment of a particular kind of modernity, a particular modern secular anthropology. The book may also be of interest to economists, although much of the exposition of their subject will not be new to them. It does show how difficult it can be to reconcile the assumptions of neo-classical economic theory with those of Christian belief.

This is a book about the philosophical foundations of economic theory and of Christian belief, not about economic 'issues' or Christian reactions to them. It is about neo-classical economics as a system of thought, not about the merits or demerits of the market system which that theory describes. This might disappoint some readers, but we would contend that a dialogue of the kind we offer here is important as a preliminary exercise before Christian ethics can proceed to draw useful conclusions about economic life. Moreover, we see this as an important part of a continuing quest for mutual understanding between Christian faith and the modern world. Should Christians regard economic theory as a friend or a foe? Or is it just part of the intellectual environment which has to be taken as read?

It is, we hope, possible to provide an introduction to neo-classical economic theory for those not already familiar with it, whilst at the same time indicating how some of its assumptions are being debated by economists at the present time. Obviously we do this in a selective way, aimed at finding points of contact with the issues of concern to theologians. Typically we then make a 'jump cut' to related themes from the Bible and recent interpretations of it, before any attempt is made at integration. We feel that each discipline should be given the chance to speak a few words in its own language before the process of reconciliation is begun. The languages are very different.

What we are trying to do is not at all easy. Our purpose is to define, and then to contrast, two very different descriptions of what might be the same reality. Ideally we would seek to combine them. But it is like getting oil and water to mix – one or the other is always trying to float to the top.

A dialogue of the deaf?

Economic theory and Christian belief often talk across each other. Within our society today there are these two systems of thought, both very influential, both mature and systematic, both being used to guide human behaviour; yet most of the time it is as if they lived in different worlds.

Economists do not often talk about religion at all. When they do, it is usually as one of the sources from which value judgements might be derived. In this model of interaction between economics and religion, the economist is a detached, scientific observer, ready to offer advice to society in accordance with any criteria that may be set. The economist knows how the world works, but has no view as to what constitutes human well being. Thus the Christian is asked, 'Show me your social welfare function'. Having provided that one vital piece of information, Christianity can, it appears, safely leave the rest to the experts.

Other economists recognise that a dialogue with Christian belief could not in fact ever take that form. There are values, implicit if not explicit, in economic theory itself. Thus Samuel Brittan, in a series of essays sympathetic to neo-classical economics, calls for the ethical debate to be more explicit:[3]

> A dialogue – suspended since the time that Dickens, Ruskin and Shaw thundered at nineteenth-century political economists – will have to resume. [...] What is needed is more critical scrutiny, both of widely accepted moral beliefs and their role in economic activity, and of the moral implications of widely advocated economic policies. The idea of technocratic value-free economics has had its day.

There are also views of human motivation and behaviour which form an integral part of Christian belief. The two systems of thought are rivals. One of the old masters of American economics, Frank Knight of the Chicago School, was very clear in his mind that Christianity

3 Brittan, S., *Capitalism with a Human Face*, Edward Elgar, 1995.

and neo-classical economic theory do not mix.[4] Christians, he believed, are unrealistic, expecting business and political life to be conducted on the same basis as personal relationships. They want to talk about love, when they ought to be talking about the distribution of power. Christians, he also maintained, cannot participate effectively in policy debate, because their minds are not open to persuasion.

Relations have not been helped by some of the incursions of church leaders and academic theologians into territory that economists think is their own. Some of these writings betray a poor understanding of economic theory; some are clearly hostile in intent. Behind the religious mask, orthodox economists often think that they can detect the features of their old enemy, Karl Marx.[5] If they wanted a debate with Marxists they would have it with their professional colleagues. Conversely, some economists have written about Christian belief in a manner which can only appear naive to a professional theologian. Add to this the sheer obscurantism which exists in all academic disciplines – economists can over-use mathematical symbols for the same purposes as theologians over-use ancient languages. Dialogue across any boundary will always meet with some resistance.

One of the most vigorous attacks on mainstream economic theory in the name of Christian belief has been made, not by a theologian but by the economist Jane Collier. She has written:[6]

> The most dominant of our cultural 'paradigms' – or intellectual frameworks of thought – is given to us by the discipline of economics. If cultures are ways of living articulated in languages, rituals and institutions, then our modern culture *is* 'economic' culture. The language of economics is the language through which the world is understood, the language by which human and social problems are defined and by which solutions to those problems are expressed.

She attacks what is called 'economism', that is the primacy of economics over other sources of meaning and value. She associates

4 See the article by Emmett, R. in Brennan, H. G. and Waterman, A. M. C., *Economics and Religion – Are they Distinct?*, Kluwer, 1994.

5 To mention just one example of many, see Gorringe, T., *Capital and the Kingdom*, SPCK, 1994.

6 Collier, J., 'Contemporary Culture and the Role of Economics', in Montefiore, H. (ed.), *The Gospel and Contemporary Culture*, Mowbray, 1992.

the discipline of economics with the articulation of that view. She calls for the conversion to a more Christian view, of society in general, and of professional economists in particular.

Many theologians would now take a somewhat similar line; they feel that they co-operate with any form of social science at their peril. Richard Roberts begins a recent survey article on theology and social science like this:[7]

> At first sight, as observed from the standpoint of the social scientist, the relation of theology to the social sciences looks somewhat unpromising. [...] Modernity *(Neuzeit)* has witnessed the long and sometimes tortuous relinquish-ment of the central role of theology in culture and society. Indeed sociology understood in terms of 'grand theory' may plausibly be understood in a certain sense as the successor to theology as 'queen of the sciences'. There is something of a natural progression from the *mentalite* of the once all-knowing theologian to that of the ambitious contemporary social scientist who aims not merely at comprehensive interpretation of human life-worlds, but also to promote the emancipatory role of social science as itself the agent of enlightened modernity. By contrast, the theologian would seem to occupy a shrunken and marginalised residual territory confronted by a hostile secular reality; such theology lives on in reduced circumstances.

Economics is not typical of the social sciences, but it may sometimes have ambitions that conflict with those of theology. For a very few people economics may actually be a form of religion. A few might subscribe to the 'economism' described by Collier. For rather more, perhaps, economic ideas provide what might well be called a 'meta-narrative', that is a framework within which different 'stories', or accounts of experience, can be brought together and unified. In one context this means that money is the measure of all things. In another, much more intellectually sophisticated, context, it means that human nature is defined by rationality and individualism, whilst the environment is defined by scarcity and competition.

In this book we shall seek to identify the anthropology implicit in neo-classical economic theory, that is to say its model of human nature. Many, perhaps most, economists would say that their aim is

7 Roberts, R. H., 'Theology and the Social Sciences', in Ford, D. F. (ed.), *The Modern Theologians* (second edition), Blackwell, 1999.

merely to explain, and perhaps to predict, certain aspects of human behaviour, not to answer any deep philosophical questions. Nevertheless a model of human nature is there in neo-classical theory, quite clearly expressed and worthy of examination. One of the most interesting questions is, indeed, the range of issues to which this model of 'economic man' is appropriate.

The Chicago School, particularly Gary Becker, is associated with a very broad definition of the scope of economics. He has written:[8]

> What economists 'do' has vastly changed during the last several decades [...] Hardly a nook or cranny of behaviour has escaped their attention. Discrimination against minorities, marriage and divorce, the legal system, addictions, the underclass, suicides, tariffs and regulations, and wars and conflict are just a few of the subjects investigated. Moreover it is now sometimes difficult to distinguish economists from other researchers, for increasing numbers of political scientists, lawyers, sociologists, and historians are also committed to variants of the economic approach. This intrusion of the economic approach into other fields has not usually been welcomed by scholars who take a more traditional way of looking at the subject matter of these fields.

Perhaps theologians might be included amongst those 'who take a more traditional way of looking at the subject matter of' their discipline. But, if there are those who would subsume social ethics within economics, there are also those who would treat economics as a branch of theology. According to Douglas Meeks,[9] God is an economist, although what he means by that word is very different from what it means to those who actually practise economics. He does look for answers to economic questions in the Bible and some of the answers he finds are certainly different from those of modern economic theory.

Typically theologians have engaged more with sociology than with formal economic theory. Some would reject the whole of social science as unchristian. The writings of John Milbank have been

8 Becker, G. S., Preface to Tommasi, M. and Ierulli, K. (eds.), *The Economics of Human Behavior*, CUP, 1995.

9 Meeks, M. D., *God the Economist*, Fortress Press, 1989.

particularly influential in British theology in recent years.[10] He describes secular social thought as either heretical or pagan. He describes the beginnings of economics and other disciplines as they broke away from their Christian foundations in the eighteenth century. He seems to be saying that we have to go right back to that period and start again, so as to get it right this time.

There have been some more constructive approaches to dialogue from the economists' side of the divide. Donald Hay, for example, has asked how a professional economist can be a Christian. He writes:[11]

> Christian economists have to learn to live with ethical tensions arising from the disjunction between their personal value system and the values implicit in the analytic tools they are using every day.

One answer might be to treat economics as a purely descriptive subject. As Hay says:[12]

> The methodology [of economics] legitimises self-seeking behaviour in every area of human life. The Christian response is to note that, while this model of human behaviour may not be inconsistent with the actual behaviour of fallen human beings, it is by no means an accurate description of what human beings made in the image of God should aspire to.

One might say that the values implicit in economic theory are indeed the values on which our secular community is built, but that we, as Christians, dissent. That is a perfectly tenable position, which many Christian economists adopt. But one might also offer a more profound criticism of economic theory, saying that it is so incomplete as to be fundamentally wrong, even if it is viewed as no more than description. Arguably, the description of human behaviour, even after the Fall, to be found in the Bible and the Christian tradition, is profoundly different from that assumed in economic theory.

10 Milbank, J., *Theology and Social Theory – Beyond Secular Reason*, Blackwell, 1990.

11 Hay, D. A., Preface to Hay, D. A. and Kreider, A. (eds.), *Christianity and the Culture of Economics*, University of Wales Press, 2001.

12 ibid.

Which economic theory?

It should be made clear at the start, if only to disarm criticism from amongst economists, that we shall not attempt to survey the whole of this rich subject. We shall examine only one variety of economic theory, and do so from our own particular perspective. There are many other varieties of economic theory and economists notoriously disagree amongst themselves on most issues. However in recent decades the discipline has been dominated by the neo-classical school. For rather different reasons, both the Keynesians and Marxists have been in retreat. A recent overview of the state of the discipline recognised that:[13]

> Many of the most outspoken critics of the state of economics complain that the profession is too hierarchical and elitist, and that it is dominated by a relatively small contingent of orthodox neo-classical economists centred in a few leading departments.

In this study we shall concentrate our attention mainly on this one school, mentioning others when this is important to our analysis of what is called orthodoxy.

The influence of neo-classical economics is now pervasive in the profession, especially in America, but increasingly in the rest of the world as well. It is the economics that students are taught, as any college textbook would show.[14] There are nevertheless active groups of economists who describe themselves as radical or 'alternative'. There are also many who criticise the neo-classical school from within, accepting its approach as a starting point, but offering criticism as well as support. This may well be the direction in which the subject is heading, neo-classical theory being gradually modified, rather than rejected or overthrown.

13 Coates, A. W., 'Economics as a Profession' in *Companion to Contemporary Economic Thought*, Greenaway, D., et al. (eds.), 1991.

14 Reference will be made throughout the book to a standard economics textbook, for example Pindyck, R. S. and Rubinfeld, D. L., *Microeconomics*, Prentice Hall 1995.

Neo-classical economics is a rigorous discipline, intellectually satisfying, even beautiful. It is relatively simple to understand, at least in its main outline. Given its clearly stated axiomatic foundations, its rich conclusions follow without doubt by a process of deductive reasoning. Its most economical expression is mathematical, leading to displays of virtuosity from some economists, but complaints of elitism from others.

Because of its logical structure, this style of theorising naturally tends to invade areas other than that in which it was originally cultivated. Economic theory has been defined, not by its subject matter – market prices, output, trade etc. – but by its method, which can be applied to most, perhaps all, aspects of human behaviour.[15] If this definition is accepted then economics can become a theory of all human behaviour, not just about things that people actually buy and sell.

Economic theory starts from individual decision-making, which it assumes to be rational. From this it deduces consequences for society as a whole. Thus the rate of interest and the rate of economic growth depend on individual productivity and thrift. Business cycles are not the result of anyone's deliberate plan, but of the way that the decisions of millions of individuals happen to interact. Sometimes the theory of individual behaviour leads directly to strong propositions about the economy as a whole. Thus the assumption that individuals and firms behave rationally leads directly to the proposition that the level of prices (and the rate of inflation, if it is fully anticipated) will have no effect at all on the level of output or employment in the long run.

A similar method can be applied, it is claimed, to politics, demography, crime and even religion. In the religious market place, for example, individuals decide, rationally of course, which of many competing denominations offers the best combination of social and spiritual benefits at the least cost in terms of time and other

15 For some excellent illustrations of this point, see Tommasi, M. and Ierulli, K. (eds.), op. cit.

commitments. Patterns of mobility between denominations, intermarriage and so on can, it is alleged, be predicted as a result.[16]

The influence of neo-classical economics extends well beyond the academic community. It is taught to business people and used by management all over the global economy; it is used by policy-makers in virtually every nation state, not only in relation to trade, industry and finance, but also to health, education, social security and so on. Those who are attracted by neo-classical economic theory in public affairs may find themselves using it in relation to their private lives as well.

What Christian belief?

There are many schools of theology, as of economics, each with its own rather special interpretation of Christian belief, and there are many different Christian views of human nature. But they would all claim to be based on authoritative traditions going right back to the origins of Christianity as told in the Bible. To find out what is the current Christian anthropology, we must look for a present-day understanding of biblical teaching on the subject.

There are, however, various different ways of using the Bible in relation to the modern world and to economic issues in particular. One approach is to concentrate on particular passages which appear to have a direct bearing on the question under discussion. For example the very precise Old Testament laws relating to the Jubilee would seem relevant to any discussion of debt remission or the ownership of land. Notoriously this can lead different commentators to opposing conclusions, even using the same texts to support incompatible beliefs or prescriptions.[17] Another approach is to look for themes and principles that run through the whole of scripture, or at least through

16 Iannaccone, L. R., 'Household Production, Human Capital and the Economics of Religion' in Tommasi and Ierulli, op. cit.

17 Gay, C., *With Liberty and Justice for Whom?*, Eerdmans, 1991.

much of it. These can then be used to throw light on contemporary problems, less directly, but perhaps with greater certainty. We shall favour the more indirect approach, whilst not refusing to use the more direct method where it seems particularly appropriate.

It is always tempting to distort the text of scripture so that it fits easily with the wisdom of the contemporary world. It can be made to say what people want to hear. But in fact it is full of what are called 'hard sayings', and it is important not to leave them out. If the expositor is allowed to pick and choose what passages to quote, then this can almost be a licence to write one's own scripture. One needs to know the context of each passage in order to get at its meaning, for the original writers and readers, and for subsequent ages up to the present day. In seeking to discover what Christianity has to say in dialogue with economics, we are very much dependent on the writings of present-day scholars and interpreters. We hope that we can thus escape the charge that we are presenting as 'Christian belief' what is actually no more than our own opinions.

Christian belief dates from the first century, a very different cultural environment from our own. Economic theory has its roots in much more recent history. This means that any engagement between them must relate to issues that are relatively timeless, like scarcity and abundance, rather than issues that are dependent on a particular institutional setting, like the form of employment contract or the management of the household. We are looking at different anthropologies. As with economic theory, so with Christian belief, it is often the method and its underlying assumptions that are most interesting, not just its application to particular subject matter. The Bible contains many passages relating to the main subject matter of economics – wages, debts, money and so on – and this is obviously very useful to the present study; but we shall also be referring to passages about broader issues like choice, trust, hope and forgiveness.

The Bible is, of course, pre-modern in its style and in its assumptions. We are comparing this with economic theory that is quintessentially modern. That is one reason why it is not easy to conduct the dialogue that we have in mind. Yet Christians have been greatly influenced by the Enlightenment – more so than many would admit. Often we shall have to say that what passes for Christian ethics nowadays owes more to the eighteenth century than to the first. This means that the ideas behind economic theory are not as strange to modern Christians than they would have been to the early church. It is important, nevertheless, to distinguish what is originally Christian, going right back to the beginning, from what has been absorbed from the secular environment over the last two centuries or so.

Some would claim that we are now moving from a modern to a post-modern world. If that is right then neither economic theory nor Christian belief will immediately feel at home there. This new world may, however, provide the neutral ground on which they can meet. Post-modernism, it is said, does not privilege any creed, or respect any meta-narrative. It lets everyone have their say, but draws no conclusions of its own. Within this pluralist society, all the same, each person must decide where their loyalty is placed, which opinion they find most convincing. There is no point in having a debate if beliefs and values are no more than matters of taste.

Christians writing about their faith face a dilemma in a pluralist society. They can stick closely to the language of the Bible and the historic creeds; in that case they risk being incomprehensible to all but a minority of their readers. Alternatively, they can try to translate theological concepts into secular terms; they then risk loosing the essence of what they want to say in the process. Sometimes Christians discuss questions of social ethics without actually mentioning God at all. Sometimes God is present, but only, as it were, in inverted commas. We do not think, however, that there is something called Christian anthropology or Christian ethics which can be described adequately if it is separated from theology.

The concept of God is not, in fact, alien to the society in which we live. We may live in a post-Christian culture, but not in a non-Christian one. The way in which most people think about human nature has been profoundly influenced by Christian teaching, and some of it is still taken for granted by many who have no church affiliation at all. Indeed we would argue that Christian ideas are so basic to our culture, even today, that no one can afford to ignore them when considering social, political, or economic questions. Thus economists, or any other social scientists, might be interested in gaining a better understanding of Christian belief, even if they do not have any wish to share it themselves.

Outline of the book

In this book we allow economic theory to set the agenda and expect Christian belief to respond. In the nine chapters which follow, the first section is written from the point of view of an economist, the second from that of a theologian, whilst the third attempts to bring them together.

The first chapter is about the cognitive status of both economics and Christianity. In the modern world, both need to define their views of reality and of knowledge relative to those of the physical and biological sciences. Both, we shall argue, can be made to provide models of human nature and our place in the world, as it is and as it should be. Both would claim knowledge of the real world, although their means of access to such knowledge are clearly not the same.

Most of the book then follows the order in which economic theory is taught in a textbook or a series of introductory lectures. Preferences and choice come first, then production, and then the market equilibrium and the role of government. A few quotations from a fairly typical textbook illustrate the way in which this material is commonly presented. In each chapter we try to identify the basic assumptions and arguments of neo-classical economics, contrasting them with the way in which similar issues are treated in the New Testament and in subsequent Christian teaching.

In the chapter on rational choice we also discuss free will, and what Christians mean by conversion. Different understandings of individual and group identity are the subject of another chapter. This is followed by a comparison of concepts of well-being, whether material, moral or spiritual. We then turn to the production side of the economy and the assumptions made by economists about the environment in which human beings live; it is an environment of scarcity rather than abundance, very different from that suggested by the miracles and the parables of the New Testament. There are then two chapters about what are called the factors of production, first labour and then capital. Obviously, Christians have plenty to say about both of these, often from very different perspectives from those of modern economics.

In economic theory, consumption preferences and production possibilities are reconciled by the market mechanism. Under perfect competition this is a totally impersonal relationship in which no one need ever know with whom they are making exchanges. The Christian critique of that system is relatively familiar. Less well explored is the case of imperfect competition, where participants have to devise strategies, of rivalry or co-operation, that take account of how others will react to their behaviour. In the real world of competition, strong emotions can be involved as well as calculation. This needs to be considered together with Christian teaching about human relationships, especially about love and self-sacrifice. Perhaps Christian ethics might make use, like economics, of the mathematical theory of games.

The book concludes with three chapters which are even more speculative in character. One is about time and uncertainty, especially the way in which the prospect for the future, such as the Christian hope of Christ's coming again in glory, determines the character of the present. Another chapter considers some issues of economics and speculates about changes of regime: these could be new rules of the game in economics, like those which follow a revolution or just a monetary union; they could also be a new covenant between God and creation. The final chapter draws together the themes of the whole book and speculates about where it might be pointing.

Chapter One

Methodology – The Real World?

Introduction

Before embarking on a study of economic theory and its relation to Christian belief, there are some prior questions of method and philosophy to be explored. In what sense does economic theory claim to be true? Is this the same kind of truth as that claimed in theology? These are very deep questions indeed, but they need to be asked. If the kind of truth claims made by the two disciplines are wholly different, then there will be no conflict between them, and perhaps not much point in the present exercise. But if both assume models of human behaviour and well-being which are supposed to be real, as well as useful, then there may well be some rivalry between them.

In modern times it is the world that is discovered by science that most people accept as real. If we can understand it, it makes good sense. It is coherent and consistent. Most importantly, it works! It is very difficult not to believe that science is telling us about something that is real. Occasionally, our ability to accept it may be stretched – quantum mechanics, for example, does not accord with common sense – but, most of the time, what scientists mean by the real world is much the same as what everyone means by reality in everyday life. It is the world that we meet when we are wide awake, not the world of dreams, of poetry or of fiction. It is a world that we discover, not a world that we invent.

Post-modernists, in more recent times, have pointed out that much of what passes for reality is in fact (in reality?) a social construct. In the study of history, for example, the selection of events to be included in the narrative depends on the culture of the community to which the historian belongs. The way that the narrative is told reflects social conventions about what relationships are important. It is possible, of course, to make simple (and real?) errors of fact, getting the date of a battle wrong, for example; but if one is asked to explain why one side won the battle rather than the other, or why it was ever fought at all, then the answers one gives cannot be unaffected by the preoccupations and prejudices of the community within which the debates take place.

The form which scientific enquiry takes is also, of course, influenced by its social context. The very words that are used to describe scientific concepts – relativity, evolution, chaos, morbidity – are all part of a language which has developed in a particular historical setting. All this is interesting, and perhaps important to remember, but it does not alter the fact that, most of the time, science works. It makes predictions, which subsequently come true. Its experimental results can be repeated. That is bound to be impressive. We would surely want to say that science works because it is true.

Both economic theory and Christian belief have, in modern times, tried to be as 'scientific' as possible. Both, for rather different reasons, have had only limited success. But their failures have not obliged them to redefine what they mean by reality. Both could say, without necessarily stopping very long to consider, that, of course, there is a reality out there which they would dearly like to grasp.

Post-modernism insists that much of what we hold to be the truth is in fact specific to our own particular culture. This must be especially the case for our views of human nature – we may treat as general what is actually specific to our time and place. But, against this, there may be aspects of human behaviour and motivation which really are universal – like most of our genetic endowments. It seems that both economic theory and Christian belief do claim to be of general application in just this way.

Throughout Christian history missionaries have taken their view of reality and preached it to people whose view is very different: to Africa, India, China or Papua New Guinea. The missionaries have been convinced that their own view is correct, and other views incorrect. Moreover, the view of human nature implicit in Christian teaching – that human beings are free and fallen, capable of redemption, capable of love, capable of evil and so on – is invariant to all differences of race, culture, class, gender, age, intelligence and education. In recent times more of an effort has been made to distinguish the Gospel message itself from the culture of the missionaries' home country. There is no need to insist that converts wear European clothes or sing to European music. But the Gospel itself is not just European, and it speaks to all humanity.

Nowadays there are also 'missionaries' taking neo-classical economics, along with democracy and respect for human rights, to all the nations of the world. Some of them are sent out by multinational companies and some by intergovernmental agencies like the IMF and the World Bank. They also go to Africa, India, China and Papua New Guinea. They offer prosperity, and they seek to win converts. Their missionary activity also implies that they have a message of general application. They know, of course, that different institutions and traditions mean that economic life is not the same everywhere. But there is also something that is always the same. Neo-classical economic theory implies its own view of human nature – capable of reason, motivated by preferences, each making choices independently – which is also invariant to all differences of race, culture, class, gender, age, intelligence and education. That was, and still is, the anthropology of the Enlightenment. It also believes that anyone who is well taught can understand and accept this perspective.

It is important to recognise these claims to real knowledge and to universal application, but at the same time one must also recognise the cultural setting of neo-classical economic theory. It is a product of modern times and of the industrial revolution. It grew up in partnership with liberal political theories that legitimised the revolt of the individual against the power of the state. It has been used to defend the rights of property owners against socialism. Its vocabulary, method and rhetoric all belong to the history of Europe and North America over the past two and a half centuries.

Christian belief has, of course, a much longer history. This may make it possible for its adherents to stand back a little further from the context of the present day. But it also had its original conditioning in the social environment of the early church, an environment that we can now only very imperfectly understand. Christian teaching in all ages, including our own, has been shaped, not to say distorted, by the many different social settings in which it has made a home. What we today instinctively think of as Christian is often no more than the conventional wisdom of some bygone age. It takes an effort to seek out what really is distinctively Christian, but that does not mean that it is non-existent, or that it is impossible to find.

Neo-classical economic theory is often described as an ideology, that is a system of thought which justifies the power of one social group. A Marxist would call it 'bourgeois' economics. This may, or may not, be accurate as a historical account of its origin and purpose. But that is, strictly speaking, irrelevant to its falsity or truth. Darwinism is also for some people an ideology, justifying the oppression of the weak by the strong. This does not affect one way or the other its validity as a theory of biological evolution. We intend to take neo-classical economics at face value, reading the text itself, not the gaps between the lines. We will be assessing its claim to describe the real world.

Christian belief has also no doubt often been an ideology. It has been used to persuade the victims of oppression that they must accept injustice without complaint, looking forward to a reward in the afterlife. It has been the excuse for persecution, aggression, barbarity and genocide. All this must be admitted, but it does not actually affect the claim that Christian belief makes to represent reality. All it means is that Christians, living as they do in glass houses, should be careful what rhetorical stones they throw.

In Section One of this chapter, we shall begin with the standard interpretation of economics as approximating to the method of sciences like physics or chemistry, before looking at some alternative accounts suggested by philosophers or by economists themselves. Section Two touches on similar issues in relation to theology, showing how very different concepts of truth and reality can be found in the Bible.

Section One: Economic Theory

Testing economic theory

One introductory economics textbook begins like this:[18]

> Like any science, economics is concerned with the *explanation* and *prediction* of observed phenomena [...] In economics, as in other sciences, explanation and prediction are based on *theories* [...] No theory, whether it be in economics, physics or any other science, is perfectly correct. The usefulness and validity of a theory depend on whether it succeeds in explaining and predicting the set of phenomena that it is intended to explain and predict. Consistent with this goal, theories are continually tested against observation. As a result of this testing, theories are modified or refined and occasionally even discarded. The process of testing and refining theories is central to the development of economics as a science.

Since the 1970s economists have been increasingly preoccupied with the discussion of their own methodology.[19] The received view is, as the textbook quotation indicates, that economic theory can, and should, be tested against observations of the real world and modified when it does not fit. The simplest view of this process is 'falsificationism', which says that theories that fail the test of observation should be abandoned. For example, Mark Blaug has written:[20]

> The methodology which best supports the economist's striving for substantive knowledge of economic relationships is the philosophy of science associated with the names of Karl Popper and Imre Lakatos. To fully attain the ideal of falsifiability is, I still believe, the prime desideratum of economics.

We should note, however, the reluctance shown in the textbook quotation actually to discard a theory, rather than to modify or refine it. Philosophers of science know well how difficult it is to devise a test

18 Pindyck, R. S. and Rubinfeld, D. L., *Microeconomics*, Prentice-Hall, 1995.

19 See Backhouse, R. E. (ed.), *New Directions in Economic Methodology*, Routledge, 1994.

20 Blaug, M., *The Methodology of Economics*, CUP, 1980.

which will really make or break a hypothesis. What actually happens, in economics as in other 'research programmes', is rather that theories get modified in the face of conflicting evidence to the point where they no longer appeal except to a minority of devotees. If a rival theory appears at this point then it is likely to win the support of the profession. Two of the best examples of the process in economics are the rise of Keynesianism in the 1930s and its decline in the 1970s. In both episodes, empirical evidence, sometimes of a very informal kind, played an important part.

There are very few areas of economics in which controlled experiments are possible. Macroeconomists do, it is true, publish forecasts of inflation rates, unemployment, and so on. It is difficult to be certain, on the basis of forecasting performance, whether the methods and models they use contain useful information. Probably, the results are rather better than might be achieved by pure chance, but not good enough to demonstrate the validity of the underlying theory. In most branches of the subject, controlled experiments are not possible, any more than they are in such undoubtedly scientific subjects as astronomy or evolutionary biology.

Testing, for most of economics, means the statistical analysis of time-series or cross-section data, often collected for some other purpose. A causal relationship is hypothesised, which is stated, in mathematical form: variable x is a function of variables y and z, together with random interference and observational errors. For convenience the relationship is very often assumed to be linear. A data set, containing observations of all the variables, is found and various summary statistics are then calculated. On certain assumptions, the values of these summary statistics can provide tests of the validity of the hypothesis in question. The correct formulation of such tests is the main task of econometrics.[21]

The real world is called the 'data generation process', the DGP. The econometrician has to work backwards from analysis of the data set to determine the character of the DGP. This requires assumptions and estimates of the random components in the data as well as the

21 As an example of econometric methods, see Harvey, A. C., *The Econometric Analysis of Time Series*, Philip Allan, 1981.

deterministic part. From this information one can estimate the likelihood that the parameters of the DGP fall in a specified range. Testing the hypothesis that y influences x usually amounts to calculating the likelihood that the coefficient in the relationship between them in fact takes the value of zero. Convention alone determines the level of statistical significance, or likelihood, that is taken as good evidence that a relationship does, or does not, exist in reality.

If all that the econometrician had to contend with was stochastic variation and observational errors then the task of hypothesis testing would be relatively straight forward. In practice things are not so easy. There is often doubt as to whether the data really measure the concept to which the hypothesis relates – what do we really mean by income, for example? Using a slightly different definition sometimes produces dramatically different results. It also matters a lot what other variables are included in the data set when the tests are carried out (the relationship between income and consumption depends on the level of interest rates for example). Yet econometricians never question that the DGP actually exists, hard though it may be to perceive it.

A fundamental problem, familiar to applied economists especially in the area of macroeconomics, is that the data sets are seldom really large enough for the analysis that the econometrician needs to make. (Microeconomic studies use much larger data sets, but the questions they ask are also more complex.) A cross-section study of national growth rates may be confined to just ten or twenty countries; a time-series study for any one country may be able to use just ten or twenty years of annual or quarterly observations. This is inadequate to distinguish between the many ways in which a hypothesis might be framed. Instead of continually discarding one data set and using a fresh one, the researchers have to work over the same numbers again and again, until any 'interesting' results that eventually get published may have no real statistical significance at all.

In practice, mainstream economic theory proves well able to survive what looks like empirical refutation. For example some very basic economic theory implies that an increase in the rate of inflation, if it persists long enough to be fully anticipated, will be fully matched by an increase in the rate of interest. The conclusions of one statistical study of this relationship were reported as follows:[22]

> The effect of inflation on the rate of interest is small, perhaps surprisingly so. An increase of a percentage point in the rate of inflation results after some time in a rise of at most a quarter of a percentage point in interest rates. This could be because the rate of inflation expected in the future is more relevant to interest rates than the rate of inflation in the past, and expectations do not adjust one-for-one to experience of outturns. If however the forecasts of inflation actually published by the National Institute are added to the analysis they do nothing to improve the explanation.

This is quite typical of applied macroeconomics. The result seems to contradict a very fundamental prediction of all mainstream economics, yet the test cannot be at all decisive. There is, amongst other problems, a question about how expectations should be measured which can never be resolved to everyone's satisfaction. In any case this is just one short time-series data set. One could go on searching until one finds a data set which gives results that accord better with the theory. These might then be the only results that are deemed to be 'usable'.

Economic models and the real world

The difficulty of testing economic theory has led some students of methodology to a reappraisal of what kind of discipline economics really is. An important contribution to that debate has been made by Alexander Rosenberg. He starts from a position very different from that of Mark Blaug. In an article called 'What is the Cognitive Status of Economic Theory?' he has written:[23]

> Though some economists still pay lip service to Popper's test of falsifiability, most students of the philosophy of economics recognise that (a) economic

22 Taken from a book by one of the present authors: Britton, A., *Macroeconomic Policy in Britain*, CUP, 1991.

23 Rosenberg, A., 'What is the Cognitive Status of Economic Theory?' in Backhouse, R. E. (ed.), op. cit.

theory is not in fact falsifiable and (b) falsifiability is unacceptable as a test for the scientific respectability of a theory. But an adequate substitute litmus test has yet to be found.

Economic theory is deductive before it is empirical. It begins from a limited set of clearly stated axioms, or assumptions about human nature and motivation, and draws some rich conclusions about what human behaviour will be. One test of the 'respectability' of a theory might be the realism of those assumptions, to be judged by introspection or by asking a sample of people whether they really think like that. Economic theory might not do well in such a test; but perhaps that does not matter.

For some economists all that matters, or so they claim, is the accurate prediction of behaviour; the realism of the assumptions is irrelevant. The most famous expression of that view was by Milton Friedman. In response to the criticism that neo-classical economics is unrealistic, he said,[24] 'This question can be answered only by seeing whether the theory works, which means whether it yields sufficiently accurate predictions.' He thought it was good enough to be able to assert that it is 'as if' the axioms of economics hold. As we have seen, however, the question cannot often be settled that way because the tests are not conclusive.

When people say that the assumptions behind economic theory are unrealistic they can mean many different things. Uskali Maki[25] has distinguished no fewer than eight different criteria for realism in economic theory: relevance to something that is itself real, capability of being observed, factual accuracy, empirical success, inherent plausibility, completeness, concreteness and practical usefulness. Some would say that mainstream neo-classical economics is vulnerable on all these fronts. At best, the assumptions about rationality, individualism and the nature of risk are useful abstractions, isolating some aspects of human experience. No one really believes that he or she is 'economic man', although few could deny that there is something recognisable in the portrait. Why not enlarge the

24 Friedman, M., *Essays in Positive Economics*, Univ. of Chicago Press, 1953.

25 Maki, U., 'Reorienting the Assumptions Issue', in Backhouse, R. E. (ed.), op. cit.

compass of economic theory to take account of other features of humanity like emotion, group identity and systematic misperception?

Some economists, usually those who are sceptical of mainstream neo-classical theory, want the subject to adopt a more eclectic methodology. Sheila Dow, for example, has written:[26]

> The alternative approach is to employ several strands of argument which have different starting points and which, in a successful theory, reinforce each other; an argument, therefore, does not stand or fall on the acceptability of any one set of axioms. Knowledge is generated by practical applications of theories to examples, using a variety of methods. Various traditions can be identified as having something in common with the mode of thought described here. [...] This style of reasoning is found typically in theological and legal argument.

If the aim of economics is to give practical advice to policy-makers and to business leaders, who may have no strong commitments to any one theoretical school, then this so-called 'Babylonian' style has much to recommend it. It might go down well in a court of law, although not necessarily in fact in an academic theology seminar. In economics it would clearly mean departing from the main stream of neo-classical tradition. For many practical economists this would not matter very much, but for the purist to compromise on the method of neo-classical economics would be to abandon the tradition all together.

We are left asking what neo-classical economics would be good for, if it cannot be defended either as realistic in its assumptions or as successful in its predictions. Rosenberg[27] offers two different end uses. We could simply redefine economics as a branch of applied mathematics. 'Both detractors and defenders of orthodox neo-classical theory have found its intellectual core in its mathematical expression.' This would certainly confirm the impression any lay person might receive on opening at random a journal of economic theory. Rosenberg compares the history of economic theory with that of Euclidean geometry. Despite the apparent refutation of neo-classical

26 Dow, S., *Macroeconomic Thought – A Methodological Approach*, Blackwell, 1985.

27 Rosenberg, op. cit.

general equilibrium theory by the events of the great depression between the wars, he says:[28]

> Many economists continued to be interested in the purely formal questions of the conventional theory, quite regardless of its irrelevance to understanding the actual world. These economists were implicitly treating microeconomics as a pure axiomatic system, whose terms may or may not be instantiated in the real world, but which is of great interest, like Euclidean geometry, whether or not its objects actually exist.

Perhaps the pay-off from studying this branch of applied mathematics may eventually come, not in understanding economic behaviour, but in some quite different field, like political theory or even biology. Mathematicians are often surprised to find where their elegant propositions prove to be most fruitful.

The other role which Rosenberg sees for economic theory is normative. The real world may not actually be a general equilibrium system, but perhaps it should be. Suppose that individuals really were free to make their own decisions, as many feel that they should be. Suppose that these individuals really were rational, as most of us wish that we were. How then would their economic life be organised? What role would there then be for government? What need would there be for a legal code? It sounds like a project to design a Utopia, but it is not altogether different from the agenda of economic theory over the past two hundred years.

Rosenberg ends by arguing that the apparent unrealism of some of the assumptions of neo-classical economics may actually be to its advantage when it is used for prescriptive purposes. He reminds us of Hume's view that political constitutions should bc drawn up, for safety's sake, on the assumption that all men are 'knaves'. Similarly economics, since Adam Smith, has demonstrated the efficacy of the market in satisfying the needs of all, even if each seeks only his or her selfish ends.

It is said that economic theory provides a model of the world. There is a nice ambiguity about that word. The *Shorter Oxford English Dictionary* offers two relevant definitions. It can mean 'a

28 Rosenberg, op. cit.

representation of structure'. The theory can identify the most important relationships in the economy and show in simple terms how they can explain much of its behaviour. As such it can be useful in predicting, and at least partly 'true'. But alternatively a model can be 'an object of imitation'. The theory can be a design, showing how the economy might work in a better world. Either way economic theory defines a set of logical relationships which may have an aesthetic appeal of their own. Either way the same question could be asked, with a different meaning: 'but is it *realistic*?'

Section Two: Christian Belief

Revelation and biblical truth: testing the evidence

Modern Christians may share the modern concern that truth should be confirmed by empirical demonstration; they may feel uncomfortable unless scientific research confirms their faith. But the Bible takes for granted much which nowadays we might want to subject to a test. This is not to deny that in some stories, in both the Old and the New Testaments, to see was to believe. The point is rather that the most blessed people are those who have *not* seen, but who nevertheless believe. Faith in the biblical narratives is not dependent on empirical observation.

Ancient Israel did not begin its testing of religious belief with disclosures of deity.[29] That is to say, it did not ask whether God might be thought to exist, and, if so, how this God could be proved to exist. Rather it was concerned with knowledge of the future which was concealed from human beings. The deity (or deities) was but one source among many of knowledge of what was hidden. It was taken for granted that there were divine beings, or household gods. The paramount questions centred on the nature and number of such beings, and their explanatory power about the future. Their explanatory power

29 Pannenberg, W., *Systematic Theology*, Volume 1, T and T Clark, 1991.

could be demonstrated in a number of ways. There was consultation of the dead, and of soothsayers, as means of revealing the divine power. The Old Testament is clear that such practices are to be forbidden, but the strength of the prohibition shows that such things were practised (Leviticus 19:31 and Deuteronomy 18:10).

Throughout the Old Testament an interest in the future remained part of the belief of Israel, and in 1 Samuel 28:6 there is a reference to dreams, the casting of lots and prophets. In these ways the power of God might be employed to understand the future. The prophetic word here is understood as an oracle, and all three means of discerning revelation are justified by the acknowledgement that the God of Israel was the only one who can be the ruler of what is yet to take place. All these attempts at foretelling the future are part of ancient practices of manticism. Manticism is the interpretation of signs, and in other religions it could include observing the flight of birds, discerning the entrails of animals, or subjecting individuals to the testing of their claims by fire or water. Israel accepted some but not all of these practices.

The giving of signs was a regular accompaniment of the miracles of Israel. In Exodus 4:2 and 7:9 Moses and Aaron carry a miraculous rod which validates their choice by God. Gideon also asks for a sign, but here the sign is one which reassures Gideon, rather than validates his commission (Judges 6:17), and Isaiah tells King Ahaz to ask God for a sign (Isaiah 7:11). When the king replies that this is a form of tempting God, Isaiah dismisses the argument as a way of refusing his message. The signs and wonders which took place before the Exodus are well known. Again the problem was that Pharaoh would not believe them (Deuteronomy 4:34; 6:22; 7:19; 26:8). Once Israel was out of Egypt it was threatened by judgement if it ignored the commandments. This was seen as a sign for all generations (Deuteronomy 28:46). Prophets could see themselves as a living sign sent by God to Israel. Isaiah refers to himself in this way in Isaiah 8:18 and Ezekiel became a sign after his wife died in Ezekiel 24:24–27.

When we come to the world of the Gospels, we find that Jesus rejects the demand for signs as tempting God. He was asked for them, but rejected the demand. The large number of references in the four

Gospels to this episode show how well attested this confrontation was (Luke 11:16; Mark 8:11; Matthew 12:38–39 and 16:3–8; John 2:18, and 6:30). Jesus did however relate more to the traditional Jewish belief in signs than this rejection might lead us to imagine. His reply to John the Baptist about whether Jesus was the Messiah was to invoke the signs of the coming of the Kingdom. The blind are given their sight, the poor have good news preached to them, and the lepers are healed. The signs of Matthew 11:4–5 and Luke 7:22–23 are given by God. They are not proofs demanded from God. The problem is succinctly put in Jesus' rebuke to the official in Capernaum (John 4:48): 'Unless you see signs and wonders you will not believe.' If the only way in which people could come to faith was by demanding signs, then for Jesus this was a lack of faith. Mark 6 shows Jesus' amazement at their lack of faith. At this point it is clear that religious truth is not to be tested by empirical means, even if signs may accompany certain events.

Religious faith and the real world

It was central to both Jewish and Christian theology that the fundamental knowledge of God was given in and through the events of history. The argument about the value of signs does not mean that the pattern of knowledge in scripture ceases to be unique. What was unique was that religious knowledge was given in and through history, above all else. Such history was bound up with the practice of worship, where the saving events of Israel were recounted and God praised for his actions. In and through such events there was a call to responsible living. One key term found in scripture is that of 'wisdom'. Wisdom becomes the central term, and the equivalent concept in scripture of the modern quest for substantive knowledge. If wisdom is the key to the fullness of life, and the knowledge of God's call to his people, then it functions in the same way as substantive knowledge does in contemporary Western culture.

Judaic teaching looked to the importance of wisdom, and the practice of life.[30] Greek philosophy preferred to specify the conditions through which knowledge could be gained. Even if this led on to the implications for social ordering, as it often did in Plato, Aristotle and other philosophers, nevertheless the difference between Greek and Judaic teaching remains profound. There is yet another complication which is that many of the early Christian thinkers after the biblical period expressed themselves in deeply Hellenistic, even Platonic, forms of thought. However, despite these nuances of the Hellenistic tone of much of early Christianity, and the interest in society in Greek thought, the unique nature of Hebraic thinking in scripture is found in its appeal to history and the demands which God makes on his people to order their society aright. 'You shall be holy, as I the Lord your God am holy', remains the basic command in scripture.

The Hebrew understanding of time and movement centres upon a belief that God would be present in the future, according to his sovereign will. Like Greek thought, the expectation was that wisdom would be present in thought and practice determining their content despite the often-flawed ability of humanity to be in fact open to its guidance. It was elaborated throughout the Old Testament in laws and in practical wisdom. That is why so much of this writing is concerned with how wisdom is to be carried out. Wisdom itself dwelled with God and it was no easy matter to describe its nature, although its agency could be described. It was not a regular process, like the regularities of the heavens, but rather depended on the way in which God was present in the operations of wisdom. John Eaton writes of the Psalmist's understanding of wisdom: 'In the Lord's guiding law he found a mighty sun. Here was rounded perfection and power to revive a dissipated soul. Here was reliability; here was enlightenment for the simplest, bestowing wisdom.'[31]

The agency of wisdom is the action of God's people. This responsible action is how the reality of God's truth impinges on the world. Materiality is not simply the vehicle for where wisdom could be expressed, but is itself the mediation of wisdom. Land, behaviour

30 Hardy, D. W., *God's Ways with the World*, T and T Clark, 1996.

31 Eaton, J., *The Contemplative Face of Old Testament Wisdom*, SPCK, 1989.

and history all mediate the agency of wisdom. 'So there are the foundations of a notion of human rationality which is proportioned to the positive content of the agency of wisdom, in addition to the notion of human knowledge assimilated to the positive content of wisdom.'[32] History is not for the Hebrew writers some time-neutral screen through which the purposes of God are to be discerned. Instead the great historical narratives of scripture all combine to present the identity of God and God's people.

The wisdom of God is found in history. It is not to be seen as an object, such as a tree or mountain, nor as an event or person. It is however to be discerned in and through the events told in the historical narratives of scripture. These events must be interpreted in the appropriate manner. A theologian cannot add up all the examples of wisdom in history described in scripture, and say that this is 'reality', for that would be to commodify it as a single thing. Reality is more fluid in its texture in biblical thought. It is, perhaps, one of the great differences between modern thought and scripture in their understanding of the real world.

The contemporary person, such as an economist or more simply someone who lives in the worldview of our modern Western society, is therefore forced to employ a 'hermeneutic of wisdom' in understanding the nature of historical narrative. S/he must attempt to interpret what the nature of biblical truth is in describing reality. Such a response relates to the Old Testament through the particular experience of praise which is found especially expressed in the Psalms. One of the deepest questions is whether this experience of praise means anything in a world where often the intrinsic value of a person or thing which makes it worthy of praise is subordinated to the instrumental or functional nature of that object.

However, if it is possible to appreciate the importance of the activity of praise, then it becomes clear that the praise of God involves the acknowledgement of what God has done, and what he will do. Praise means that there is no fixed relation between human beings and wisdom, but rather an opening up of truth through the praise of the Lord of history. This understanding is continued in the accounts of the

32 Hardy, op. cit.

life of Jesus, and the Epistles and narratives of early Christianity. What matters is the presence of wisdom in his followers, where the agency of wisdom is once again the responsibility which his followers are prepared to live out in their lives. This leads inevitably to the necessity of interpretation (or hermeneutic) in the life of the Christian community. It is by this lengthy road that biblical Christianity answers the challenge of the modern empiricist as to how the truth of its beliefs is to be tested. There is a fundamental difference about the nature of reality, found in the appreciation of history and responsible action, in response to an 'other' which is called wisdom.

The question which one is left with is whether this discourse about religious language can have its own coherent unity as well. One of the problems which scripture wrestles with is the consistency of its beliefs. As we have seen, Sheila Dow has appealed for an eclectic methodology in economics. However it will be inadequate to impart this eclecticism into neo-classical economics, and the same is true of scripture. Rowan Williams confronts this issue, when he writes:[33]

> If there is one god, the acts of that God should, prima facie, be consistent; the community established by the divine speech should have some unifying points of reference; and reflective speech of that community should in some way articulate the divine consistency, or, at the very least, be able to deal with and contain what seems to make for fragmentation.

There are undoubtedly great moments of division in the history of Israel, and this meant that the unity of divine action, the community and the beliefs of the community all had to be reconstructed again and again. The stories, law and prophecy were revised, through that interpretation (or hermeneutic) of history which is fundamental to the methodology of Israelite belief. This in turn rested on a conviction that the promises of God would endure despite the storms of history. The New Testament is no different. Again the acts of Jesus, and the actions of God in Jesus, were assimilated to the Old Testament stories of creation, Exodus and the return from exile.

One of the fundamental ways of establishing unity is by the use of analogy between Old and New Testaments. There is an analogue in

33 Williams, R. D., *On Christian Theology*, Blackwell, 2000.

the Jewish Scripture, where the community is seen as Israel in the desert, or the Babylonian captivity. The use of analogy in those writings is itself an analogue for the Christian appropriation of individuals, and events in the Jewish Scripture as they are set out in the New Testament. As Abraham stood before the God of Israel, so a Christian may stand before the God of Jesus. The roles created in the early Jewish writings are set out again as paradigms of hope in the Epistle to the Hebrews. Both the patriarchs and the Christian set out for lands unknown. As we have argued previously, it is in particular the responsible living out of the life of faith as a form of wisdom that allows the analogy to be made at all.

This enables a few concluding remarks to be made on the relation of religious belief, whether Jewish or Christian, to the question of the real world. The issue will not be settled by appeal to an object, or by intricacy of argument in itself. Instead it is by looking at the 'compatibility and coherence of the roles made available, the patterns of life opened up in the speech that witnesses to the foundational events of the Jewish and Christian communities'.[34] Such an answer is to be sought in humility, for the awareness which is central to the wisdom tradition outlined in this chapter is that the 'real world' is a world that goes beyond human understanding.

The German theologian who pioneered work on the wisdom tradition in the post-war period was Gerhard Von Rad. He wrote of the wise man that his search was always conducted with this awareness of humility as the only frame of mind which would lead to understanding: 'This fear of God has trained him to openness, to readiness for an encounter with the inscrutable and the imponderable; it has taught him that the sphere in which definite, verifiable systems of order can be discerned is a very limited one.'[35] Such a concern with humility can be found repeatedly in the literature. As two examples among hundreds which could be cited, these quotations from Proverbs (15:33 and 21:30) make the point about the value of wisdom as eloquently as possible:

34 Williams, op. cit.

35 Eaton, op. cit. and Von Rad, G., *Wisdom in Israel*, SCM, 1972.

> The fear of the Lord is the discipline leading to wisdom, and before glory is humility. [...] There is no wisdom and no understanding, and no counsel over against the Lord.

Section Three: Summary and Discussion

In this book we contrast the 'anthropologies' of economic theory and Christian belief. To do this we need to make two assertions, neither of which will go unchallenged. The first is that economic theory assumes a view of human nature which is both positive and normative. Many economists might say that all they require is a model of human behaviour that actually works. We find this 'as if' philosophy unsatisfactory for two reasons: firstly because economics does not in fact 'work' so well that it can stand on the basis of empirical demonstration alone; secondly we would say that when economics, or any other would-be science, does 'work' well, that indicates that it is really true and its assumptions are at least approximately correct.

The second assertion which is crucial to our study is that Christian belief entails a view of human nature which is positive as well as normative. This view is about human motivation and behaviour now, in a fallen world, as well as being about the potential for human perfection in the kingdom of God. We shall be discussing this in the rest of this book, under such headings as rational choice, individualism, relationships and work. It is very different from the view of human nature assumed in economic theory.

In modern times the most impressive advances in knowledge and capability have come from the application of scientific methods. This has influenced profoundly the way that people think about the real world and assess our knowledge of it. The world, they conclude, is fact rather than fiction; and our knowledge of it corresponds, they would maintain, more or less accurately to how it really is. This confident claim has been applied, not just to the physical world, but to human beings as well. The model of learning is the same for all kinds of knowledge: collect the data series, form hypotheses as to the processes that generates them; test those hypotheses by experiment or statistical analysis; if any test fails then reject the hypothesis in question and try again with another one. If we find that we can forecast correctly, then we know that we know something about the real world.

Economists like to describe themselves as social scientists and they aspire to scientific knowledge. As we have seen, however, there are severe difficulties in applying the methods of science to the subject-matter of economics. Much of what economists believe and teach is not based on the kind of enquiry typical of sciences like physics, or even medicine. It seems rather to rest on assumptions about human behaviour and motivation which are not subject to empirical refutation, and which are sometimes regarded almost as articles of faith. The separation of values from factual statements, which is taken for granted in science, becomes problematic when human behaviour itself is the subject of investigation. Thus, the proposition that rational individuals will use resources most efficiently when they are left free to make their own choices can be interpreted in both a positive and a normative sense.

The pre-modern view of the world did not even try to make this sharp division between facts and values. Certainly the two run close together in the Bible. The very nature of things is defined by their purposes: it is of the nature of rain to water the ground and it is the nature of human beings to worship God. God knows everything, both how things are and how they ought to be. To be wise is to be in accord with God, knowing his purposes and supporting them. Indeed, the invisible world of God may be regarded as more real than the world that we can see. Truth comes to us, not by enquiry, but by revelation.

It is important to stress that religious belief today includes positive as well as normative statements, now that the distinction is much clearer than it was in pre-modern times. It is about how things are, as well as about how they ought to be. Thus the question of empirical verification is not irrelevant, even though it may be impossible in practice to provide. For that reason, the different views of human behaviour implied by different 'anthropologies' are differences of view about 'the facts' as well as different judgements about values.

Perhaps the nearest one comes to an empirical test of religious belief in the Bible is the contest on Mount Carmel between Elijah and the prophets of Baal (1 Kings 18). This is not an experiment that many Christians would wish to repeat! There are examples in the New Testament (especially in the fourth Gospel) of miracles being used as demonstrations of God's power and as evidence in support of Christian belief. It seems that the miracles were not done to compel belief, yet supported Christian claims, after the event. The temptation to 'put God to the test' is quite explicitly rejected by Jesus at the start of his ministry.

Pre-modern wisdom is enshrined in stories, and especially in the sacred stories of the Bible. Events, whether real or mythical, are given an interpretation as the story is told. It is the inner meaning of the story that is important, rather than the detail of what actually happened. The modern mind is left wondering what is intended literally, and what is just a metaphor. Modern Christians do not cease to be modern when they read the Bible. Many would like to find the key events in the Christian story confirmed as historical by archaeology or biblical criticism – and they are left puzzled when the evidence conflicts.

One way to escape from such perplexity is to question the need for consistency between the pre-modern narrative and modern standards of proof. A thorough-going sceptic would regard any perspective as no worse than any other, since none corresponds to an objective reality. A post-modern Christian might claim the right to be modern or pre-modern according to the context. The Bible might be taken literally for the purpose of worship, but metaphorically as a description of human nature and destiny. This is the way many people resolve their difficulties today, but it will not satisfy the aspiration to unify human experience. Truth, we sense, even today, is one and indivisible.

Economic theory, unlike theology, has been little affected so far by post-modern philosophy. Although interest in questions of method is certainly on the increase, the mainstream of the subject remains located, quite comfortably, within 'modernism' – that is to say in the dominant philosophy of the nineteenth century. This does not mean, necessarily, that it is now outdated. Perhaps post-modernism is just a name for a late-twentieth-century loss of nerve. Science continues to progress and technologies continue to enlarge human capabilities; economies continue to grow, making us richer and more prosperous all the time. At the start of the twenty-first century we may be, in some ways, back where we were at the start of the twentieth century. The free market system is working rather well again, the threat of nuclear war has receded a bit, the gloomy view of human nature associated with the likes of Marx and Freud is at least a little discredited. Perhaps the twenty-first century will see modernism back in vogue.

In this book we shall adopt a 'realist' view both of economic theory and of Christian belief. The two systems of thought will be used to define alternative models of human nature and fulfilment, or one might say of human behaviour and well-being – the choice of terminology is not unimportant. In both of them there are normative as well as positive propositions closely bound up together. These two systems of thought are clearly not the same, and where they differ fundamentally they cannot both be right. Our main task is to identify where they are similar and where they are not. Some of the real differences ought in principle to be resolvable by some kind of test, at least by a 'thought experiment'. In practice, nothing of the kind is available to us. We are attempting to do something else. We are asking in effect what revision would be required to economic theory for it to be consistent with Christian belief, and conversely what it is about Christian belief that makes it incompatible with the way that economists describe the world. We are seeking to show what they have in common, and also the profound differences between them.

Chapter Two

Rationality, Preference and Choice

Introduction

In this chapter we begin our exploration of neo-classical economic theory and a Christian reaction to it. As explained above, we seek to extract the 'anthropology' implicit in it, that is to consider it as a possible model of human behaviour and motivation. One of the most important characteristics of 'economic man' is his ability to make rational choices. In a standard economics textbook, this might first be considered under the heading of 'Consumer Behaviour', but its significance is not confined to this topic. The same model of rational behaviour can just as well be applied to producers, or indeed by extension to individuals as citizens, parents or government officials.

In seeking to explain human choice and actions, we have two quite different sources of evidence: the observation of human behaviour and our own experience of taking decisions. We can see life both from the outside and from the inside. Looking from the outside we seek to identify the causes of human behaviour, as we might study animal behaviour, or even the behaviour of inanimate objects. Looking from the inside, by the method of introspection, we seek for reasons which will explain, or even justify, our own behaviour or, by analogy, that of others. Some philosophers and scientists would dismiss introspection as 'subjective' and therefore unreliable. One thing which economic theory and Christian belief have in common is that both take notice of accounts of human behaviour as we might describe our own motives to ourselves.

To distinguish his own school of behavioural economics from the main stream of neo-classical economics, Herbert Simon has written[36] that the latter 'generally eschews a detailed empirical study of human choice in favour of deducing the behaviour logically from axioms of perfect rationality'. He then goes on to argue that, 'actual choice behaviour commonly departs widely from the behaviour predicted by the axioms of perfect rationality'. To this the neo-classical economist would respond that the divergences from rationality at the individual level are in fact slight, or that they do not greatly influence behaviour at the aggregate level, or indeed that the implications of rationality are of interest in their own right.

To avoid depending on 'subjective' explanations of behaviour, some economists within the main stream of neo-classical economics use the concept of 'revealed preference'. Choice can then be described in terms of its motivation, but evidence is sought in what people do, rather than in what they say that they think. In criticising this approach, Amartya Sen comments thus:[37]

> The idea that behaviour is the one real source of information is extremely limiting for empirical work and is not easy to justify in terms of the methodological requirements of our discipline. There is an old story about one behaviourist meeting another, and the first behaviourist asks the second; 'I see you are very well. How am I?' The thrust of the revealed preference approach has been to undermine thinking as a method of self-knowledge and talking as a method of knowing about others. In this, I think, we have been prone, on the one hand to overstate the difficulties of introspection and communication, and on the other to underestimate the problems of studying preferences revealed by observed behaviour.

If we see behaviour from the outside then the distinction between description and prescription is sharp and clear. Once we get inside our own heads as it were, the distinction, whilst it is still there, is much easier to miss. What we in fact choose to do will, in general, be what seems good to us. The process of choice involves evaluations of

36 Simon, H. A., 'Behavioural Economics', in Kuper, A. and J. (eds.), *The Social Science Encyclopedia* (second edition), Routledge, 1996.

37 Sen, A., *Choice, Welfare and Measurement*, Blackwell, 1982. Chapter 2: 'Behaviour and the Concept of Preference'.

alternative actions and of their consequences. The description of our own behaviour therefore depends on a normative assessment. The more we describe the behaviour of others by analogy with our own reasoning, the closer the threads of 'is' and 'ought' will run together.

The process of choice can be evaluated as well as described. The concept of rationality is itself often used in a value-laden sense. Hausman and McPherson, in their valuable survey of the interface between economic theory and ethics, make the point forcefully:[38]

> Despite the fact that utility theory makes no substantive claims about what people should prefer, it remains a normative theory concerning how people ought to choose, rather than a positive theory of how people do choose or merely a model or a definition. It lays down conditions that choices and preferences *ought* to satisfy.

Thus economic theory describes rational choice, as we understand it from our own conscious experience of taking decisions; it is normative because it takes account of our own perceptions of what wise decisions require. The same could be said about Christian belief. But what Christians believe about human experience has always to be interpreted in relation to belief about God. Calvin said that, 'without knowledge of God, there is no knowledge of self'. In the book of Genesis, ch 1, God created man 'in his own image'. That verse can be given many different meanings, but one given to it by most Christians over the centuries is that human beings are capable of making rational decisions, just as God did in the process of creation. The Christian economist Brian Griffiths makes the connection very directly:[39] 'The Creator is revealed to us as a rational, moral, feeling person, capable of making choices'; and: 'God's image in man implies that he too is a rational, moral, feeling person capable of making choices.'

This is indeed one aspect of Christian belief about human decisions, but it is not the whole of it. The choices with which men and women are confronted in the New Testament require something more than just rationality. They certainly do not require subtle

38 Hausman, D. M. and McPherson, M. S., *Economic Analysis and Moral Philosophy*, CUP, 1996.

39 Griffiths, B., *Morality and the Market Place*, Hodder and Stoughton, 1980.

reasoning or difficult calculation. They do not involve foresight or 'taking thought for tomorrow'. What is needed is a personal response to a calling; it may appear foolish rather than wise; a child could make it more easily than an adult. Christians can write about the 'Foolishness of God'[40] and describe their own experience as being 'Against all Reason'.[41]

Christian belief is also full of paradoxes about choice and predestination. God chose us before we could choose him. This might seem to imply that human choice as it seems to the introspective view is an illusion. Yet we are held responsible for the choices that we make. Philosophers debate the freedom of the will in contrast with determinism, asking much the same questions. Economists certainly believe in free and rational choice, but they also believe that behaviour can, in part, be predicted. It can, indeed, be predicted precisely because it is rational.

In Section One of this chapter we begin with rationality as it appears in the standard theory of consumer choice. We then elaborate, using some recent literature on topics such as 'meta-preferences', that is rational choice between alternative ways of choosing. We also reflect on the question of free will versus determinism in the context of economic theory. Then in Section Two we turn to the theological treatment of some related issues. These include pre-destination and the rationality of conversion. (Can it be likened to an expression of meta-preferences, a decision to change the shape of one's own utility function?)

40 Baker, J. A., *The Foolishness of God*, Fontana, 1970.

41 Moorhouse, G., *Against all Reason – The Religious Life in the Modern World*, Weidenfeld and Nicholson, 1969.

Section One: Economic Theory

Utility maximisation

A textbook account of consumer behaviour begins from a set of assumptions about personal preferences.[42]

> The theory of consumer behaviour begins with three basic assumptions regarding people's preferences for one market basket versus another. We believe that these assumptions hold for most people in most situations.

Thus these assumptions are put forward almost as articles of faith, based presumably on introspection. They are not logically necessary, self-evident or obviously true.

> The first assumption is that preferences are *complete* which means that consumers can compare and rank all market baskets [...] The second important assumption is that preferences are *transitive*. Transitivity means that if a consumer prefers market basket A to market basket B, and prefers B to C, then the consumer also prefers A to C [...] The third assumption is that all goods are good (i.e. desirable), so that leaving costs aside, *consumers always prefer more of any good to less* [...] These three assumptions form the basis of consumer theory. They don't explain consumers' preferences, but they do impose a degree of rationality and reasonableness on them.

Consumer choices then consist of ranking all the combinations of goods and services that can be purchased within a given budget. The combination with the highest ranking is the one selected. Within that combination it can be proved that the rate at which the consumer is prepared to trade as between any two commodities, both of which are purchased, must at the margin be the same as their relative prices in the market. If that were not true the consumer could move to a higher ranking of satisfaction by giving up a little of one commodity so as to be able to have a little more of another. In effect the normal result is a compromise, in that the consumer buys a little of everything on offer. When, at the other extreme, all the budget is allocated to just one

42 Pindyck, R. S. and Rubinfeld, D. L., op. cit.

commodity this is termed a 'corner solution', because the position lies in a corner of the standard textbook diagram, and it is treated as a rather special case.

It might seem obvious that a rational consumer will always increase the proportion of his or her income spent on a commodity when its price falls. This is what one might expect from naive introspection or from casual empiricism. Economic theory, on the contrary, can demonstrate that this will not always be the case. This example shows rather well how theory can correct the errors in 'common sense'. Consider the choice between bread and meat made by a very poor household. The diet will consist almost entirely of bread; when the price of bread falls the family income will go further and they will be able to afford a little more meat which for them is a luxury item. Consider also the choice between income and leisure facing a part-time worker: when the hourly wage rises, he or she may decide to work fewer hours, not more. Similarly when the rate of interest rises, some people will save less, and add little or nothing to their prospective income in the future.

We have described consumer theory in terms of preferences and rankings, not in terms of happiness or standards of living. When the theory of consumer choice was first formalised it was described as utility maximisation.[43] Utility or happiness was imagined to be measurable on a cardinal scale. In other words it was thought to make sense to say that I would be twice as happy in one situation as I would be in another. Some economists would still defend such language today, but others regard it as meaningless and irrelevant to the choices which people actually have to make. This becomes important when one wants to speak of the sum of happiness over several periods of time, or the expected value of utility over a range of many possible contingencies.

43 See, for example, Farina, F., Hahn, F. and Vannucci, S. (eds.), *Ethics, Rationality and Economic Behaviour*, OUP, 1996 and especially the papers in it by J. Broome and P. Hammond.

Rationality

This is how choices are described at the most elementary level within the standard framework of economic theory. The limitations of the model are obvious, not least to economists themselves. The concept of rationality has been explored in much greater depth than that. We can just indicate some of the directions in which the model can be extended, particularly those most relevant to the themes of this book.

One might ask whether it actually adds anything to say that rational choices depend on preferences. If preferences cannot be described independently of the act of choosing, then they are nothing more than an alternative way of describing the same events. For preferences to *cause* choices they must have prior existence; people must be able to make hypothetical choices, to know how they would choose in circumstances that they have never met. Indeed for preferences to be complete, as the standard theory requires, people must know how they would react in all possible situations which seems quite unrealistic. Actual introspection does not reveal a full set of preferences; what it tells us is that we discover, or indeed invent, many of our preferences in the process of choice. Choice is not an effortless task. It requires calculation, imagination and will power. We often keep our options open, not just to reduce risk, but also because we really do not know what we want to do.

Some economists have argued that the process of choice described in the standard theory is not just difficult but actually impossible. The consumer, or more generally the economic agent, cannot know what all the results of a decision will be. The standard theory says that the consumer will calculate the expectation of satisfaction using a probability distribution. Even using an ordinal rather than a cardinal measure of utility, one can have preferences between alternative risks, but to make a rational choice one needs to know the extent of the risks one will run. The difficulty is that, so often, one has no objective measure of the probability distribution at all. In situations of great uncertainty people may use quite different methods of choosing, for example repeating their behaviour from some previous occasion or copying what they see other people do. This is not fully rational as the standard theory requires. Economists call it 'bounded rationality'.[44] It is often the most sensible approach one can actually adopt.

The standard model assumes that all choices can be made afresh from first principles on every occasion. But this is to ignore the value of precommitment and planning. In economics rationality is sometimes extended to include decisions which will constrain future choices. David Gauthier concludes an article on commitment and choice with the following words:[45]

> Effective planning requires commitments to choices that are not directly supported by preferences for their outcomes. Taking this as a starting-point leads us to a better understanding of both rationality and morality, as having a pragmatic foundation in the temporal and interpersonal relations that give shape and substance to the lives of human beings as planning animals.

Economists often define rationality much more narrowly than the use of the word in normal speech. To be rational, for most people, means no more than to be able to gave a coherent account of the reasons for one's acts, to be capable of modifying one's behaviour in the light of new information, and to be open to persuasion by others who share the same culture and values. To be irrational is to be blind, bigoted, inconsistent or incoherent. There are not many people who would describe their own behaviour as irrational.

In popular speech to be reasonable is to conform to expectations, to follow norms, to respect conventions and to co-operate with those whose interests and views are not identical with your own. Most people, in practice, choose what others like them have chosen in the past. In an uncertain situation this may be the best strategy to follow. It may be followed for that reason, or simply because it is the custom, and one has never had occasion to question it. If rationality is so broadly defined we need some other words to describe the different kinds of 'rational' procedures that people might adopt.

44 van Raaij, W. F., 'Economics and Psychology', in Greenaway, D., Bleaney, M. and Stewart, I. (eds.), op. cit.

45 Gauthier, D., 'Commitment and Choice', in Farina, F., Hahn, F. and Vannucci, S. (eds.), op. cit.

In ethics the distinction is made between theories which evaluate the consequences of actions and those which evaluate the actions themselves in some other way. In describing, rather than prescribing, choice a similar distinction could be made. There is, for example, a theory which says that consumers merely seek a 'satisfactory' combination of commodities, rather than spending the time and effort required to be certain that they have found the best combination that they could possible have. That is a consequentialist theory, and most people would call it rational. Another theory would be that consumers have a self-image of the kind of person that they are, and seek to reinforce that image by the choices that they make. The choice itself is what matters, not any calculation of its effects. 'My friends would expect me to buy that hat.' That may, or may not, be described as a rational way to choose. It is, in any case, how many decisions are made.

Choosing how to choose

In economic theory the preference orderings of individuals are exogenous, facts which the theory takes as given rather than something to be explained. People know what they like. Indeed it is a small step from this to saying that people know what is good for them, or at least usually know better than anyone else could know. As the quotation from the elementary textbook showed, there is not much curiosity in economics at that level about how preferences are formed or how they might change as a result of experience. This does not mean however that no economists are interested in the question.

In one variety of consumer choice theory the actual goods and services purchased are considered to be packages containing combinations of more basic ingredients a sheep provides wool for clothing and mutton to eat; a car provides speed of transport, comfort and prestige. It is these more basic ingredients which enter into the consumer's utility function. To choose wisely one needs information about the ingredients to be found in the goods and services for sale. This is one purpose of advertising: the more that consumers know about the commodities on offer, the more effectively they will be able to satisfy their wants and needs.

Advertising, undoubtedly, also seeks to persuade, to change people's preferences and hence what they choose. It would suit the economic theory of consumer choice best if all advertisement could be presented as an appeal to reason, but that is not always the form it takes. It often appeals to the emotions directly, to desire or envy or fear; the aim is often to associate the product with pleasures and satisfactions quite remote from anything that the product itself could provide; this is done at a level of thought below that of full consciousness. Consumers are not just being informed, they are also being influenced, even manipulated. The image of a product may be at least as important as its quality; the packaging may matter more than the substance it contains.[46]

Individual consumers are, of course, greatly influenced by what their friends and neighbours are buying. One way of analysing this is in terms of peer-group pressure. The choices we make, what we wear, how we spend our time, the teams we support, the music we listen to, the newspapers we buy, the political parties we vote for, the churches we attend – all these make up a lifestyle which we display to the world around us. We crave approval and we fear contempt. That is perhaps the sociological approach to fashions and group dynamics; the approach suggested by economic theory is different.

The neo-classical Chicago school can provide an account of fashions which is consistent with the standard model of rational individual choice. David Hirschleifer writes:[47]

> *Learning by observing others* can explain the conformity, idiosyncrasy, and fragility of social behaviour. When people can observe one another's behaviour they very often end up making the same choices; thus, localised conformity. If the early movers erred, followers are likely to imitate the mistake; hence idiosyncrasy. If later on a few people start behaving differently for whatever reason, then a sudden phase change can occur in which the old convention is swept away by the new; hence fragility. Such imitation can explain either

46 Jhally, S., 'Advertising' in Kuper, A. and J. (eds.), op. cit.

47 Hirshleifer, D., 'The Blind Leading the Blind – Social Influences, Fads and Informational Cascades', in Tommasi, M. and Ierulli, K. (eds.), op. cit.

> transient fads or permanent choices among alternative products, sexual and marital options, scientific theories, and religious beliefs.
>
> My first crucial point is that imitation can be sophisticated, being based upon rational weighing of pros and cons. Even if the blind are leading the blind, as in Breugel's painting the followers need not be fools – each individual realises that he is somewhat ill-informed and that his predecessors are also.

This account may well explain what happens when individuals with similar preferences copy one another in the choice of products. But something more than that is needed to explain why people's preferences themselves are so similar. It is not just information about where satisfaction can be found that passes from one individual to another, it is also opinions as to what kind of satisfactions should be sought. Economists, working with the standard model of consumer behaviour, would have difficulty in analysing essentially ethical choices of that kind.

What has been said about advertisement above in relation to consumer demand could be repeated about education in relation to life in general. Schools and colleges, parents and teachers, do not only seek to transmit information; they also hope to help to form the minds of the young, to persuade them, consciously or unconsciously, to adopt certain norms of behaviour, certain preferences, standards and values. The older generation certainly has views about what the views of the younger generation should be.

It is also possible for a person to have wishes as to what his or her own wishes should be. At the borderline between economics and philosophy there is now active discussion of the concept of 'meta-preferences'. Thus Hausman and McPherson write:[48]

> It may be useful to suppose that individuals have different preference rankings or utilities depending on whether they consider matters from a self-interested or a moral perspective or to suppose that individuals have 'metapreferences', that is, preferences concerning what their preferences should be. Multiple-preference systems very naturally model internal conflict concerning such personal choices as whether to smoke, as well as more clearly moral choices such as whether to contribute to charity. Some have argued that the choices of morally influenced persons are better represented in such models. However this

48 Hausman, D. M. and McPherson, M. S., op. cit.

> approach also raises difficult questions, for it is not clear within the multiple-preference framework how to explain which ranking will prevail in which circumstances. If that determination is itself made by a consistent preference ranking at a higher level, then it may make sense to re-invoke standard utility theory.

The Chicago school has also introduced an interesting theory of what is called 'rational addiction'. Michael Grossman describes it as follows:[49]

> In economic analysis of addictive behaviour, the consumption of a certain good is termed to be an addiction or a habit if an increase in current consumption of the good leads to an increase in future consumption. [...] A harmful addiction is one in which current consumption has detrimental effects in the future, such as reductions in health and therefore in utility caused by cigarette smoking and excessive alcohol use. Similarly, a beneficial addiction is one in which current consumption has favourable effects in the future, such as increases in future utility from attending and acquiring additional information about operas today. Other examples of beneficial addictions are attending church, jogging, or playing tennis on a regular basis.

Rational consumers (and worshippers) will take account of the consequences of their behaviour today for their preferences, and hence their happiness, in the future, in deciding whether to become addicted or not.

Choice and freedom

To the extent that economic theory makes use of introspection, it describes a process of conscious and deliberate choice. Economic man knows what he is doing. Other people's choices are also assumed to be conscious and deliberate, because however different their culture or values may be they are nevertheless 'people like us'. In this economic theory differs from other social sciences which often regard anyone's description of their own motivation with acute suspicion. Marxists sometimes say that people suffer from 'false consciousness' such that

49 Grossman, M., 'The Economic Approach to Addictive Behavior', in Tommasi, M. and Ierulli, K. (eds.), op. cit.

they misunderstand their own inner lives. Freudians attribute behaviour to unconscious motives which their owners would strenuously deny.

We describe decisions in the way we do because we can make them consciously. This certainly influences the concepts and language of economic theory quite fundamentally. Nevertheless we know that decisions can be made by agents who are not themselves conscious of what they are doing. An animal confronted by alternatives clearly selects one rather than another, although any consciousness it may have is not accessible to us. A computer programme can be written to make decisions, and no one will seriously suggest that it knows what it is doing in the sense that a human decision-taker does. It just follows a procedure specified for it in logical or mathematical form. It is interesting to reflect that the description of human choices in mathematical form, as developed by economists in the 19th century, actually predates the development of machines capable of behaving just like that. It is also interesting to reflect that economic man as described in the textbook, if he existed would be indistinguishable from an intelligent robot.[50]

The behaviour of economic man in the textbook is clearly predetermined. Given full knowledge of an individual's preferences, and the constraints he or she faces, there can only be one answer to the problem of choice. It may be difficult to predict behaviour in practice, but in principle the issue is not in doubt. The use of the theory of games in economics actually depends crucially on the assumption that each player can understand and predict the behaviour of the others.

It is surprising then that economists in practice attach as much importance to human freedom as they usually do. The association of economic theory with libertarianism is close and of long standing.[51] Is this only because human brains are such efficient calculating machines, or because information about preferences is difficult to

50 The 'Turing Test' for intelligent robots requires their answers to written questions to be indistinguishable from those of a 'real person'. See, for example, Humphrey, N., *A History of the Mind*, Chatto and Windus, 1992.

51 See Shand, A. H., *Free Market Morality – The Political Economy of the Austrian School*, Routledge, 1990.

share? On the contrary the respect for human freedom is sometimes expressed in religious language. Hayek, in defending economic freedom from the encroachment of the state, quotes from de Tocqueville, 'I should have loved freedom, I believe, at all times, but in the time in which we live I am ready to worship it.' The impression is given that most economists, like most other people, value freedom for its own sake.

Section Two: Christian Belief

We now move, quite abruptly, from the language of economics to that of theology. The transition is sharp, and deliberately so. But the subject matter under discussion is the same or similar. In this section the argument will move from the alternatives to utility maximisation into the nature of choice.

Clearly the biblical account does not see this choice in the context of consumer behaviour. It is choice in the context of religious faith and allegiance. But concepts available to economists, such as meta-preferences or 'rational addiction' may not be unrelated to the concepts which some theologians might use. What lies at the heart of the discussion of the biblical account is how choices might be structured, and sustained. Thus we move back to the economist's interest in choosing how to choose, only from a different perspective.

Finally at the end of this section, there is a quite different argument. This introduces the thought of Al McFadyen on the nature of freedom in itself, prior to any discussion of choice. Of course it may well be argued that such a move about the very reality of freedom is invalid. Does this not move the argument onto a metaphysical plane? But the theologian will want to reply that it is the relationship between God and human freedom that must always be at the very heart of the discussion of freedom. So the theological conversation will end by describing what a non-competitive freedom might look like. If that is a strange notion, then it only shows the extent of the differences that exist between economic freedom which expresses itself in the market, and the freedom which rests in the nature of God's own being.

Biblical choices: salvation and destiny

The perspective of the New Testament on choice is very different from that of an economist deducing the implications of utility maximisation. The New Testament presents choices which can result, not just in 'preference satisfaction', but in salvation. Salvation means the fulfilment of human destiny which is seen as having an ultimate end or goal. Choices, therefore, become decisions made in a perspective of the final goals of human existence. Such salvation creates wholeness in human life.

One of the greatest differences between an economic (or, more generally, a consequentialist) model and a theological one when thinking about choice is that for a religious person, such as a Christian, or a Jewish believer at the time of the Old Testament, choice is constrained by the prior reality of God's saving action. Before we choose, God has intervened on our behalf. The literature of the Bible is saturated with this belief in the prior (technically prevenient: going before our choice) grace of God.[52]

What is distinctive then in both the Old and New Testament is that the essence of humanity comes not from who we are, but as a gift from God, given from the future. The essence of humanity is a destiny that lies beyond the empirical reality of the existing life of a person. So human beings move beyond what surrounds them at the moment. Salvation takes on a more precise meaning. It occurs when the future destiny of a person is united with her past and present existence. In human terms, such salvation is not obtained in this life. As St Augustine put it (*Sermon 103*): 'Thither we make our way, still as pilgrims, not yet at rest; still on the road, not yet home; still aiming at it, not yet attaining it.'

52 Fergusson, D. and Sarot, M., *The Future as God's Gift*, T and T Clark, 2000.

There is no way a person is then able to rank the combination of goods (material or otherwise, such as happiness, peace, or joy) and decide which combination of them they want in salvation. Nor can one decide to have a little more of one commodity and less of another, as was described in the previous section on utility maximisation. Neither are consumers in the religious world (if such a term may be allowed) able to compare baskets of salvation. One cannot rank love, joy and peace, and place them in an order of personal preference, thus choosing love above joy, joy above peace, and so love above peace. Such suggestions show the absurdity of introducing preferential terms into the search for God, and the gifts of God. This puts a severe warning, incidentally, against the way some churches do promote their wares on the media, in contemporary society, but a discussion of modern evangelistic techniques is a digression from the argument which must remain a comparison between economics and theology.

Is the choice (in the language of the Gospels of the New Testament) of the disciple to seek first the Kingdom of God able to be described then as rational in any meaningful sense? Certainly, as we have seen above, Brian Griffiths believes that Christian behaviour can be described as made up of choices which are rational as well as 'moral and feeling'. Nevertheless, the account given above about Christian salvation is not one about calculation, and the expectation of satisfaction. The New Testament ethicist Schrage distinguishes between discipleship and self-interest. Although there are passages in the New Testament written in the style of an appeal to self-interest, with an emphasis on rewards and punishments, Schrage argues that such passages are only a prolegomenon to a new vision of the Kingdom of God.

The Kingdom of God is that action by God which will bring salvation to human beings and which in the New Testament is linked with the life and fate of Jesus of Nazareth. The essence of humanity lies in the fulfilment of her destiny which is given by God. Humanity finds its ultimate meaning in being open to God, and this too is the real meaning of the structure of being human. Only when there is true openness to God is there a possibility of fulfilment of one's destiny.

The revelation associated with the New Testament turns these general points about salvation, and openness to one's destiny, into a specific set of claims about how God has acted. At this point it is important to spell out the claims made above about how God's grace is always prior to human action. First, the actions associated with Jesus are ones of forgiveness, healing, reconciliation and love. Through these actions Jesus promises community with himself during his life. Nevertheless, the claims which the New Testament makes, are such that it may be that this community or presence with Jesus can endure beyond his death. Secondly, the significance of Jesus is that his fate reveals the destiny of human beings themselves. Such claims are controversial, and can be made in an imperious and exclusive manner. Nevertheless, the New Testament argues first that there is such a thing as an ultimate choice; secondly, that this can be made in a religious manner, and is therefore construed as salvation; thirdly, that such a choice can be a gift of God in and through particular events.

The New Testament describes these events as about the Kingdom, or eschatology. Schrage writes:[53]

> For Jesus, ethics is a consequence of eschatology, not merely in the sense that it serves to prepare humanity [...] It is also an inescapable consequence in the sense that it is the only reasonable response to the Kingdom of God already at hand in Jesus.

Eschatology thus determines all choices in the perspective of the New Testament. The mystery of Jesus is that he claims the moment of truth has intersected time. The encounter with the Kingdom is described in such a way that the Kingdom can be entered. It is a realm into which one can move, both in terms of meaning and existence.

Economic theory describes how people plan ahead. In this perspective there is an evaluation of alternative actions, and of their likely consequences. The actions follow one after another, and the meaning which they have for the agent, depends on how far they fulfil his or her preferences. The biblical viewpoint is different. Pannenberg argues that in the biblical tradition the new and surprising events occurring in history are seen as fundamental to the ultimate reality which is history. Events do not follow on in a meaningless way. Yet, neither are these events given meaning by the choices of the agent.

53 Schrage, W., *The Ethics of the New Testament*, T and T Clark, 1996.

The biblical account sees the God of the Bible as giving a fundamental historical continuity within the series of events. Each action by God is related to earlier actions. Furthermore, the later event sheds light on the earlier happening. This is not a form of early evolutionary theory, but rather a belief in an active presence within history. Such a presence is known as the faithfulness of God. Faithfulness relates present and past events in a particular way.

This is because the Bible argues for the activity of God as being determined by his adherence to certain principles. Within the sweep of historical events there are choices made by God, in which the principles of the election of Israel and the creation of humanity remain firm. Hence human choices are placed within the parameters of divine choice. As argued above, this choice is expressed in the gift of salvation to God's people, and the actions of forgiveness and healing.

Rationality and biblical choices

In the section on economics and rational choice, the argument then moved after the discussion of utility maximisation to that of rationality. As we saw, rationality in economics can be extended to include decisions which will constrain future choices. The theological account of utility maximisation is very different from that of economics. Equally distinct is the way theology might approach rationality.

What distinguishes a biblical perspective on choice is that it presupposes a particular view of rationality. The way choices are made in the Bible does not turn on (quoting from earlier in this chapter) a calculation based on 'the expectation of satisfaction using a probability distribution'. Rather, choices depend on what the New Testament describes as perception, insight or vision. This analogy of seeing is used to illustrate the fact that sight may be more or less clear. In so far as there is true insight, choices can be made correctly. The economist may concede (again to quote from this chapter) that 'we really do not know what we want to do [...] Choice is not an effortless task. It requires calculation, imagination and will', but a theologian would say that the right choice depends on illumination.

The New Testament makes a strong claim that if the vision is correct, then the choices will follow in the right way. The vision of the Kingdom, or of salvation, is predominant in the Synoptic Gospels. In the Epistles the language varies. Paul in 1 Corinthians 13 argues that we have 'put away childish things'. We move towards the light of day, in which God will be seen as he is. This knowledge is not a conceptual grasp, but rather a sharing in the divine life. When this sharing is complete, then choices will be made in a way that is synonymous with the life of God.

Yet, even in this life which is lived now, there is a change in the person which affects the choices made. The reference to 'liberty' in 2 Corinthians 3:17 means that the Christian life is not a possessed state but a changing reality. Life in the Spirit is 'a straining forward to what lies ahead' (Philippians 3:13) or a transformation into glory by the action of God. What, however, most marks these biblical passages is an awareness of suffering, failure and rejection. The motivation for choice is described as sharing in 'newness of life' (Romans 6:4), and a new capacity for love.

This means that rationality is reconceived as an enlargement of the understanding's scope, where there is an awareness of the presence of God in history. This led the early Christian community to a rejection of norms, expectations, and conventions. Their experience became extremely risky, and they frequently experienced persecution. Many New Testament scholars have explored the nature of this 'alternative culture' in the past few decades. Yet it would be a grave mistake to portray this as a cult mentality, in which the only rationality is that of the leader, and there is a fidelity to the demands of the cult. Rather, the New Testament places both choices and rationality within the perspective of a belief in a greater spiritual reality. The presence of the Kingdom and the demands which a response to this kingdom make on spiritual self-awareness means that the language is broken and episodic. Nevertheless this formation in love is a process of deeper understanding. Only on the basis of such understanding can choices be made. These choices are not the weighing of preferences (though they may involve deliberation about different actions) but rather are about the attempt to embody a particular style of life. Rationality is embraced by the religious tradition in which the goal is a more comprehensive understanding of reality.[54]

Choosing how to choose

The neo-classical account of imitative behaviour is able to reconcile it with rational decisions made by individuals. Such a model is not sociological, but instead one based on economic theory. We have also seen how addiction, whether to drink or to religion, can be interpreted as a rational choice. One model suggested by Christian theology is somewhat different again, and turns on liturgy or participation in worship. This is different from the experience of conversion, in which a binary model of choice or judgement is presented. Instead, the participation in worship socialises the religious person in particular ways which are neither reducible to peer-group pressure (the sociological model) nor learning by observing others (economic theory). The dynamics of the liturgy are internalised within the participant, so that the choices become an expression of the person's character or 'being'. In the language used by some economists, it changes not only one's preferences, but one's 'meta-preferences' as well.

Choices can be formed by the act of participating in the worship of the church. The Anglican theologian Christopher Jones uses the sociological concept of 'structuration' to show how individuals can be shaped both by rules and resources from a particular community.[55] This is akin to the Christian understanding of tradition, especially since the sociological meaning refers to 'rules and resources which focus relations of mediation and transformation in social systems'. Their 'structural properties' are 'the institutional features which give solidity to their life across time and space'. Jones points out that

54 Placher, W. C., *Unapologetic Theology*, Westminster, 1989.

55 See his article 'Loosing and Binding: The Liturgical Mediation of Forgiveness', in McFadyen, A. and Sarot, M (eds.), *Forgiveness and Truth*, T and T Clark, 2002.

examples of such resources and properties within Christianity would be scripture, liturgies and creeds.

Rules have a normative character within a community. They make possible how individuals can learn (and be conditioned to accept) social roles. Such rules need not be explicit and articulated, but are rather more often generalisable procedures that embody meaning. As Jones says, believers encounter in worship the presence and activity of God. Here, Jones refers to another philosopher, Michael Polanyi, who suggests how personal knowledge is structured in ways that can guide our actions. We indwell our frames of knowledge, so that we understand and act through them. Polanyi refers to this process as 'indwelling'. As we monitor this process, we modify our knowledge, so that it becomes more adequate and universally valid. Frameworks of knowledge are similar to tools. They are assimilated to our bodies as instruments of perception and action. Polanyi argues that knowledge has a practical dimension, or in other words, is a skill to be acquired in its use, application and orientation. There are two forms of awareness which human beings employ. Focal awareness is where attention is brought to bear on the object of our perception. Subsidiary awareness is where we indwell the framework of knowledge through which we perceive.

By using the sociological understanding of structuration (the shaping of individuals into roles within a society by a communal process) and the philosophy of Polanyi, Jones argues that choices are shaped in a particular way for a religious person. Participation in the liturgy focuses attention on the activity of God. This provides a link back to the eschatology described earlier, and the coming of the Kingdom of God in the life, death and resurrection of Jesus. The liturgy recounts this in a particular way. However, worshippers are aware in a subsidiary manner of the words and actions which make up the liturgy. The words and actions are only the means by which we indwell the account of eschatology, and the activity of God in the life of Jesus Christ.

Liturgy, therefore, serves two crucial roles. It links the believer with the past actions of two thousand years ago, making them present in the life of the individual here and now. Theologically, Christianity speaks of the action of God in the Spirit making this possible: there is no such thing as 'mere memory', either in the Jewish or Christian tradition. Secondly, liturgy shapes the choices which an individual Christian makes in her life, so that there is a pattern in the behaviour adopted. Such behaviour is a response to the perception of the eschatology made present once more (or re-presented) in the liturgy, and it is a formed, or structured, behaviour.

Much could be said about how liturgy functions to shape human activities. One example must suffice. In the service of Holy Communion (otherwise called the Mass, Lord's Supper or Eucharist) the believer is taken back to the Last Supper of Jesus, on the night of his betrayal. Jesus enacted a symbolic meal which was both the liturgy of the Jewish Passover, and also the inauguration of a new liturgy. What was novel was precisely the eschatological element embodied in this meal. The Passover commemorated the inauguration of a covenant between God (Yahweh) and the Jewish people. It referred to a unique redemptive act of God which was the exodus from Egypt of the Jewish people. Jesus, by celebrating the Passover, as any Jewish person would have done, links the meal to his forthcoming death. This death is done 'for the forgiveness of sins' (Matthew 26:28) and it also looks forward to the anticipation of feasting when the Kingdom of God comes fully. As Paul puts it in 1 Corinthians 11:26, 'we proclaim the Lord's death until he comes'.

In this act of worship, the believer is re-incorporated into the action of God. Choices are made because of the renewed acquaintance of the believer with the presence of Jesus in judgement, forgiveness and hope. The intended choices which should be made are those of reconciliation between God, humanity and the environment. How the Church can embody forgiveness and reconciliation in the actions of its individual members is the task of its lived discipleship.

This chapter has set out two entirely different accounts of choice. One is based on preferences, utility maximisation and rationality. It is deeply individualist, value free and a-historical. At any time in human history, in any society, a neo-classical economist could predict by what processes of reasoning an individual might make a choice. Political, social or cultural forces might constrain her imagination, but in principle, her actions are free. The Christian account could not be more different. It presupposes a different understanding of rationality, and of history. It turns on the memory of certain events, but the primary focus is not one of memory. Rather participation in communal practices engenders a sense of hope for the future, and Jesus offers the gift of forgiveness and new life. Choices are made within a value-laden tradition in which all activities are filled with the quest for reconciliation and peace.

Free will and predestination

We come finally to a very different type of argument. Freedom in economics means that choices are really made by agents who know what they are doing. The choices made by an agent may constrain the choices open to another, but no one can be compelled to choose anything other than what (in the circumstances) they actually want.

Al McFadyen[56] has pointed out that we 'have been culturally attuned to regard divine and human freedom as competitive'. It appears as if God and humanity both have freedom. There is a different sort of competition here. If God has more of anything, then humanity must have less. It seems as if we are faced with a dilemma. It has often been argued, even by those who defend Christianity, that it is necessary to obey God's will and sacrifice our own, so that our freedom is swallowed up in God's. We can either become the servants of the divine will and reject our own freedom, or we can assert our freedom in a Promethean way against God. There is, it appears, a fundamental dichotomy between autonomy of the self and heteronomy of a transcendent other. Pride is at the root of this opposition to God.

Why does this argument matter? Ultimately the liberal sceptic will have a shrewd suspicion that religious people do not really believe in choice or rationality at all. There is only the will of God and the choices which flow from God's will. The true description of rationality is the rationality which God decrees as rational. If God decrees killing someone, then that is what is meant by rationality. Such an argument will strike the sceptic as bogus, and pulling the

56 McFadyen, A., 'Sins of Praise: The Assault on God's Freedom', in Gunton, C. (ed.), *God and Freedom*, T and T Clark, 1995.

ground out from below the feet of the Christian, who up to now has been discussing the nature of free choice in apparently the same way as a secular philosopher or a neo-classical economist. In the previous theological sections on the nature of choice it is true that the conclusions are unlike those of economic theory, as are the values in the argument, but the overall discussion seemed the same. But if free choice is only doing the command of God, and God decrees everything, then the whole argument seems at risk.

It is true that there certainly are theologians who have gone down this road, and appear to be determinist. Nevertheless, it is important that the argument is refuted, so that Christians can enter the debate on the nature of choice alongside secular disciplines. The debate about the relationship of God and humanity turns on how their relationship is understood. The determinist argument sets up an antagonism between God and humanity. There is God, and there is a human being. One must 'give way' to the other. But this is only so if God is like a physical body and humanity like another. Two bodies cannot occupy the same space. Like the cuckoo in the nest, one must force the other out. Nor can one body be in two spaces at the same time.

Even if God can 'dwell in me' this assertion of divine power nevertheless subjugates my autonomy. The liberal sceptic does not believe that it is possible to have freedom if God comes along, for God will take over. Freedom in this view is a protection of one's own space. The reason for not believing in God is to protect ones own space, or freedom. The biblical account is not really about choices and preferences at all.

It is possible to rephrase this in far more abstract language, drawing on philosophical definitions of personhood. Freedom is an exclusive orientation to an asocial or autonomous centre through which autonomy is guaranteed in self-possession. Freedom in many secular disciplines, including neo-classical economics, must first be found within one's self before one enters into any relationship. This is true even before a person enters into a commercial, or market, relationship. But Christianity will not let one do that, for God must have his due first. The self is not allowed to protect its freedom first, for God will not permit this. So in this argument, Christianity is a threat to freedom.

However there is a substantial reply to this criticism of Christianity. It is that orthodox Christianity holds together God and humanity in a non-competitive manner. Whatever the conceptual difficulties, this is where Christianity must begin. Only then can the ambiguities and paradoxes in such discourse be explored, and a means found of responding to the issues of rationality and coherence. McFadyen refutes the determinist argument by insisting on seeing freedom as a relational form of freedom.

The central point of his argument is that the analogy of physical space for God's transcendence and God's presence must be replaced by social conceptions of space. The incarnation is not an[57]

> invasion of our space, but an invitation into freedom. For in Christ, God is present in an orientation towards and radically for us all. And in that being for us and movement towards us, we are taken seriously in our integrity and freedom and called freely to participate.

The space occupied by God and humanity is one which they both can share together.

The reason for this claim cannot simply rest on a bare assertion that true human freedom is not in competition with divine freedom. Nor does the argument turn on the fact that even if as religious believers we must apparently give up freedom, nevertheless there was a time when we were free to make that decision. For there must be recognition that freedom certainly existed at the point of decision to respond to the call of Christ.

Instead the claim that God and humanity are not in competition starts from a different point. McFadyen justifies his argument by a reconception of the nature of God. He spells out his case. God is a community of persons in movement towards and present in creation. In God's inner life, there is the giving of space to one another, in the mutuality of three Persons. So it is because of the Trinity that there can be a different understanding of freedom. If God is different, then the relationship between God and humanity can also be different. If that can be different, then in turn the understanding of freedom can be different from the modern liberal. It is possible to appeal to the nature

57 ibid.

of God in any argument without also having to surrender one's freedom in the way which the liberal believes is necessary. So the whole argument is transformed. Because of the Trinity, it is possible to have a richer, deeper account of freedom, which does not involve giving up one's space to the celestial cuckoo.

The argument about the Trinity can be spelled out in depth. Each member of the Trinity gives and receives their very being and their individuality from one another. Each has personal integrity, and the giving of space is interpersonal. There is no competition for space. There is an indwelling of identities in mutual love, joy and freedom, so that each is present with one another in 'creative recognition of their autonomy within the relationship'.[58] This divine reciprocity of giving and receiving of being sustains the whole life of creation, and therefore human existence.

Transcendence, by which is meant the existence, nature and presence of God's own being, becomes more analogous to personal co-presence, in which the dynamic of the divine life offers human beings a new and more fulfilling life of freedom. The dichotomy of heteronomy (the demands of another) and autonomy is superseded. Instead, there is an ongoing transformation of the world at the point of its greatest damage and brokenness.

The argument advanced above is for a reconceptualisation of freedom, similar to, yet subtly different, from the freedom which modern liberals respect, or even take for granted as absolutely fundamental. Autonomy indeed can be prized on this account, but it is a different kind of autonomy. This freedom, or autonomy, is a gift of God. However just because one says that freedom is a gift of God it does not follow that this giving puts the recipient in a threatened or dependent relationship which undermines their well being. God's freedom and sovereignty are not threats to this human autonomy. Our freedom is then in the end a freedom to respond, and this leads into a celebration of the appropriate, and still free, response. Response leads in due course into our recognition of our responsibility before the call of God, which can be a dialogue of partnership. It is a relational form of autonomy which is intensified in praise and thanksgiving.

58 ibid.

Christianity argues for the need for conversion. What is important is that in this account of conversion the Christian account of free will allows for the presence of an 'other' that is called God. That 'other', or the Trinity, for that is who God is, has a dynamic all of its own. This stems from its own nature which moves toward us. So conversion is a move to a new, but not coercive, kind of freedom. It is the ultimate affirmation of our free choice, and how we learn how to choose. It is appropriate to use the language of re-centring, in which our spirit is reoriented to a centre where there is a relationship with God. So the self finds a centre, an identity and a reality at the heart of its own being. God is present at the heart of our being.

Sin also remains central in this reformulated account of self. The critique of self is expressed as the discernment of other values than the ones presently expressed in behaviour or attitudes. Sin is the inability to image what a response to this movement might be, either because of a disbelief in the reality of 'the other', who is God, or (more commonly) because of an unwillingness to accept that 'the other' can determine one's own action. This more earthed disbelief is made up of a mixture of incredulity that there is anything transcendent to one's self which could influence our own being, and a reluctance to accept that there are implications of the existence of a transcendent reality. So, as Al McFadyen says, there is a danger of the abandonment of faith and hope. He writes:[59]

> If the further condition is not met, that one believes oneself to be forgiven, affirmed, upheld, given, worth something – precisely in the integrity and particularity of one's being the belief in God, and praise of God, become impossible.

It is possible to spell out this answer to the sceptic in another way as well. This is to turn to the New Testament account of the life of Jesus. The story of the cross and resurrection is one of making the death of Jesus an event in which evil, sin and death are overcome. Death is not disallowed, but rather the finality of that death becomes the means by which there is an anticipation of the final victory of life over death, and freedom over evil. This story cannot again be construed in terms

59 ibid.

of physical space, in which one (greater) body, who is God, occupies the presence of another (lesser) body, who is Jesus on earth. The analogy of transcendence/humanity as physical bodies is inadequate. This is because the New Testament sees a unity between God and humanity in Christ. There is an integrity of divinity and humanity together in which neither the transcendence of the divine sovereignty nor the freedom of humanity is compromised.

All this may seem far removed from the earlier discussion of utility maximisation, rationality and freedom, and so in a way it is. Yet it is worth demonstrating how God as Trinity enhances the freedom of the Christian, and how the suspicion that God and humanity are in competition is fundamentally a false notion.

Section Three: Summary and Discussion

Human beings are rational creatures, able to foresee the consequences of their actions, and to choose what they will do. In modern times this has been essential to our definition of human nature. Enlightened by reason, we can free ourselves from the limitations of instinct, tradition, ignorance and authority, so as to achieve our self-selected goals. It is a brave vision of human potential, rather than a sober assessment of what we are really like.

Economic theory takes this ideal as its model of actual behaviour. The standard model explains what people do in terms of their aims, not in terms of their genes, their upbringing, their emotions, or the norms of the society to which they belong. In the standard model, all depends on calculation and on preferences between alternative outcomes. This is choice as seen from the inside, the way that we might explain or defend our own decisions, not the way that they might be described by an outside observer.

In the Bible human beings are different from the rest of creation in that they are made in the image of God. It follows that we are free to make choices, and responsible for what we do. But we find our fulfilment in serving God, not in going our own way. The need to choose is a challenge that confronts us, a call which must be answered one way, or the other. It involves much more than just our actions; it requires also a change of our values, our objectives, our preferences; and it means we must repent of our past. It is a choice between different ways of life. It may be a once-for-all conversion, or it may be a slow process of discovery. We redefine ourselves by the choices that we make, and our subsequent behaviour will confirm our new identity.

It is tempting, especially in modern times, to model religious choice within a rational framework. There are many different religions to choose between, or we can have no religious allegiance at all. The consequences of that choice may depend in fact, or at least seem to depend, on which religious belief is actually correct. They may include prosperity rather than hardship in this life if our prayers are answered; they may involve heaven rather than hell in the life to come. It can be seen as a matter of placing one's bets, and the stakes are very high indeed. There are, indeed, passages in the Bible which encourage this kind of calculation, and it was made famous by the philosopher Pascal. But this model of religious choice might be questioned, on different grounds, both by economists and by theologians.

The standard model of choice in economic theory can be applied only when the probability of different outcomes can be estimated by some means. With limited information, one can still be rational; but with no information at all what is required is more in the nature of a leap of faith. Arguably this is the position of the true agnostic when confronted by the claims of many rival religions. The reasoning behind a leap cannot be rational in quite the sense that economic theory uses that word.

Christian belief may be happy enough with the notion of reasonable faith, but it may be unhappy with a different aspect of the Pascal model. It does not easily concede that correct religious choices can be made for essentially selfish reasons. Those who believe in God may want to deny that there is any fundamental conflict between the service of God and our true self-interest. But one has to believe in God before one can accept that proposition. In modern times it does not seem self-evident, as it might have done when the Bible was written.

We therefore may feel that there is something unacceptable about the concept of the eternal payoff, to which earlier generations had no objection. We have perhaps become more fastidious in this respect, believing that virtue should be its own reward – a view which is never expressed in the Bible.

A more fundamental question still would be whether this account of choice, based on introspection, is anything more than a flattering illusion, a rationalisation after the event. Can we really choose at all, or is our behaviour predetermined? There is discord on this matter within modernism itself: on the one hand there is a strong attachment to liberty – moral, political and religious; on the other there is the ambition of science to explain and control human behaviour alongside all else. There is a kind of social engineering, a kind of psychological medicine which treats human beings as objects instead of subjects. Some economists have been attracted by that model, and the political philosophy which goes with it. But this is not the spirit of mainstream neo-classical economics, which has been associated with a very high regard for individual freedom and deep distrust of any programme, however well intentioned, that could prove to be 'The Road to Serfdom'.

Christian belief raises similar questions about predestination, and the relationship between God's choices and our own. If God knows, and determines in advance, what we are bound to choose, then are we really free at all? One way of describing this is in terms of creation and incarnation. There is a tension between the relationship between God's gift at creation of freedom to humanity, which puts a distance between humanity and God, and the indwelling of God, as spoken of in the Pauline letters where the Spirit indwells in the Christian. Yet somehow these two perspectives are both correct.

Clearly there are great differences between the ways in which economic theory and Christian belief describe the process of choice. We do not seek to minimise them or regard them as unimportant. But we would wish also to emphasise the elements that both have on common. Both take seriously the motives of which we are conscious, and our ability to foresee what the consequences of our actions will be. In this they contrast with the suspicious approach to self-awareness encouraged by post-modern philosophy. They are also united in opposition to the Marxist notion of false consciousness, and the Freudian analysis of unconscious motivation. Currently they are both at odds with the latter-day Darwinians. Human beings are fundamentally different from other animals. Rationality, however bounded it may be, is a very important part of that difference.

Chapter Three

Individualism and Group Behaviour

Introduction

In his monumental work, *Foundations of Social Theory*, James Coleman describes individualism as:[60]

> A broadly perpetuated fiction [...] that society consists of a set of independent individuals, each of whom acts to achieve goals that are independently arrived at, and that the functioning of the social system consists of the combination of these actions of independent individuals.

Neo-classical economic theory takes this for granted. One way of describing its purpose would be to say that it seeks to explain social (or aggregate) outcomes in terms of the decisions taken by individuals. That is its approach to questions about how the economy works. With this is associated an approach to normative issues which is equally individualistic. The well-being of society consists of the well-being of its members. These views are perhaps most often stated in opposition to 'holistic' accounts of political life, the behaviour and well-being of class or nation. But individualism is also in sharp contrast with religious beliefs, not least with Christianity. How could one speak of 'independent individuals' within the church if it is described as the body of Christ? There is not only an ethical issue here, but also an ontological one.

In this chapter we shall be examining these issues. Clearly, in doing so, we are not just comparing economic theory and Christian belief. We are looking at the political and social philosophy to which neo-classical economics belongs. But economics is a good place to begin such a debate, because the precision of its reasoning makes the

60 Coleman, J. S., *Foundations of Social Theory*, Harvard UP, 1990.

contrast particularly sharp. It even poses the difficult question as to what a rigorous alternative to the assumption of individualism might actually be.

Individualism is an assumption about the way in which decisions are taken and not about their motives or purposes. It does not mean that individuals are selfish, or even that they are self-interested; they may be altruistic or idealistic if that is what they want to be. It does mean that individuals think for themselves, in the sense that they make up their own minds what they want to do. This, as the quotation from a leading proponent of individualism recognises, is a 'fiction', an assumption that is made in the knowledge that it is untrue. It might even be called a myth.

As individuals, of course, we interact with the communities to which we belong. Our tastes, our values, the rights we claim, even the needs we feel, depend on the social norms which we adopt from the social environment in which we live. No one could seriously pretend that the preferences of individuals are their own unaided invention. We have each become who we are now as a result of the relationships that we have had in the past. Our genetic inheritance is that of a social animal, designed to function as part of a group. Neo-classical economics adopts an essentially reductionist programme. The fact that society also has a cultural, moral and political life is not so much denied as ignored.

But the question remains whether society really is no more than the sum of its parts. Do people in fact take decisions together? When they meet do people in fact each make up their own mind in advance and then seek to persuade one another? Or do they think differently just because they are deciding on behalf of a group which would suggest that the group has purposes and interests of its own? Fundamentally we are asking whether groups actually exist in the same sense that we all recognise the existence of individuals. Is it biological identity that matters, or is it something else?

It is easy to see the normative issues just below the surface of this debate. The attachment of individualists to their methodological position is not unrelated to the moral and political belief that individuals should be free to take their own decisions wherever possible.[61] Somewhere in the back of the mind there is a citizen protesting against oppressive laws, an artist with the courage to break free from convention, the slave in revolt against the master, the child struggling to escape from domineering parents. The self has to be realised and asserted; individualism asserts that it is real.

In an encyclopaedia article on 'Individualism', Alan Macfarlane writes:[62]

> Although it is usually conceded that there was a long individualistic tradition in western civilisation, somehow linked to Christianity, it is often assumed that the eighteenth century with the rise of market capitalism, saw a new order of things.

This quotation brings together the religious and economic foundations of modern individualism. Today, it is the community side of religion that is most often stressed, in contrast to the extreme individualism of the free market and its supporters. Christianity is becoming more consciously a group activity, but it also remains, as it always has been, an individual relationship as well. The feeling that each person is unique and precious, and the belief that each person is responsible for their own destiny – both of which are elements of modern individualism – are both, as the quotation says, 'somehow linked to Christianity', and always have been.

In Section One of this chapter we describe how standard economic theory approaches group behaviour within the assumption of individualism, for example its treatment of inequality. The theological material in Section Two is necessarily more elaborate since the reality of both individuals and groups has to be maintained and reconciled to one another. Thus one individual, Christ, can stand for many, and the church can be called his body.

61 See for example, Brittan, S., *Capitalism with a Human Face*, Chapter 4, Edward Elgar, 1995.

62 Macfarlane, A., 'Individualism', in Kuper, A. and J. (eds.), op. cit.

Section One: Economic Theory

Social capital and social contracts

An elementary textbook of economics is unlikely to include much discussion of individualism. It is simply assumed that the choices with which it is most concerned will be the choices made by individuals seeking their own interests. The theory of consumption is presented in terms of individuals, not of households; the theory of production is presented as being about firms, but there will be little or no discussion about how a corporate body reconciles the preferences of its members. This does not mean that economists are not interested in such issues, just that they are seen as rather too difficult or 'advanced' to include in an introductory course, and perhaps not essential to a good enough understanding of how the economy works. To an individualist the decision processes of groups are not easy to model at all.

It is possible to attach great importance to social relationships whilst remaining a methodological individualist. In the 'Foundations of Social Theory', Coleman develops the concept of 'social capital'. The idea is that relationships between individuals are a necessary part of the productive economy, like machinery and the skills of the workforce. Business needs a network of social contacts with suppliers, customers, financial institutions, employment agencies, research institutes and so on, in order to engage in profitable economic activity. The better these business relationships, the more efficient the business will be. This network is like a kind of capital because it takes time and effort to build up and to maintain, but when it is in being it makes a good return.

A network is a concept familiar to economists in many different contexts. A telephone system is a network enabling the subscribers to talk to one another. A transport system is a network enabling people to meet face to face. Each person who has access to the network gains, at least potentially, from the decision of all the others to link up with it. As the development of the Internet has shown, the growth of a network does not require a master plan or complex regulations. People make their own decisions whether to join. The more people there are who have joined already, the more advantageous membership becomes. Thus a social organisation develops spontaneously once it passes a critical stage. The commitment involved in joining a network is very limited, and membership can be terminated at any time.

At the other extreme there is the family, another kind of community with an economic function to perform. Family members know each other very well, and they usually trust one another better than they would trust anyone else. This is the basis for the family business. Notoriously, the quarrels within such close social units are proportionally bitter when they do occur. Families are not very flexible units: they are difficult to join and difficult to leave. Economic production often requires larger and less close groupings, whether these are tribes or villages or, in modern times, the company or firm. Although the sense of belonging is not as strong as it is in most families, these larger units are still bound together much more tightly than is the case with a network. They usually share a common culture, some common norms of behaviour, often local loyalties and perhaps a common religious allegiance.[63]

Individualists, including mainstream neo-classical economists, would, of course, acknowledge the importance of all these communities; but they would not ascribe to them any distinctive group identity. They are there to serve the interests of their members; society as such has no interests of its own. Obviously, there are goods and services which are enjoyed in common, like defence or clean air; but it is still individuals who do the enjoying, not some corporate being with thoughts and feelings of its own. Somehow the existence of any society at all needs to be explained – and indeed needs to be justified – as the result of individuals rationally pursuing interests of their own. In this way of viewing the life of all communities we can find the origins of the social contract myth.[64] It is a model which fits well with

63 The effects of social organisation on economic efficiency are addressed in Fukuyama, F., *Trust – The Social Virtues and the Creation of Prosperity*, Hamish Hamilton, 1995.

64 The design of social contracts, explicit or implicit, is well discussed in Chapter 3 of Dasgupta, P., *An Inquiry into Wellbeing and Destitution*, OUP, 1993.

neo-classical economics because it is about the social outcomes of rational decision making by individuals. There is, indeed, an overlap between economic theory and the political theory of democracy and human rights.

The social contract is a myth in the sense that no one seriously suggests that the first human society was founded in this way in the remote past. It may however be a necessary myth to give legitimacy to social institutions, and especially to the state. If only individuals have rights, or duties, or interests, or responsibilities, then how do social institutions come into existence with powers to coerce? Part of the explanation is that respect for the law, and the rights of property, are necessary for the foundation of a market economy.

Group decisions

If one starts from the assumption that only individuals have preferences, then it becomes a real problem to work out how groups can make decisions at all. We must begin by ruling out all notions of consensus, group loyalty or team spirit. Each individual knows perfectly well what he or she wants the outcome to be; the question is how those individual rankings can be reconciled with one another. This is the subject matter of the theory of social choice, a branch of economics or political theory with a strong appeal, both because of its potential use in policy-making and because of its mathematical rigour.[65]

This rigour was demonstrated in the 1950s when Kenneth Arrow produced his 'impossibility theorem'.[66] He specified five principles which seemed appropriate to any process of social choice in an individualistic world. They were:

1. If everyone prefers A to B, then A is better than B.
2. No one individual should be able to dictate group decisions.
3. The choice between A and B should depend only on individual preferences as between them.

65 See Chapter 12 of Hausman, D. M. and McPherson, M. S., op. cit.

66 Arrow, K. J., *Social Choice and Individual Value*, Wiley, 1951.

4. Social decision-making should be able to rank all alternatives.
5. If the social ranking says that A is better than B, and also that B is better than C, then it should also say that A is better than C.

Arrow was able to demonstrate conclusively that these five principles, all attractive in themselves, are mutually incompatible.

In practice, groups have to adopt other methods of reconciling individual preferences. One method is by majority voting. Many decisions are successfully made in this way. It is well known however that the outcome often depends crucially on the way in which the questions are put. As an extreme case, it is quite possible for majority decisions to be inconsistent. A majority may prefer A to B, B to C, but also C to A.

Voting on individual preferences is, in reality, the exception. Elected representatives take most group decisions. The representatives will sometimes be expected to vote according to their own preferences, sometimes according to what they think would be the preferences of the people they represent. The process of forming preferences for the group of constituents then has to go on in the mind of the representative. In a strictly individualistic world what the representatives will actually worry about is only trying to guess what pattern of voting behaviour is most likely to ensure their own re-election.

Representatives, or indeed economists giving policy advice, may adopt their own criteria of group welfare as a method of decision making on behalf of a community. They will invent for themselves what they regard as a 'social welfare function', that is to say a means of ranking alternative outcomes on behalf of the community. The task of policymakers is then one of optimisation, similar to that which faces the individual consumer with reference to a choice between alternative baskets of goods.

One very common approach is strictly utilitarian. This begins with two very strong and questionable assumptions: that individual utility is cardinal rather than ordinal; and that the utility of the group is the sum of the utility of its members. Utility or happiness is treated exactly like money income, or the intake of calories. The aim of group decisions is to maximise total group utility which is regarded as a measure like national income or national food consumption.

The most that can really be said for this procedure is that it provides a reasonably sensible answer to some practical questions. An economist advising a government whether to build a new road, for example, has to have some system of accounting in which the various costs and benefits can be scored. Even then there will usually be 'intangible items', like the need to pull down a unique historic monument, or to destroy the habitat of some rare species of snail.

Economists are continually confronted by the need to assess alternatives on behalf of a group or community. It is partly a matter of reconciling the interests of individuals, but sometimes there has also to be an appeal to a set of standards which are not thought of as purely subjective. That ancient building, for example, might be said to have value in its own right, even if most members of the community do not recognise it. When the choice is one of life and death, as it can be in health economics, then these external moral absolutes can dominate all other considerations.

There is another approach to group decisions which does not presume that a social welfare function exists at all. One can treat decision-making as the outcome of a process of bargaining amongst members. Thus the decisions made by a household can be seen as reflecting the preferences of its members, in particular the husband and the wife, but also the relative strengths of their bargaining positions. This will determine who goes out to work, and who gets most to eat; it will also determine the circumstances in which the marriage breaks up. Here we have an account of family life which may take account of feelings of mutual affection, but which is nevertheless uncompromisingly individualistic in its approach. Thus one interesting discussion of the contribution that bargaining theory can make to understanding household decisions, especially amongst the poor, ends with a reminder that, whatever model is used, the criterion for public policy choices should always be the well-being of individuals and not of households. In particular, even if household decisions are weighted in favour of husbands, policy should give equal weight to the well-being of wives.[67]

Social cohesion

Economists in the neo-classical tradition do not take easily to such concepts as social cohesion or social inclusion, because they do not think of society as a unit at all. They would need to redefine them in terms of individual opportunities of access. Thus poverty may exclude one from access to social networks and social capital. One great advantage of a market economy may indeed be the ability of everyone to participate in it. Tightly cohesive societies can be very effective in excluding non-members from economic opportunities, and economists are not slow to point this out.

It is often maintained that a society cannot be cohesive if the distribution of incomes within it is too wide. This is not, however, the usual justification for economists taking an interest in measures of inequality. A utilitarian economist might justify such an interest by a very simple, individualistic, argument. Suppose that the marginal utility of income declines as income itself increases; in other words income is subject to decreasing returns as a means of creating more happiness. Then taking income from the rich and giving it to the poor will always increase the sum of human happiness, right up to the point where everyone has the same level of income, and all are equally happy.

Those who think of complete equality as the ideal nevertheless acknowledge that it cannot be achieved without destroying the incentives which drive production. There has to be a compromise between the level of national income and its distribution.[68] The problem is to maximise total utility, subject to the constraint imposed by individual behaviour. A mathematical model can be built to calculate the optimum system for redistributing income through

67 Dasgupta, P., op. cit., Chapter 10.

68 Mirrlees, J. A., 'An Exploration in the Theory of Optimal Income Taxation', *Review of Economic Studies*, April 1971.

taxation and social security payments. At each point on the scale of original income a rate of net payment is set, taking account of the incentive effects of the marginal rate as well as the redistributive effects of the average rate. The model uses the calculus of variations to calculate the rate all along the scale simultaneously and consistently.

In fact many people who care about inequality mean by it something quite different from this:[69] they mean inequality of opportunity rather than inequality of outcomes. Nature is not fair in the distribution of innate abilities, but at least society can avoid adding to that unfairness by restricting access to sources of income. This appeals very strongly to an ethical kind of individualism. Each person is of equal importance, whatever their race, creed, sex or social class. It is individuals that count; and they each count the same. They should all have the same rights before the law, and they should all compete on the same terms in the market economy. The result will not, of course, be equality of income, but some would say that it is the process that is morally significant, not the outcome.

Section Two: Christian Belief

Individualism of the kind assumed by neo-classical economics is a modern idea, dating back perhaps two or three hundred years. Pre-modern societies, including many in the present day, would regard such autonomy as unnatural or unreal. Modern Christians in the pluralist societies of Europe or North America may find individualism appealing, but the assumptions of the Bible, and of earlier Christian centuries, are very different. Here then we find one fundamental contradiction between the views of both human behaviour and well-being which are found in the two systems of thought being compared in this book.

69 See Hausman, D. M. and McPherson, M. S., op. cit., Chapter 10 for a discussion of both equality and egalitarianism.

The Christian response to the economist's assumption of individualism will follow the same outline as Section One above. First, social contracts and capital will be examined. Secondly, there is the question of group decisions. Thirdly, social cohesion will be examined. Social cohesion in biblical theology is expressed as the representative individual or group. Group decisions focus in the covenant. Then there are the demands which follow from keeping the covenant. The covenant is enshrined in the Torah or law, and here we find a parallel to social cohesion.

However the theologian has something more to add. Even if we do not mention the biblical history, with its representative groups, its covenants and law keeping, the theologian would still not be an individualist in the way presupposed in neoclassical economics. This is because the theologian sees the world as relational from the beginning of creation. Methodological individualism is foreign to the theologian, and even from the creation of the animal kingdom right through to human kind there are inherently relationships. After exploring the theological account of social capital, we shall turn finally to the centrality of relationships for the individual in biblical theology.

The representative individual

It is not unusual in any social setting for one individual to represent a group. A salesman is the representative of a firm, a diplomat represents a government, and a legislator represents the electorate. The words and the decisions of the representative are supposed to be those of the group being represented. It is as if an individual could take on another identity, and play a different role. This may be very problematic for methodological individualism, but it is absolutely central to biblical theology.

The concept of the representative individual begins with that of Adam. Adam stands for the whole of humanity. Adam is created to be God's partner, and is entrusted with tasks. Adam in Genesis 5 is able to produce future generations which are described in detail. Thus the whole of humanity is seen as bound up in this one being Adam. In

Jude Enoch is described as being 'in the seventh generation from Adam'. Genesis 5 sets out the generations of Adam, since the divine likeness is transmitted through Adam. Adam names his son Seth, as God named him. This mythological narrative shows the power of corporate imagery, in which a particular individual (mythically endowed with the power to procreate at an advanced age, beyond human powers) is representative of all humanity. It demonstrates graphically how distinct the biblical view of the individual is from the one postulated by neoclassical economics.

It is above all in the calling of Israel that the representative comes to the fore. Israel stands before God as the one people whom God has called. The prophets recount the love of God for Israel, and it is clear that salvation is only found in and through belonging to the chosen people of God. In the demands that are given to Israel, God endows his people with a unique status in the world. Israel's sense of election was so strong that its chroniclers traced its election back to the creation of the world.[70] Here the sense of a group having a unique salvific status is far stronger than any modern individualist could ever give to a group.

The Jewish concept of the Son of God took this idea of being a representative further still. It was this concept on which the representative nature of the rulers of Israel had been built. The Judean king was called the Son of God in 2 Samuel 7:14 and in Psalm 89:26. Nathan makes a promise to David and the formula of enthronement and legitimisation in Psalm 2:7 expresses the same idea. In the Exodus tradition all the people of Israel are called the children of God (Deuteronomy 14:1).

Jesus saw himself as representative of his people, embodying in some sense the whole of humanity before God, and fulfilling in his short life the destiny of Israel. Contemporary theologians such as Pannenberg have laid great stress on the way in which Jesus was representative of humanity before God, both in his life and his death.[71]

The question whether Jesus himself ever used the title 'Son' centres on the interpretation of Matthew 11:27 which runs 'No one

70 Pannenberg, W., *Systematic Theology*, Volume 2, T and T Clark, 1994.

71 Pannenberg, W., *Jesus God and Man*, SCM, 1968.

knows the Father except the Son'. This text has been much argued over as to whether it represents the authentic words of Jesus, or a reworking of them. However this discussion is resolved, it is clear that the unique Sonship of Jesus means that the sonship of Jesus carries representative status for Christians. He is the Son for all those who are sons of God. The representative nature of Jesus is seen at this point. Equally the even more problematic set of sayings which concern the words 'Son of Man' show, in the words of the German Roman Catholic theologian Walter Kasper, that Jesus is the representative of all humanity. He writes:[72]

> The complex and mysterious phrase 'Son of Man' indicates that Jesus is the eschatological representative of God and his kingdom, and also the representative of man. The cause of God and man is decided in him and through him. He brings God's grace and God's judgement.

This is a much more clear-cut assertion of representation than most modern thought would find comfortable. 'Son of Man' in Ezekiel or in the Psalms is a term which sums up the whole of humanity, and at the least Jesus is drawing on this tradition. There is a complex set of additional meanings which could be adduced, but at the very least the way in which Jesus represents humanity, when that title becomes his, must be noted as defining the reason for his mission.

It is no surprise therefore that he was soon seen this way in the letters of the New Testament. Christ is seen in the New Testament as humanity before God, the 'first-born of many brothers' in the words of Romans 8:29. As such he represents humanity before God, and the claim to be the final expression of the truth of humanity is unsurpassable. When Paul calls the followers of Christ children of God, he is reworking that idea, but it is possible because believers receive the Spirit of sonship[73] where in the New Testament the sense in which Jesus represents both God and humanity becomes stronger yet. This is clearest in the fourth Gospel where Jesus says, for example, 'Anyone who has seen me has seen the Father'. The very least that this means is that Jesus represents God to humanity. At the

72 Kasper, W., *Jesus The Christ*, Sheed and Ward, 1976.
73 Pannenberg ,W., *Systematic Theology*, Volume 2, T and T Clark, 1994.

same time the whole sacrificial interpretation of his death implies that Jesus represents humanity to God. He died 'for us'. As compared with modern ways of thought, the idea of a representative individual is central to biblical thought. Christians can say that they 'share in' the death of Jesus, hoping therefore to share in his resurrection.

Indeed Pannenberg sees his death as a substitute for Israel and for humanity.[74] Out of this death comes the church as the body of Christ, in which representative body individuals participate in the new life inaugurated by Christ's death and resurrection.

From covenant to church

The question is raised in Section One above as to how groups make decisions at all. There are representatives who are elected to this task, but the representation is only by election in a democracy: in no sense do the representatives 'stand' for the people. Once again we see how different the ideas of group decisions were in biblical theology, whether in the Old Testament or the New.

The covenant is a central theme in both the theology of the Old and New Testaments. The identity of the Israelite community rested on the covenant, as it was celebrated in worship.[75] Much of the worship of Israel was carried on in ways not very different from other religions and cultures. What was distinctive was the covenant itself. It was the relationship between Yahweh (the Old Testament description for God) and Israel during the departure, or exodus, of Israel from Egypt. In Exodus 20 the core features of the covenant were given. The moral concern of Yahweh, and the manner in which historical actions were ascribed to Yahweh, show the covenant as being central to the identity of Israel. The community of Israel felt itself bound by this covenant, and those who were born into Israel equally accepted the demands of the legal framework. Here is an example of a decision

74 Pannenberg, W., *Jesus God and Man*, SCM, 1968.

75 The classic expression of this theology is Eichrodt, W., *The Theology of the Old Testament*, Volumes 1 and 2, SCM, 1967 or, Rowley, H. H., *The Biblical Doctrine of Election*, Lutterworth, 1950.

ascribed to the group as such, as if the group had a collective mind of its own – a concept quite unacceptable to an individualist.

Although the religious order in the Old Testament is often seen as one covenant, the use of the Hebrew word *berit* appears especially in the Deuteronomic history, including the second book of Kings and the book of Jeremiah. It would appear that in the late seventh and sixth centuries BC the term came into popularity. It may well have been that an older idea of covenant was reordered at this time. The covenant with Abraham in Genesis 15:18 gives him possession of the land of Canaan. Some recent theologians, such as Keith Whitelaw, have argued that this is a theological device to legitimate the silencing of Palestinian history.[76] Other theologians have argued that the origin of the covenant may well lie in the vassal treaties which were made in the ancient Near East at this time between victorious powers and other conquered states.

The framework is spelled out in Exodus 20. Imageless religion meant that the worship of Yahweh could never be located in a particular focus. Yahweh was seen as transcendent and active. Nevertheless, since this was a highly moral relation, the next provision was the ordering of the Sabbath. Time was seen as having a regular structure which remembered the creation of the world and Yahweh's rest on the seventh day, and gave thanks for it. Although Yahweh was an active deity, nevertheless rest was an important part of his relationship to his creation, and rest was therefore honoured as part of the natural order of the world. The third aspect of the legal framework is an ethic of respect for property, image, life and above all relations within the family.

Social cohesion

All this meant that the individual was placed within the demands of a particular social framework. In the previous chapter on rational choice there was a reference to the Passover which was based on the unique

76 Whitelam, K., *The Invention of Ancient Israel: The Silencing of Palestinian History*, Routledge, 1996.

redemptive act by Yahweh in liberating the Jewish people. In the Israelite understanding of social cohesion the demands of keeping the Passover, and the rest of the Torah, become paramount.

Jewish theologians have argued that what it means to be Jewish is to accept the demands of their faith. Being a faithful Jew is to live with an awareness of the demands of social cohesion uppermost in one's mind. This of course means that it is difficult for this community to change, and it becomes inevitably a conservative body. However the point at issue is not how much a community might change, but what the theological analogue to our modern concern with social cohesion might be. Inequality and equality in this respect become subsumed into the demands of being faithful to the calling of the covenant.

Michael Wyschogrod is one such Jewish scholar who has argued that Jewish theology can never be about individual self-consciousness, but about living out the embodied being of Israel. He says that the true glory of Israel is not found in the individual acts of heroism but in the actions of ordinary men and women. It is a moving quotation which pays tribute to the unknown masses who are not recorded in history:[77]

> Also the mute and heavy masses who have suffered for the covenant with a minimum of understanding and who have sinned because they responded to the craving of their flesh and the tiredness of their exile, whose significance they understood very little.

Other Christian theologians have taken up this idea of social cohesion. For example, Stanley Hauerwas quotes Wyschogrod with approval. The way in which the Christian Church is conceived by Hauerwas is significant. The church is seen as a social body constituted by practices and disciplines which shape the lives of its members. Hauerwas explains 1 Corinthians 6:12-20 as expressing the presence of God's Spirit in the community called the Body of Christ. Hauerwas

77 Hauerwas, S., 'What could it Mean for the Church to be Christ's Body? A Question without a Clear Answer' (unpublished paper given to the Society for the Study of Theology) citing Wyschogorod, M., *The Body of Faith. God in the People of Israel*, Harper, 1983, p. 26.

tackles individualism of the kind assumed by neo-classical economics directly. The understanding which is characteristic of liberal societies, is one in which my 'body' is an instrument for expressing my 'true self'. The New Testament perspective is very different. Hauerwas puts it as follows:[78]

> Such practices require community disciplines through which the story of our baptism is embodied in all that we do and are. We require practices through which we learn that we do not know who we are, or what our bodies can and cannot do, until we are told what and who we are by a more determinative 'body'.

The example given is that of the saints. It is we, that is the communion of saints, who tell them who they are. The living of lives on the basis of communal knowing is a practice which is lifelong. This is not a simple appeal to communitarianism, for the church is called rather to be a body 'constituted by disciplines that create the capacity to resist [...] the economic habits that support the state'.[79] In such a body the crucial point is that success is defined not by the achievement of certain ends, as in modern politics, but rather by embodying the ends in the means. This leads to an emphasis on the practices of the church as embodying the life of the spirit. The church does this by rethinking the nature of community and authority in terms of the spirit of Christ. The implication of this is to emphasise the importance of community in the understanding of individuals within Christian theology. If faith is seen in terms of responsibility, then it creates not only individuals who are faithful to God and to each other, but also the church as a corporate body.

In the three areas which we have examined so far, we find that the idea of the representative individual, the covenant and thirdly the corporate body are very different from the understanding of social life exemplified by neoclassical economic theory. However as mentioned above, the theologian has another way of arguing. This is not opposed to the biblical narrative, but rather compliments it. This is the

78 ibid.
79 ibid.

conception of the individual as created in a relational way of being. It is to this understanding we now turn.

The biblical concept of the individual

The presentation of human beings as individuals in the Bible is irreducibly relational. The theological way of putting this is that each individual is seen as 'made in the image of God'. What does this phrase mean? Even in the Judaic understanding of creation, individualism is put in very different terms from those of a modern social scientist. At the creation in Genesis, humanity is seen as incomplete without the creation of Eve. The creation of Eve does not merely complement Adam, but rather ensures that Adam's full humanity becomes complete. Therefore relationships matter in the Genesis account because only within relationships does each individual reach their fullness of being. The narrative presentation begins with Adam and then moves on to Eve, but in reality subordination is not an intrinsic part of the relationship. The creation of human beings in Genesis 1:26–27 is the final work of creation. It is the whole existence of human beings which makes them the 'image of God'. The image of God, or *imago Dei* (in Latin) is a fundamental concept of both Old and New Testament.

At this point the discussion could turn to the question of the dominion, or rule, of human beings over creation. Needless to say, this has been much disputed in recent years. However the issue of dominion is not our concern here. Rather it is the nature of relationship which we must explore. The term 'image of God' describes both dominion and relationship. Human beings in Genesis 1:26 are given the power to rule: 'Let us make human beings as our image, as our very form. They shall rule over.' Biblical scholars ascribe this passage in Genesis to the Priestly (or P) writing, and references to the theology of the image are found also in Genesis 5:1, and 9:6. The same theology also underlines Psalm 8:5, Wisdom 2:23 and Ecclesiasticus 17:3. It has often been read mistakenly, as if the likeness to God was found only and solely in the commission from God to rule and subdue the earth. However the divine image is also a way of revealing God through relationships, so that God is revealed through humanity. Psalm 8 refers to the reflection of the glory of God, found in human relationships.

What then might be meant by a relational view of the individual? This is a holistic viewpoint, in which the complete existence of human beings is important. Such a viewpoint includes relationships between the sexes, as in the creation of Adam and Eve. It also includes the whole person, and not simply a reference to the soul, or the person over against nature. Central to all this is the relationship to God. It is not as though human beings have certain qualities, such as reason or the power of using language which animals lack, and on the basis of these superior qualities human beings resemble God. Rather the biblical argument ignores the issue of both reason and language. It argues that God creates human beings in relationship to himself, and by that creation human beings are both given tasks (to represent God) and so to reveal him. Moltmann describes the theology of the image of God in these terms:[80]

> The nature of human beings springs from their relationship with God. It is this relationship which gives human nature its definition – not some characteristic or other which sets human beings apart from other living things. The God who creates for himself his image on earth finds his correspondence in that image. So human likeness to God consists in the fact that human beings, for their part, correspond to God. The God who allows his glory to light up his image on earth and to shine forth from that image is reflected in human beings as in a mirror.

This relational theology is also continued in the New Testament. The Pauline argument in Romans 1:23 is that human beings have broken their relationship with God. However Paul argues that we can grow into a new image which is the 'image of the Son'. Once again the qualities of reason, intelligence and language are set aside. What matters is the relationship to God, only this time it comes through the new revelation found in Christ. The theologian Alan McFadyen describes this relationship to Christ in terms of a 'call' by God through the person of Christ.

80 Moltmann, J., *God in Creation*, SCM, 1985.

McFadyen argues that God's relationship to us does not depend on how intelligent we are. Equally it does not depend on the possibilities which we possess for future existence:[81]

> The individuality reformed in response is dependent upon the creativity of the call; the call is not dependent as such on the pre-existence formations and possibilities of the persons called. [...] This does not mean that their previous identities play no part in the transformation, but that the transformation is wrought in the creative power of the call.

This relational nature of humanity is also connected to the concept of freedom. Throughout history, especially in recent European history, the ideal person has been displayed in art, literature or other cultural forms. At the same time political leaders have claimed to epitomise what it means to be a person, by summing up in their unique greatness what humanity can be. Again and again the true nature of a person has been found in kings, emperors, or even in the revolutionary heroes of modern times. Sometimes this can be taken to a degree which virtually divinizes rulers as quasi-Gods, as in the Nazi belief in Hitler as the Führer (or chosen leader) of Germany. The biblical account fears that such a belief will destroy the unique nature of the individual's relationship with God. Individuals are not only always in relationship, but are also seen as persons who are open to the constructive criticism of another, which is at the heart of any relationship.

This belief in a particular value of relationship, where the person cannot be divinised, is established in the Old Testament by the prohibition of the image of God. Human beings cannot be represented by visual representations of anything else as the image of God. By this prohibition the freedom of humanity is established as their freedom under God.[82]

> Belief in the destiny and value of man has a pre-eminently critical function. It forbids the divination of rulers, leaders and geniuses. It makes impossible for him the divinization of his nation, of his people of his society or of his race.

Individualism here is seen as free because the Bible forbids the glorification of a particular leader or community. The distinctive

81 McFadyen, A., *The Call to Personhood*, CUP, 1990.

82 Moltmann, J., *Man*, SPCK, 1974.

nature of Christian freedom lies in the freedom established by God in which they enter into relationships.

As described above, modern political philosophers set up social fictions of contracts, in order to give legitimacy to social institutions. Such a tension between methodological individualism and the importance given to social relationships is also inherent in modern economic thought of the neo-classical school. The biblical account instead emphasises relationships and responsibility, through the concept of the image of God. However these relationships must be tested and scrutinised. Nevertheless this critical, negative approach is only there to preserve the freedom of the individual in relationship to the call of God.

Individuals experience a personal call by God in many different ways. These could be through a description of God's being shining through the nature of humanity at its most open and obedient. It could be through the acceptance of responsibility, vocation and particular tasks. It could be through the portrayal of the church as a community with a relationship with God which is called the covenant, and with its 'peculiar practices' which discipline it in a communal living before the authority of God: throughout all this we find that individuals experience a personal call by God. The response of individuals to such a calling is, of course, of tremendous importance in both the Old and New Testaments. But it is never discussed in terms of modern individualist philosophy. This means that the biblical understanding of reality which we explored as wisdom in the first chapter issues in a vision which shapes our freedom. The practice of religion, or as a theologian would say the living out of faith shapes our preferences and gives us roles and responsibilities which we must live out. We define ourselves by our response to God's call of our selves. We define ourselves by the choices which we make. The theological argument of these first two chapters casts the remaining theological exposition in the succeeding chapters in a particular light. Much of the exposition of the individual, well-being and the nature of work follows with a certain logic from these opening accounts of wisdom, truth and the nature of God.

The non-believer or the sceptic may see the individual in this third chapter as a being whose life is not her own. However the

Christian will want to point to the way in which individual call and the life of the community are mutually enhancing. Social capital (personified as the representative individual), the covenant as the fundamental context for all decision making, and social cohesion are realities for the Christian which are expressed in the community in which he or she stands.

This could lead to a very static view of social cohesion, and this has certainly been the case in Christian history on many occasions. It has sometimes loosely been described as an appeal to the value of tradition. The family in its traditional patriarchal form was one such example, and political authority was another. This means that the modern reader of the Bible is met by a theology which has often entirely legitimated and justified a particular form of social coherence, and traditional group practices. Indeed there are times when the immobility of the Christian story seems its most familiar feature. Nevertheless it is not quite that simple. The belief that it is God who establishes these social realities means that such institutions can change.

There are innumerable stories in scripture and in church history of individuals who experienced the call of God in ways that remade the communities from which they came. Social cohesion is therefore something which Christians can articulate as the outcome of decades, even centuries, of tradition and custom which has been shaped by ways of responding to the call of God. Indeed as we move into the next chapter and its account of wellbeing, we shall discover the remaking of tradition by individual Christians out of loyalty to what they saw as God's concern for the poor, the marginalised and the needy is a constant corrective to the justification of traditional social life.

Section Three: Summary and Discussion

Human beings are social animals, living together in families, tribes, cities and nation states. As a species we have been successful because we have hunted together and shared our food. Individual consciousness, it is suggested, developed from our use of language to communicate with each other. Individual characters are formed by relationships. Yet we each feel ourselves to be autonomous, independent and on our own. We value ourselves and one another as unique and very special personalities. Society can be seen as a threat to our individuality, as well as a support.

As a question of philosophy one could ask whether the individual or the society is more real. Do we exist as persons only by virtue of our social interaction? Or does society exist only because we have chosen to pursue some of our individual activities together? Neo-classical economic theory takes an extreme position: it attributes values, preferences, choices and well-being only to individuals. In that sense individuals exist, and society does not.

The assumption in the Bible is towards the opposite end of the spectrum. Social relations are defined by a covenant between the whole people and God, not by a contract between individuals. The church is described as a single body – the body of Christ – of which individuals are just members – that is to say limbs or organs which cannot possibly manage on their own. Israel is personified as an erring wife; the church is the bride at a wedding feast. There is a story to be told about the group as such which encompasses the stories of the men and women who belong to it.

Individualists must explain how and why social co-operation happens at all. The mutual benefit of exchange is at the heart of economic theory; more tentatively it examines the foundations of mutual trust and the circumstances in which selfish individuals may find it in their interest to work together. Group decisions, in this context, may be best understood as the outcome of a bargaining process within the group, rather than a search for a 'common good', which is somehow different from the good of individuals in it.

Christian belief cannot embrace such thorough-going individualism, but it should not be placed so far to the other extreme that it is indifferent to the lives of individuals altogether. On the contrary, the relationship of each person to God, and to Christ, is central to the message of the whole Bible, and especially to the New Testament. The new society of the church was formed as a result of many individual experiences of conversion. The witness of individual saints and martyrs was celebrated. Later the monks and nuns struggled to overcome individual temptations and to win their personal salvation, leading isolated lives even as members of religious communities. The modern literature of biography or popular fiction, so intensely concerned with individual character and motivation, can be seen as a natural development from the lives of Christian saints.

In modern times, Christians have taken the biblical belief that human beings are made in the image of God and applied it to individuals rather than the species as a whole. From this they have deduced support for such secular causes as human rights, equal opportunities and democratic government – none of which feature much in the Bible itself. At the same time, however, Christians have also been attracted to modern corporate ideals that exalt the community above its members. They have identified themselves with their nation or their class, applying to it the biblical texts that originally referred to Israel or to the church. Thus the persistent tension between the individual and the community which is characteristic of modern times, has been felt acutely by Christians and led to some sharp differences of political stance, with markedly different interpretations of scripture to go with them.

Increasingly the societies we live in are pluralist in culture, ethics and religion. The individual is free to select from a wide range of lifestyles, thus approximating towards the autonomy presupposed by economic theory. But the consequence is not always the splendid isolation which individualism expects. It may be confusion and anxiety in the face of so much choice. The personality may itself begin to fragment. Post-modernism may rejoice in this flexible, unstructured, new world, but many of its inhabitants experience nothing but loneliness and disorientation. One response is to seek out a very tight community in which the rules are all laid down precisely so that everyone knows where they stand. Such a community may be a church.

Chapter Four

Ethics and the Concept of Well-being

Introduction

Choice, in neo-classical economic theory, is rational and individual. That has been the subject matter of the last two chapters. They have been primarily descriptive, concerned with how people in fact make choices, rather than with how choices ought to be made (although we have found it difficult to keep the two questions apart). In this chapter we shall address ethical questions directly, comparing the view of human well-being (or welfare or utility) commonly taken in welfare economics with that adopted in the Bible and in the subsequent development of Christian ethics.

In modern philosophy a sharp distinction is made between statements which are positive, describing how things are, and statements which are normative, prescribing how they should be. Within economics there is a separate branch of the subject called welfare economics which is strictly normative, whilst the other branches are all supposed to be positive. One can imagine oneself as the policy adviser to a government. Consumer demand, productivity, international trade – these are all types of behaviour that one has to study, much as an engineer would study hydrodynamics or nuclear physics. Before giving any advice, however, the economist must be able to define a system of values as well. Welfare economics makes those values explicit and considers what kind of policy recommendations might follow from them. The viewpoint is important. The distinction between normative and positive policy analysis would be different if one imagined oneself to be advising a business how best to react to government regulations.

The borderline between ethics and economic theory is now a very active area of research. Mainstream neo-classical economics grew up in close association with utilitarianism. Some economists still defend that theory of ethics, even in the strictest form which has been abandoned by most moral philosophers. Others recognise the need to consider a wider range of values, but no simple alternative to utilitarianism is at hand.[83] It might seem that Christian ethics could offer some clear and objective standards. However the relationship of Christian ethics to Christian belief can itself be problematic. There is no simple answer to the demand for a Christian social welfare function.

In Christian ethics, the good life is not just a matter of consumption, not just a matter of satisfying preferences indeed. Yet, Christian teaching is not always opposed to the enjoyment of plenty. The Old Testament promises that the righteous will prosper in a very material way. The images of heaven in the New Testament are full of feasting and celebration. His enemies accused Jesus himself of over-indulgence. The Christian Gospel says that it is better to be poor than to be rich, but this is not because it denies the value of all worldly enjoyment. What it says is that enjoyment should be accepted as a gift from God; it is not something that we should strive to obtain.

To explore the differences between Christian ethics and the utilitarian basis of neo-classical economic theory it is not enough to ask what are the factors which should be included in a welfare function. The whole idea of such a measure of well-being has to be questioned. One might imagine paradise in terms of utility (and economists sometimes use the word 'bliss'). But surely Heaven is something quite different from that.

In Section One of this chapter we begin, as before, with the treatment of the subject in an elementary economics textbook. We then explore the distinction between necessities and luxuries, the problems of measuring economic well-being, and the problems which arise in economic theory when it makes contact with systems of ethics which are not utilitarian. In Section Two we find a very different set

83 See Sen, A., *On Ethics and Economics*, Blackwell, 1987; Sen, A., *Choice, Welfare and Measurement*, Blackwell, 1982; Farina, F., Hahn, F. and Vannucci, S. (eds.), op. cit. and Hausman, D. M. and McPherson, M. S., op. cit.

kind of ethics in the Bible, such that poverty may be a blessing. This leads to a concern with happiness that is not confined to this life.

Section One: Economic Theory

The way in which economists make the transition from positive to normative can be illustrated from two college textbooks. In *Microeconomic Theory* by Henderson and Quandt, first published in 1958, there is a separate chapter on welfare economics. It begins[84] 'The objective of welfare economics is the evaluation of the social desirability of alternative social states.' The second paragraph begins: 'The welfare of a society depends, in the broadest sense, upon the satisfaction levels of all its consumers.' To which a footnote adds:[85]

> Statements of this kind are based on ethical beliefs or value judgements and cannot be proved. It is reasonable to postulate that the concept of social welfare transcends the more restricted notion of economic welfare. For obvious reasons the present analysis deals only with the latter.

A much more recent publication, *Microeconomics* by Pindyck and Rubinfeld (1995 edition) does not treat welfare economics as a separate subject, but it draws the distinction between positive and normative analysis right at the beginning of the book.[86]

> Sometimes we want to go beyond explanation and prediction to ask questions such as 'What is best?' This involves *normative* analysis, which is also important, both for managers of firms and designers of new public policies. When value judgements are involved, microeconomics cannot tell us what the best policy is. However, it can clarify the trade-offs and thereby help to illuminate and sharpen debate.

84 Henderson, J. M. and Quandt, R. E., *Microeconomic Theory – A Mathematical Approach*, McGraw-Hill, 1958, Chapter 7.

85 ibid.

86 Pindyck, R. S. and Rubinfeld, D. L., op. cit., Chapter 1.

A footnote says that most of the value judgements in economic policy are about the trade-off between equity and efficiency. This is indeed one kind of ethical dilemma associated with economic policy, but it is by no means the only one, as more advanced economic texts would certainly admit.

Preferences, freedom and utility

Theories of well-being can be either 'substantive' or 'formal'. A substantive theory identifies certain states as being good in themselves – for example happiness. A formal theory defines well-being as the outcome of a process – for example the satisfaction of individual preferences. Hausman and McPherson say:[87]

> One reason why economists are attracted to a formal theory of well-being is that formal theories appear to involve fewer philosophical commitments. In particular, economists are reluctant to make substantive claims about what is good or bad for people. [...] The preference satisfaction view of well-being also appeals to the anti-paternalist values of many economists.

But the authors go on to identify a formidable range of problems associated with this formal approach, not least the well-known fact that many people clearly do not actually know what is good for them.

Hausman and McPherson also make a very significant connection between the content of the positive and normative aspects of neo-classical economics:[88]

> Given economists' commitments to utility theory in *explaining* human choices, it is natural that they would look to levels of utility – that is, preference satisfaction – as the fundamental measure of human well-being for evaluative purposes as well.

All we need to assume is that individuals are self-interested and well informed, and it might appear that all ethical problems for the economist would disappear.

87 Hausman, D. M. and McPherson, M. S., op. cit., Chapter 6.
88 op.cit.

It is worth setting against this argument a point well made by the economist Frank Hahn in a discussion about the ethical principles that people actually hold. He recognises that people can derive their behaviour from a great variety of motives:[89]

> For much of economics concerned with 'ought' questions, one form or another of utilitarianism is the organising principle. But what if citizens are not utilitarians? For instance, history may have left them with absolute religious foundations of right and wrong. Would not the underlying principle that it is the individual's assessment of his or her own satisfaction count against the application of a utilitarian ethic.

It has been suggested that the values which many economists themselves most cherish are 'anti-paternalistic'. Behind their talk of preference satisfaction there lies a much more real commitment to human rights and the freedom to choose. Is it really better to be a well-fed slave or to be hungry but free? Human beings are not just passive observers of their own mental or bodily states. Happiness involves doing as well as being, achievements as well as gratification. Alongside any measure of material living standards one would wish to place an index of rights and freedoms before saying, for example, which economic or political system one would regard as better than another.

We can all readily agree that well-being is complex. Simple theories are easy to reject. The difficulty is that economists feel the need of something that they can measure so that they can go beyond the most general statements and actually say that one outcome is preferable to another in concrete examples of policy choice. Economics always seeks clarity of thought and precision of statement. Many non-utilitarian theories of ethics are somewhat vague and impressionistic. The ideal would be to find an index like temperature or weight, which could be read on a scale to show whether people are getting more or less happy, whether their living standards are rising or falling. It is easy to say that no such index actually exists. Yet people in fact do make choices which a utilitarian might say they could not rationally make unless they had some such index in mind. It is hard to

89 Hahn, F., 'Some Economical Reflections on Ethics', in Farina F. et al (eds.).

imagine questions of welfare economics being addressed in any other way.

Needs and wants

The ethics of welfare economics is not the same as the 'common-sense' ethics of every-day life. In common speech there is certainly a difference between wanting and needing, although the difference is not always the same. The difference can be that wants are subjective whilst needs are objective: you want what you think that you need. However the difference can also be that needs are compulsory whilst wants are optional, or that needs are urgent whilst wants can be delayed. None of these are distinctions commonly recognised by consumer theory or welfare economics. There are no breaks or discontinuities in the welfare functions or scales of well being usually imagined by economists; it is all a matter of degree. But this does not mean that the distinction could not be made, if a sufficiently precise definition could be found.

Most of contemporary economics is written with the rich countries in mind, where the basic economic essentials of life are taken for granted. In that case it seems right that most of economics should be about wants rather than about needs. It is not so all over the world, of course, neither was it so in Europe and America when classical economics was invented. Certainly it was not so in biblical times, or for much of Christian history.

One approach is to treat the basic necessities of life as contributing to production as well as to consumer satisfaction. There are studies, extensively described for example in Dasgupta's study of well-being and destitution,[90] of the actual requirements of diet to maintain life and to work efficiently. Similar estimates could be made of needs for clothing and shelter which would vary greatly from one place to another. This would then tell us what, strictly speaking, we need – all else is, in a biological sense, superfluous.

90 Dasgupta, P., op. cit., part four.

When economists talk about necessities and luxuries they usually mean something very different. A necessity in consumer theory is a commodity for which demand increases less than in proportion to income. As consumers become more affluent they spend a larger share of their resources on luxuries and a smaller share on necessities. Some items are uncontroversial: bread is a necessity on this definition, and foreign holidays are a luxury. Others do not agree so well with common parlance: beer and cigarettes are necessities, whilst fresh fruit and vegetables are luxuries. Paradoxically most poor people would say that they actually need to have just a few small treats.

Moralists, not least Christian moralists, have said that the good life is to be found in sufficiency, not in excess. Greed is one of the seven deadly sins, and the cause of much fruitless anxiety and strife. 'Enough is enough.'[91] In practice the definition of 'enough' will vary from time to time and place to place, but the sentiment is the same. Economic theory is familiar with the idea that the added value of each successive increment, the marginal utility of income, or total expenditure, declines; it is right to give priority, once an adequate living standard has been reached, to other aspects of life: to leisure, family and friends, or indeed to religion.

There may even come a point when further consumption is pointless or counter-productive. When an individual commodity is free, the demand for it is not infinite. The same might be true for all commodities considered together. Many people who are rich find it impossible to spend all that they could, simply because they already have all that they want. Economists do not necessarily believe that consumption is the only goal of life. Many would want to say that that is not only unethical, but also unrealistic.

Economists have a reputation for being materialists who attach importance only to satisfactions that can be bought. This is not altogether fair. Economic theory does not claim that consumption always makes people happy, or that only consumption ever makes people happy. All it really claims is that, other things being equal, most people are happier with a higher, than with a lower, standard of living. They simply devote most of their attention to marketable

91 Taylor, J. V., *Enough is Enough*, SCM, 1975.

commodities because that is where their professional expertise mainly lies.

The most telling criticism of the consumer society is one which many economists would accept in principle. It concerns the existence of what are called 'positional goods'.[92] Such goods are valued, not for any intrinsic satisfaction that they can offer, but because their possession is a matter of pride. It is good to know that you have something that other people do not have. The converse is that others actually suffer from knowing that you have something which they do not. On the one side there is pride, and on the other envy – both deadly sins. On the imaginary index of total utility it is quite possible that the pleasure of pride and the pain of envy net out at zero. Total expenditure is increased, but total well-being is not. Looked at from any detached point of view, resources are being wasted.

The income of nations

Economists would like to be able to measure, not just the well-being of individuals, but also the well-being of whole societies or states. The word 'wealth', used by Adam Smith in the title of his book, originally meant welfare or well-being, rather than riches. It is now used by economists for an accumulated stock, a store of value, and not a flow of income or a standard of living. Statisticians do sometimes attempt to value the whole wealth of nations in this sense, constructing a national balance sheet to include the infrastructure of buildings and works as well as productive equipment and net financial claims. The definitions and estimation methods have sometimes to be very imprecise. Much more attention is paid to figures for national income, or gross domestic product. Sometimes this is treated as if it were a measure of national success or failure. It is sometimes taken for granted that the aim of economic policy should be to maximise its level or its rate of growth, although economists are well aware of its limitations.

92 See especially, Hirsh, F., *The Social Limits to Growth*, Routledge and Kegan Paul, 1977.

National income can be measured in three different ways:[93] as total income, total expenditure and total output. In a closed economy they would all be the same; in an open economy adjustments have to be made to account for foreign transactions. Total income includes wages and salaries, rent and profit; total expenditure includes consumption, investment and net trade; total output includes goods and services, in the public as well as the private sector. To make comparisons over time, and to calculate growth rates, everything has to be measured in real terms or valued at the prices which ruled in some base year.

As indicators of economic well-being, the national accounts statistics are clearly incomplete. They do not, for example, include the value of unpaid work. This seriously understates the value especially of housework and childcare within the family which would add greatly to measured national income if it were done on a commercial basis. Another qualification to the use of national income as a measure of living standards is that it takes no account of relative needs, across different nations or across periods of time.

Serious consideration has been given to the possibility of including wider estimates of depreciation in the national accounts. The physical deterioration of the capital stock is, in principle, measured already. The concept could be broadened to cover the depletion of natural resources, even if these are not included in any national balance sheet estimates. Changes in the quality of the environment could also be treated as positive or negative investment. Logically that would suggest that the estimates of consumption should also include the imputed benefits or losses resulting from environmental improvements or deterioration in the past. It is difficult to know where to stop. The fact that a measure is incomplete does not mean that it is useless. The concept of well-being will always prove elusive, but that does not mean it is mistaken.

One alternative method of measuring well-being is to ask people directly how happy they are feeling. That has been done for many

93 See Johnson, C., *Measuring the Economy – A Guide to Understanding Official Statistics*, Penguin, 1988.

years and in several, relatively rich, countries.[94] The results show some variation across countries, but it does not correlate well with measured income. The results also show some fluctuations over time, but no upward trend. People who are asked how happy they feel need some point of reference. Probably they compare themselves with their neighbours, or with their own situation in the recent past. If that is the way that they answer questionnaires, then they will tell us little or nothing about international comparisons or about longer-term developments.

More serious questions are posed if this is how happiness really should be defined. Perhaps, for those not in real need, their feelings of happiness really do depend on relativities and not on levels of consumption at all. In the extreme case, if happiness depends on nothing but one's ranking relative to others in terms of income, then there is no possibility at all of making one person happier without making another more unhappy in similar degree.

Health economics

Most people would say that health is more important to well-being than is wealth. It is particularly interesting therefore to see how economists in the neo-classical tradition treat the economics of health care.[95] Where money can contribute to the prevention or cure of disease it is commonly given a very high priority, compared to all but the basic necessities of life. When we compare our lot with that of previous generations, it is the increase in the expectation of life, and the relief of suffering caused by ill health, that gives us most cause for gratitude. The spread of modern medicine throughout the world is one of the most evident benefits of the spread of western culture. When health care is provided free of charge, the demand for it sometimes appears to be insatiable. It is difficult to set any limit to the funding of

94 See Oswald, A. J., 'Happiness and Economic Performance', *Economic Journal*, 107(445), 1997.

95 Maynard, A., 'Health Care' in Kuper, A. and J. (eds.), op. cit.

the Health Service, or to deny resources to any project which is justified on medical grounds.

Value judgements must be involved in any method of setting priorities. Economists are particularly concerned that these judgements should be made overtly, and consistently from one situation to another. It is to be an exercise in rational choice, a constrained optimisation with the same logic as that of consumer theory. Thus health economists find themselves trying to answer questions which many doctors, and most of the general public, would rather not think about at all.

Resources are scarce, so not all sickness can be treated, still less cured. There has to be a quantitative measure of well-being, so that outcomes can be compared. It is called the QALY (Quality-adjusted Life Year). Different treatments will offer different prospects for longer or more active and comfortable life. The most difficult choices require the prospects for improvement in one patient to be compared with those for another.

Some economists would go so far as to say that the resources available to the health service should be allocated so as to produce the maximum possible number of QALYs, even if that means, for example, concentrating on preventative medicine and being unable to treat many of those who are actually ill. In practice, however, no one seems willing to press the argument to its logical conclusion. Faced with a real patient in severe pain or danger, medical staff do all that they can to help.

Medical ethics is one area in which the tensions between the utilitarian approach of welfare economics and popular, not to say Christian, ethics become particularly acute. The same issues arise in relation to safety in transport economics. Economists have tried to estimate the 'price' of a life saved by reducing the speed limit on roads, by improved signalling on the railways, and so on. It seems illogical that the 'price' should be so different in different contexts. Resources ought, surely, to be reallocated to those areas where the cost of saving life would the least, so that the number of deaths could be minimised. If society does not in fact do that, does it mean that society is ignorant, foolish or non-utilitarian?

Well-being is a moral concept and for most people the good life would be one which observed moral norms. These rules of conduct are problematic for any utilitarian, not least for economists of the neo-classical school. This applies to positive as well as to normative questions. Thus, Hausman and McPherson complain that economists do not take enough account of moral norms in explaining human behaviour:[96]

> Unless norms are of no economic importance, which is very hard to believe, economists need to broaden their theory of economic behaviour to find a place within it for a discussion of when norms will form, of how much influence they will have, and of what their consequences will be. If the existence and influence of moral norms depends on the strength of moral reasons (as we have argued), then economists will not be able to treat moral norms as mere sociological facts that need not be understood or assessed.

One way of introducing norms into the theory of economic behaviour is to include them in the preference orderings of individuals. Some people are happier when they think that they are being good. A guilty conscience can be the cause of misery. The norms, in other words, are internalised, or, in biblical language, 'written on the heart'. The economist need not get involved in any moral debate if norms can be equated with tastes, about which there is, proverbially, nothing to dispute.

The implication could be that everyone's conscience has its price. Most preferences, in economic theory, are subject to diminishing marginal rates of substitution when traded off against other sources of satisfaction. If this is true also of ethical norms, then it may be possible to be 'too good'. Moral rules will be broken when the alternative is to go hungry. Being good is a matter of more or less, and how good one is will depend on circumstances as well as on values. Those who find these implications unrealistic – and not everyone will – can instead describe moral rules as constraints on choice, like the constraint of a fixed budget or a given technology. If

96 Hausman, D. M. and McPherson, M. S., op. cit., Chapter 5.

moral rules are like that, then one is either good or bad, with no intermediate gradations. It is like keeping the law; there is no point in works of supererogation.

But economists may still want to ask, as Hausman and McPherson suggest, about the content of moral norms. Rational individuals decide whether to keep the law because of the sanctions, whether internal or external.[97] But are the rules themselves in any sense rational? It is not difficult to show that the ban on speeding serves the interests of the average road user. Equally the ban on stealing seems to serve the interests of the average property owner. This does not explain, however, how such rules emerge in the absence of political authority. There are also rules which do not seem to serve anyone's private interest at all.

To take up the suggestion that economics should seek to explain moral rules would be to widen considerably the agenda of the subject. One is inclined to say, in this case and some others mentioned in this book, that neo-classical theory should play to its strengths and not to its weaknesses.

Section Two: Christian Belief

Well-being in the teaching of Jesus

The response which the biblical theologian will make to the economist's account of well-being denies the centrality of consequences. In the Bible there are of course accounts of well-being which are concerned with material wealth. Job is stripped of his herds of animals and is cast into poverty and ill health. This tests him greatly, but he struggles to find a relationship with God which can endure

97 Economic theory can be used to examine the incentives facing both criminals and the police, see Friedman, D., 'Rational Criminals and Profit-maximising Police – the Economic Analysis of Law and Law Enforcement', in Tommasi, M. and Ierulli, K. (eds.), op. cit.

despite his loss of wealth. Nevertheless it is clear that wealth in its fullest meaning in both the Old and New Testament is a metaphor for a relationship with God.

The economist's understanding of well-being may be that it is the formal outcome of a process which need not adopt any standpoint in ethical theory, although in practice normative aspects of economics are usually utilitarian, or at least consequentialist. The biblical perspective is, in an argument which will by now be familiar, entirely different. It is determined at every point by the existence of a God who is involved with the life of his people. Well-being is only to be seen in the light of following in the way of God's commandments. In the next chapter we will see how production in economic theory can be correlated with the biblical concept of blessing as the fundamental term for divine creation. For the moment, without getting ahead of the argument, it is sufficient to note that the biblical account of well-being is determined by what it means to be blessed. Such an understanding was common to the period of the Bible. As Anthony Harvey argues:[98]

> To most of us the best known 'beatitudes' are those in the Bible. But once again we must not imagine that the Jewish culture stood apart from the rest of the world in this respect. [...] The form, that is to say, was universal; but it emerged in Hebrew writing first in writing that has a wisdom character.

Again there has already been a reference to wisdom in the first chapter, where the dwelling of wisdom with God meant that it could be present as guidance to the people of Israel. The theological response to economics is a cumulative one: it takes up concepts, such as blessing and wisdom, and develops them in an exploration of their deeper implications. Wisdom and the gift of the law enabled the guidance of the divine will to be present to God's people. Well-being, to put it at its most simple, occurs when a person responds to wisdom and is blessed. The account of the divine economy in Paul's second letter to the Corinthians uses metaphorical language about the divine economy to make the point as clearly as possible. We shall return to an exposition of this argument in a moment.

98 Harvey, A. E., *Strenuous Commands: The Ethics of Jesus*, SCM, 1990, Chapter 4.

The New Testament account of well-being defends an understanding of needs and wants which is entirely dependent on substantive moral values, and is non-materialist. The Sermon on the Mount, for instance, in the Lukan form attributes blessing to those who find themselves in cases of poverty, hunger and grief. They did not choose them, and it would have been difficult for them to have avoided them. The values in the Old Testament wisdom tradition depend on a basic assumption which bears little relationship to the worldview of the economist. This wisdom tradition assumes a morally ordered universe, where virtue obtains its reward, and God blesses those who live well. Harvey argues that what the Jewish and Christian tradition did was to compensate for the apparent failures of this life by the blessings of the next life. The response to the preaching of Jesus rested on the presuppositions held by his hearers, which expected an intervention by God in the lives of his disciples.

What is new in the teaching and the behaviour of Jesus was his identification with the poor. As Harvey says 'Jesus demonstrated the "blessedness" of the poor by showing that actions of profound moral import lay within their powers.'[99] No longer is material prosperity something which is to be seen straightforwardly as a gift from God. Instead it is the poor who are blest. In both cases, whether it is the blessing of material prosperity or the assertion that blessings are the preserve of the poor, there are no reasons given to substantiate the argument in the biblical (or indeed ancient, secular) texts. There is neither reasoning, appeal to any law or superior authority. The usual justification of the blessings of prosperity is the prudential or moral assumptions of the hearer or reader. It is self-authenticating because of the familiarity of the background values or beliefs of the recipient.

Jesus goes against this morality. His argument is unfamiliar. Above all his followers do not yet explore the full force of his teaching. This is why the writings of the New Testament exemplify the response of a community to the teachings of a charismatic leader who taught familiar truths (the blessing of God on his followers) in strange ways. The implications of what he taught are however fleshed out in other ways. They are never justified by rigorous argument, but

99 Harvey, op. cit.

his conduct, his parables and his style of teaching are always related to the implications of his understanding of blessings. It is by observing his life that self-authentication happens, and the challenge of this self-authentication is that it is also self-involving. It pulls those who listen into its realm of discourse and understanding.

The greatest tension lies within the Christian tradition itself, rather than between economics and Christianity. To put it over simply, Christianity has been assimilated to the conventional morality which Jesus was challenging by his teaching. It lies beyond the scope of this study to explore why, and how, the Christian church found Jesus' teaching too difficult to assimilate into its style of life. What is clear is the direct impact made by the words and actions of Jesus on his followers. Luke 4:18 quotes Isaiah's promise of good news to the poor explicitly. However there seems to be no intention of making the poor richer in material terms. Nor does Jesus highlight the suffering of the poor in the style of a modern appeal to induce greater generosity. Although Jesus does command selling possessions and giving alms in Luke 12:33 and 18:22 that is not the main thrust of his teaching. Rather it is the blessings, which will come in the future to the poor *(those who hunger will be filled)*, that represent the note of urgency in his teachings. There are clear indications in the Magnificat that the future reality of a life lived in the fullness of the Kingdom will be one without poverty. The attempts in the early church to realise this ideal are seen in Acts 4:34 where there was a community of goods. However even where the teaching of Jesus was not embodied in the social relationships of a community, what remained was something emphasised by Harvey:[100]

> We have found that, as in other areas of moral teaching, so in the matter of the proper use and disposal of worldly goods, Jesus adopted themes that were already familiar in traditional moral teaching; his characteristic contribution was not to turn them into exact standards or rules of conduct for the community but to challenge the mentality that introduces exceptions or limitations into moral action by taking the extreme case as the norm.

100 Harvey, op. cit.

Few people have been able to live up to this ethical rigour of well-being exemplified by Jesus, but the impact on the ethical thinking of generations who followed him has been incalculable. This is not to turn Jesus into a contemporary revolutionary, but rather to restate the paradox once more. There are great differences between the economist's understanding of well-being and a religious approach such as that of the Christian church, but the greatest challenge is to the teaching of the church by the foundation documents themselves.

The economy of God in the early church

The attempts to live out the teaching of Jesus are shown clearly in the life of the churches founded by the apostles and evangelists. David Ford finds one example in the church at Corinth which has been the subject of several studies by him.[101] He argues that the language of this Pauline letter is deeply metaphorical, in a manner that is often not appreciated in the modern world. The implication of reading Paul's writings in this way is both that the understanding of well-being which he presents is expressed in deeply metaphorical language, and that personal well-being is inseparable not only from the Christian community but also from a whole 'ecology' of relationships. In this ecology there is a particular understanding of time and the meaning of history, of God and of wisdom; in short, and this must be familiar now, we are circling back to the world view expressed in the previous chapters.

What is intriguing is that Paul uses the economic language of his day in a daring move to capture some of the riches and depth of the Christian life. The economy of Paul's society was a subsistence one, in which goods were in short supply. The elite dominated their society which meant that for 98 per cent of the population there was a shortage of goods. Paul was not part of the elite, so for him as for everyone else stability was the aim in a subsistence economy. This leads inexorably into how one protected and held onto one's right to subsistence. This right was only protected if one belonged to a family,

101 Young, F. and Ford, D. F., *Meaning and Truth in 2 Corinthians*, SPCK, 1987.

for the place which the family held within a society by virtue of its custom, or inherited rights, was the guarantor of one's right to subsistence. Within this steady state economy there was an ideal of no change, no challenges, but only the preservation of the hard won subsistence that was the economy of the ancient world and its peasants.

Paul however contrasts this poverty of expectation in a startling way. The divine self-giving ensured well-being in a metaphorical description of the economy. In chapter 5, Paul speaks of the exchange brought about by the death of Christ, where the death of one for all leads to the death of all. Equally Paul sees his life, although continually encountering the suffering of persecution, as filled with the exchange of the power of Jesus' resurrection in Paul's body. The reconciliation is seen as *katallage*, or reconciliation. (2 Corinthians 5:18). This Greek word originally meant a moneylender's profit, or the exchange of money and goods. Then the term is widened from its commercial usage to include the exchange of anger for friendship, and this is how Paul uses it as meaning reconciliation. It is a costly exchange, and the economic metaphor is pressed further when the Christians are spoken of as becoming rich through poverty (2 Corinthians 8:9).

The result of this exchange is shown in financial generosity, and the collection for the church in Jerusalem in chapters 8 and 9 is the direct result of the (metaphorically expressed) exchange of Christ's life for our own. At this point well-being financially is the result of the metaphorical financial exchange in the spirit. Yet it would be wrong to conclude that economic generosity is the acid test of this exchange of love, as though economic well-being won out after all as the fundamental determining factor. For Paul sees the collection as itself a living symbol of partnership, sharing and fellowship, or in another Greek word almost impossible to convey fully in English, *koinonia.* (8:14 and 9:13). Ford is worth quoting on this development:[102]

> The chapters are certainly about money and basic attitudes to possessions and prosperity, but these are inseparable from the character and glory of God, the

102 op. cit.

> practice of faith and love in the church and the dynamic reality of grace. The metaphorical application of economic terms to the Gospel is given a new development, as key Gospel concepts, including economic ones, are in turn directed at reconceiving financial attitudes and relationships.

What was Paul arguing for? Benevolence at this time was endemic in society, and was identified with the patron-client relationships which dominated Hellenic cities of this period. The escape from subsistence living came through talents which were recognised by one of the wealthy elite and taken up in a benevolent manner. Grace, or *charis* in Greek, was a secular non-religious term for the patron's generosity, and the reciprocal act of generosity in return. Paul alters this relationship in two different ways. First, he will not himself become economically dependent on anyone, thus safeguarding his independence. Secondly, the tradition of reciprocity was negated by the overwhelming generosity of God. In the face of this, one cannot give back a reciprocal act of thanks, but rather one is called to a way of life which is similarly generous. It is of course possible to set up the relationship to God as though one was in the position of being a lifelong client of God, always owing him generosity. However a better analysis is to see well-being as set free from the conventional, social attitudes of life with the required acts of gratitude. Instead there is the symbolic sharing in the 'new creation', where a deep unity in the life of the spirit is expressed through the collection of one congregation for another.

The hope of happiness

There is a strong commitment to well-being in the Bible, but we have seen how the teachings of Jesus and Paul change the meaning of the term dramatically. The life of Christ issued in death, and involved taking up a cross, but in the final analysis the end is to glorify God forever through enjoyment of his being. We search not for our negation, but for what Jesus called the pearl of great price. Paul expressed this as striving for a heavenly prize, and we seek fulfilment of our lives in following Christ. This is not a platitude, but rather the expression of a delight in God's love which echoes down the tradition. This should be kept separate from the attempts to formulate an ethics of how people should behave. Much early Christian morality is conventional enough, and is no doubt lifted from the communities in which the early church was placed.[103] Nevertheless Paul also expected that by participating in Christ they would become full of the life of the Spirit.

The fruit, then, was not really theirs, but Christ's; and they were a part of Christ. The theory of participation in Christ helps explain Paul's perfectionism and gives it a theoretical basis; Christians should bear fruit and only such fruit. He did not, however, regard effort in doing good as being in any way opposed to membership in the body of Christ.[104]

The wellbeing of human happiness in Christ, and our glorification of God in the life of the Spirit, lead inevitably to one quite distinctive aspect of Christian belief. This is the belief in renewed life in a spiritual body. The Greek term for this existence is *pneumatikon*, and it is found in Paul's writings in 1 Corinthians 15: 36–44. Some theologians in recent years have made a distinction between this theology and the bodily conception found in Matthew 27: 52–53 which expresses the Jewish theology of the reanimation of dead bodies. It is not clear that this distinction can be made, for Paul was struggling to express his understanding of the way in which Christians are resurrected in the power of the Spirit, as a corporate body in Christ. This inevitably used mystical language of incorporation, but it is a mistake to see this language as being opposed to the earlier Jewish understanding of resurrection.[105]

There can be no way in which even the most extensive conception of deferred gratification can encompass such a radical transfer of wellbeing to a different state of life. Economic theory is very familiar with the notion that wellbeing in the present will depend on the sum of expected utility in the future (discounted to allow for

103 Oppenheimer, H., *The Hope of Happiness*, SCM, 1983.

104 Sanders, E. P., *Paul*, OUP, 1991.

105 Hick, J., *Death and Eternal Life*, Collins, 1976, or for a more traditional view, see Baillie, J., *And The Life Everlasting*, OUP, 1934.

uncertainty or impatience). But this is the anticipation of a future little different from the present, not a complete transformation of the self and its absorption into a greater whole. Some philosophers have pointed out that if the future life is entirely different from with this one, then it is difficult to see how any continuity can be predicated at all. It is certainly true that it is important to assert the continuity of personal identity in a transformed state of wellbeing, lest the discontinuity overwhelm the personal self-altogether. However the biblical language speaks of a mystery, in which the action of God is so dramatic that the person begins a new life radically different from the old. The new state of being resists measurement and even description but theologians will wish to assert that this does not make the language of resurrection meaningless, for the meaning is extrapolated from the resurrected life of Jesus as described in the Gospels, and the experience of Paul.

It is also clear that Christians do not act in the way that they do because of the existence of a future reward, pure and simple. They do not, in the language of economic theory, seek to maximise the present value of their expected utility in the future. That would be to invalidate the love which they are commanded to show to all people, because this is what was shown by their Lord. Such future wellbeing is a state of being into which Christ calls his followers. It is not a carrot that motivates action, as a reduction in the rate of discount might cause a consumer to take more thought for the future. Nevertheless, the fact that such a future state is not determinative of action does not mean that it is epiphenomenal, or perhaps an 'add-on' to Christian belief for those who like to believe such a thing. Rather it expresses the profound truth that nothing can separate Christians from the love of Christ, and death is therefore rendered powerless in the face of the Spirit after the resurrection of Christ.

Section Three: Summary and Discussion

Modern science gains understanding by means of measurement. For the same purpose, utilitarian welfare economics seeks to measure the well-being, or happiness, of individuals. It reduces all life's pleasures and pains, all that we aim for, to a single index, like that of temperature or of weight. It would be unfair to accuse economics of equating happiness with consumer spending, but there certainly is a presumption that an increase in spending will result in a higher standard of living which is more or less the same as a higher level of happiness, welfare or 'preference satisfaction'. In modern times, well-being in this sense has increased tremendously in a large part of the world, and most people would regard this as a great gain. Utilitarianism may be out of favour as a moral philosophy, but it is not a bad way of describing one aspect of the values on which our present-day society is built.

At an early stage of economic development, higher levels of consumption reduce hunger, improve health and meet basic needs for clothing and shelter. Few would question that this is worthwhile. Beyond a certain point, however, the moral evaluation of consumption becomes more debatable. Economic theory may not recognise a difference between needs and wants, but popular morality always has done. Utilitarianism may not be such an appropriate philosophy for a society at an advanced stage of economic development.

Perhaps a very rich society can take a more 'post-modern' view of well-being. Nowadays shopping seems to be enjoyable in itself, not just as a means to the end of consumption. The fun comes in the choosing, the expression of personality rather than the satisfaction of need. Buying is wish-fulfilment, play-acting, and self-definition. Well-being in this setting is about exploration, realising potential and setting the imagination free. This takes us a long way away from the more pedestrian concerns of economic theory. Nevertheless it could still be classed as a 'materialist' view of human well-being.

The distance between this and the monastic ideal of poverty, chastity and obedience could hardly be greater. The modern view of poverty is that it ought to be abolished. The general assumption is, moreover, that sexual satisfaction is a necessary component of well-being – and the more of it the better. Above all, there is no great value in obedience which is regarded as no better than servitude. The life of the Christian religious orders is not just unattractive to most modern men and women, it is totally incomprehensible.

Yet few people would say, or ever have said in the past, that material well-being is the only thing that matters. In the Bible the good life depends on wisdom, and on the blessing of God. In the Old Testament God's blessing means health as well as wealth, a large family and a long life. In the New Testament it is, paradoxically, the poor who are blessed and not the rich. But this is in anticipation of a reversal in their fortunes which is promised for the future. In both the Old Testament and the New Testament the greatest joy comes from the worship of God, delight in his perfection and trust in his love.

The idea that well-being depends on relationships has no place in economic theory, but would be widely regarded as obvious enough. In modern times it has been turned into a kind of science of mental health, as well as the subject of poetry and drama. It is part of what everyone believes. It is also close to the heart of Christian belief, summed up in the formula that God is love.

Economic theory, by contrast, may appear dry and unemotional. It is also, in many respects over-optimistic. It may acknowledge human weakness and ignorance, but it knows nothing of human evil or sin. There is no need for repentance, just for enlightenment. So there is nothing at all in economics corresponding to the Christian belief that our well-being depends on forgiveness and the grace of God. We can, it seems, work out our own salvation.

Economic theory is very innocent about the evil side of human nature. Economic man has often been accused of selfishness, although even that charge will not always stick; there is nothing in the standard theory which prevents him from being altruistic if that is what he wants. It would be more to the point to accuse him of pride. Individualism assumes, or else encourages, self-sufficiency which is the opposite of Christian dependence on God. But even if he is selfish and proud, economic man is not cruel, malicious or vindictive. When economists imagine themselves in battle it is against the forces of privilege, prejudice and misguided philanthropy, not against the Prince of Darkness and his human allies.

Economic theory was born in the age of the Enlightenment, when reason was expected to overcome ignorance, and so to bring humanity closer and closer to perfection. In economic terms there really has been progress almost all the time for the last two centuries and more. Living standards, measured in any material terms, have advanced phenomenally in many parts of the world, despite the vast increase in population. Some of the optimism was justified. Whether there has been moral progress is much more debatable.

If Christianity were concerned only with 'doing good', then it could easily be brought into harmony with economic theory. All that would be required would be to recognise altruism as an element in the preferences of the individual. (The nineteenth century utilitarians were nothing if not benevolent.) But this would still be to miss the main point of Christian belief which concerns God's love and our response to it. There are two very different methods of evaluation implicit in the two 'anthropologies' that we bring together in this book. We need to recognise these differences for what they are, and resist any temptation to gloss them over.

Chapter Five

Production and Economic Growth

Introduction

Most of economic theory is about constrained optimisation, achieving the best outcome in given conditions, making the best, one might say, of a bad job. The consumer maximises his or her utility subject to a budget constraint; similarly the producer maximises output or profits subject to the constraint of a given technology. In the next three chapters we shall be looking at the supply side of the economy, at production, work and capital accumulation. Here too we shall be contrasting a modern with a pre-modern view of the world, as well as contrasting a secular philosophy with religious belief.

Economic theory paints a well-defined and distinctive portrait of 'economic man'. That figure is set against a background which is also essential to the compete picture – like an eighteenth-century portrait of a country gentleman set against the broad acres of the land that he owns and cultivates. The two belong together: the rational, calculating, prudent man and the finite, productive and predictable environment in which he lives. The theory of consumption and the theory of production complement one another. Economics is not just about human choice and well-being; it is about the human predicament as well.

The eighteenth century was, of course, the era of the industrial revolution. New technologies, and the investment of capital, resulted in a rapid and sustained increase in productivity. We have come to take such progress for granted, but before modern times it was never experienced or expected. There were good years and bad years but no continuing trends. The country gentleman in the portrait would be an improving landlord, harnessing the power of water or of steam. He was rejecting old ways of doing things, no longer relying on tradition, but on the application of new knowledge and the spirit of enterprise. Such behaviour is still celebrated in our own times. Modern Christians pray for 'wealth creation', and see the process of economic growth as co-operation with the creative work of God.

There is quite a substantial literature which examines the assumptions of rationality, self-interest and free will which underlie economic theory. We have referred to some of it in the last three chapters. The same is not so true of the assumptions about the nature of production and the resources that it requires.[106] Yet this should be just as important an issue in any dialogue between economic theory and Christian belief. There are questions to be addressed about the concept of production, about the availability of resources and the development of technology. Some aspects of these issues have been discussed extensively in recent years. For example ethical questions of stewardship and the sustainability of economic growth have been debated both by economists and by theologians. The theory of production also suggests questions about the nature of God's creation and providence which the Bible describes in a variety of different ways.

One might be tempted to say that economic theory is about scarcity, whilst the doctrine of providence is about abundance. Is the cup of life half empty or half full? We all know that human experience includes both poverty and riches, starvation and excess. The real question is rather what it is that makes the earth fruitful or barren. Does it depend on careful planning, hard work and thrift? Or are the good gifts around us sent, in the words of the harvest hymn, from heaven above?

Section One of this chapter covers the economic model of production by firms which maximise their profits. It then considers the theory of economic growth, first on the traditional assumption that technical progress is exogenous to the economy, and then using more recent work which makes such improvements dependent on research and development. Section Two contrasts the production process with God's act of creation out of nothing. It then explores the biblical belief

106 But see Lovell, C. A. K., 'Production and Cost Functions', in Kuper, A. and J. (eds.), op. cit. and the works referenced there.

that prosperity comes from the blessing of God and the sense in which human beings are stewards of God's world.

Section One: Economic Theory

Inputs and outputs

A textbook of economics, having described consumer behaviour and the demand side of the market, typically turns next to the supply side and the behaviour of producers. This is how the subject is approached in one textbook of microeconomics:[107]

> In the production process, firms turn *inputs* which are also called *factors of production* into *outputs* (or products). [...] The relation between the inputs to the production process and the resulting output is described by a production function. [...] The production function allows for inputs to be combined in varying proportions to produce an output in many ways. [...] Note that the equation applies to a *given technology* (i.e. a given state of knowledge about the various methods that might be used to transform inputs into outputs). As technology becomes more advanced and the production function changes, a firm can obtain more output for a given set of inputs. [...] Production functions describe what is *technically feasible*, when the firm operates *efficiently*. [...] The presumption that production is always technically efficient need not always hold, but it is reasonable to expect that profit-seeking firms will not want to waste resources.

What is being described is a process of transformation. It is natural therefore to think of these mathematical functions as describing natural laws like the equations used in physics or chemistry. But the analogy must not be pressed too far. The equation that describes a chemical reaction has fixed coefficients: the relative quantities of hydrogen and oxygen which combine to form water, cannot, of course, be varied. It is very different to specify the quantities of wheat or cloth which can be produced while varying the relative quantities of

107 Pindyck, R. S. and Rubinfeld, D. L., op. cit., Chapter 6.

labour and capital used by different methods of production. Such information requires experimentation and repeated observation. The producer usually will have only the most inexact notion of what are the options open to the firm.

The same form of production function is used to describe activities which might seem totally different in character. The classical economists were much concerned with the productivity of agriculture. They came to summarise the inputs as land, labour and capital. A plot of land could be farmed more or less intensively and experience could accumulate about the effects of varying the employment of men and of machines. Many other variables would be involved, not least the weather at harvest time, but with a large enough sample estimates of a production function might be made.

In manufacturing the production process is generally easier to control. For any combination of inputs the quantity produced might be relatively easy to predict, although there are still unknowns in the equation like the proportion of the output which has to be scrapped as below standard. Productivity in fact varies considerably across plants using the same process to make a standard product. Moreover the production function becomes more difficult to estimate or even define as each firm varies its product slightly so as to gain a competitive advantage.

In the service sector there is no tangible product, but there is still a transformation taking place which can be described by a production function. (A gardener, with or without a mechanical lawn mower, is keeping the grass looking tidy; an economist, with or without a computer-based model of the economy, is forecasting the next recession.) But the concept of a production function begins to break down when the definition of the product itself depends on the method of production. (A home-baked cake is not the same as a shop-bought one, or a live performance the same as a recording.) Some services depend on the identity of the individual who performs them.

The theory of production begins with the behaviour of the individual firm, just as the theory of consumer demand begins with the individual household. When interest switches to the production of a whole nation then a problem of aggregation arises. One cannot say that an aggregate production function exists just because there is a well-defined production function for each firm. A strictly neo-classical model of general equilibrium recognises this and does not seek to explain national output in terms of national inputs. Economists who nevertheless want to have something to say about total output have to be content with an approximation.

Efficiency and stewardship

Economic theory is concerned with the efficient use of scarce resources. But to know what is efficient one must first know what is of value. The theory of production cannot be separated from the theory of demand because only when the purpose of production is defined can we say what is worthwhile. The simplest form of efficiency to define is the technical efficiency which the production function assumes. If the product is of any value at all then it is desirable to use the available resources to produce as much of it as one can. This is the first task of management.

Production theory takes little account of entrepreneurship because it assumes that the technology is known and that the remaining risks of production can be calculated and hedged. In practice management requires many gifts, like creativity and leadership, which do not appear explicitly in the standard neo-classical model. The main task assigned to management in the elementary theory is to choose the mix of inputs and the scale of production. (A more advanced treatment of the theory would be closer to the world of strategic choices over product design, production location and marketing with which industrialists are familiar. Economists are not naïve in these matters.) In any case, the motive force is assumed to be the maximisation of profits.[108]

One part of the task is to compute the minimum cost of producing any given level of output. In the short run it may not be possible to vary the input of all the factors of production, for example because the firm owns the buildings and equipment; in the long run

108 For a more formal presentation of the theory, see Pindyck, R. S. and Rubinfeld, D. L., op. cit., Chapter 8.

when capital is due for replacement there is more flexibility. It is assumed that the process of adding units of any one factor of production is subject to diminishing returns. This is very like the assumption of diminishing marginal utility from the consumption of any one commodity. The efficient combination of inputs will usually include some of each kind, some labour and some capital. The ratio of the marginal products of two factors of production should be equal to the ratio of their marginal costs.

The other part of the task of management, as described in an elementary textbook, is to select the scale of production. Typically, it is assumed, unit costs initially fall as the scale of production is increased, but beyond a certain point they begin to rise. The initial economies of scale may arise from physical relationships; for example the amount of steel needed to build a ship does not rise as rapidly as its carrying capacity. Often there are indivisibilities which make small-scale production expensive. To produce a book it is necessary to type the whole text; once that is done the cost of producing more copies is little more than the cost of the paper they are printed on. It may be true that 'small is beautiful', but many goods and services which were once the luxuries of the rich have become available to all in the last hundred years as a result of mass production. In many activities the scale of production is limited, not by an increase in unit costs of production, but by the size of the market for the product

If firms maximise profits then they will expand production up to the point where the marginal cost of production is as great as the marginal revenue from sales. Any production above that point would add more to costs than to revenue and hence be sold at a loss. If the efficient scale of production is large, then the industry is likely to be dominated by one firm or, at least, by a small number of large-scale producers. Neo-classical economists tend to assume that returns to scale are typically constant or diminishing. They are then able to assume that markets are competitive and efficient. Those economists who are more sceptical about the benefits of free markets sometimes rest their case on the assumption that increasing returns to scale are normal at least in manufacturing industry. The assumption of profit maximisation is defended as follows:[109]

> For smaller firms managed by their owners, profit is likely to dominate all the firm's decisions. In larger firms, however, managers who make day-to-day decisions usually have little contact with the owners (i.e. the stockholders). [...] Managers may be more concerned with goals such as revenue maximisation to achieve growth. [...] Even so, managers' freedom to pursue goals other than long-run profit maximisation is limited. If they do pursue such goals, shareholders or the boards of directors can replace them, or the firm can be taken over by new management. In any case firms that do not come close to maximising profits are not likely to survive.

It is part of stewardship to use resources efficiently, so that nothing is lost. This may be a reason to support the market system. However there is also concern that the market system does not ensure that the productive process is truly sustainable in the long run. Resources may be used up, the environment may be damaged in ways that threaten the prosperity, the health or even the existence of future generations. This is a possibility to which economists have devoted a great deal of attention in recent years.[110]

As resources become scarcer their prices will rise, encouraging the production of substitutes. The whole of production theory is based on the assumption that some substitute can always be found. In the standard economic model there is no such thing as an essential ingredient. If there were such a thing its price would rise without limit and the stocks of it would never be used up. To that extent the message of economic theory should be somewhat reassuring. The problem, according to economic theory arises when there are no property rights and no markets in which scarce resources can be traded. Whales will be hunted to extinction, like many large mammals before them, if the hunters are not forced to pay more for hunting them as the stock diminishes. Rivers will be poisoned unless the polluters are made to pay. If there is a market then prices will

109 op. cit.

110 For a recent survey by a leading expert on this branch of economic theory, see Pearce, D. W., 'Economics of the Environment', in Greenaway et al (eds.), op. cit.

determine how much pollution is justified and how many whales should be killed each year. If a market cannot be organised then an administrative regime should be set up which will produce the same result.

Economic growth

Efficiency is a static optimum, concerned with the best use of a fixed quantity of resources; it does not produce persistent growth. In the standard neo-classical model of production, growth results from exogenous technical progress, that is from an increase in knowledge which the model does nothing to explain. The process of capital accumulation, which the model does seek to explain, will continue only until the stock reaches its optimum level, or ratio to output. As the capital-intensity of production increases, the return to capital must fall, because of the diminishing marginal rate of substitution which characterises all production functions in the standard model. When the return to capital is no higher than the rate of time preference the incentive to save disappears. Persistent growth cannot be explained by rational thrift.

This means that the most significant economic development of the modern world is left unexplained.[111] Growth is attributed to the advance of science and technology which is left to be explained by such non-economic factors as natural curiosity, the accumulation of experience or research which was originally motivated by political concern for public health or defence.

Clearly it would be wrong to treat knowledge as an input just like labour or capital. It is difficult to measure the quantity of knowledge available, or even to define what that means. Moreover the use of knowledge does not seem to be subject to diminishing marginal

111 There are also empirical studies comparing growth rates across countries to see how much of the difference can be attributed to differences in factor inputs. Again it is not measured fixed investment that shows up as significant so much as the unexplained residual. See Denison, E. F., *Why Growth Rates Differ*, George Allen and Unwin, 1967

returns like the factors of production; on the contrary the more knowledge one has the easier it becomes to acquire more. Knowledge does not get used up in the process of production, so its opportunity cost could be zero. Property rights over knowledge are difficult to define, although some knowledge may be protected for a time by patent. This is required to provide an incentive to research, since the creation of new knowledge can indeed be costly and subject to diminishing returns.

Economists are starting now to develop the standard theory of production in ways that are appropriate to the present age and technology. The main focus of interest is on the use of information, its storage, transmission, processing and application. Physical transformation of inputs into outputs is becoming of secondary importance. The neo-classical theory of production was developed in the nineteenth century and reflects the technology of its time. Sooner or later the concepts of scarcity and abundance will have to be redefined.

The standard model of economic growth cannot, on its own, explain why the growth of productivity, and hence of living standards, varies so much from one country to another. Indeed it would predict that all countries would converge in terms of growth rates and even levels of output per head. A recent survey of the state of growth theory by one who has made a considerable contribution to it reads like this:[112]

> The neo-classical model states that the long-run growth rate of output per worker is given by the growth rate of labour-augmenting technical progress, which is treated as exogenous. It would seem to follow that all national economies with access to the same changing technology should have converging productivity growth rates. [...] Something like convergence may be detectable in the recent record of the advanced industrial countries. However, it is almost impossible to see convergence in a comparison of those economies with the nations of Latin America, Africa or most of Asia.

The survey article goes on to describe the development in the last ten or twenty years of neo-classical models with endogenous growth. Typically they involve some concept of shared knowledge and

112 Solow, R. M., 'Growth Theory', in Greenaway, D. et al (eds.), op. cit.

experience which is generated as a by-product of research or training motivated by private gain. This public good benefits all the producers within a country or economic region, but does not readily diffuse to other parts of the world. As a result economic success breeds success, so that growth rates diverge, perhaps forever.

These developments might be seen as formalising the long-standing views of many historians and political commentators. Advocates of the market economy have not based their case purely on its static efficiency. They have also claimed that competition stimulates research and innovation from which the whole economy will ultimately benefit. For example:[113]

> Capitalism has proven far more efficient than centrally planned economic systems in developing and utilising technology, and in adapting to the rapidly changing conditions of a global division of labour, under the conditions of a mature industrial economy.

It is an open question whether technical progress can continue forever. Knowledge once it is acquired does not get used up, but it can be forgotten, as the history of the Dark Ages demonstrates. Any one technical advance, for example electrification, does eventually exhaust its potential for stimulating further growth. Persistent growth requires an unending sequence of innovations which of their very nature we cannot predict. Perhaps there is only a finite amount of useful knowledge to which we can ever have access. There may exist, still unknown to us, the true and definitive production function which shows where the ultimate limits of technical progress really lie. But such a function would take the character of output as given. In fact, as new and better means are found of satisfying existing human wants and needs, experience suggests that new wants and needs will be discovered or invented.

As society gets richer one might suppose that the imperative to improve our standard of living yet further would become less urgent. Economic theory itself would predict that the marginal utility of consumption would decline; some other source of well-being, perhaps family life or even religious observance, would take up more of our

113 Fukuyama, F., *The End of History and the Last Man*, Hamish Hamilton, 1992.

time. But the habits of mind developed in a world of scarcity die hard in a world of abundance. Efficiency in the use of resources still seems very important, even to those who have enough and to spare.

The new theories of endogenous growth seek to explain why some societies are rich and others are poor. They suggest that the market system need not be equalising. Accidents of history may result in persistent and even growing disparities. They do not show however that this inequality is unavoidable and may suggest how it might be reduced. This is not a matter of saving the poor from exploitation: there is nothing in the theory of endogenous growth to suggest that the rich flourish at the expense of the poor. It is simply that those who get a good start may see their advantage amplified over time.

Economics was at one time called 'the dismal science'. It claimed that scarcity was inevitable and predicted that efforts to relieve it would be counter-productive. This dim view of life is associated particularly with the name of Thomas Malthus (who was incidentally an Anglican clergyman.) He believed that population would always grow up to the limits set by subsistence, and hence that poverty could never be reduced. Since his time these predictions have been proved wrong, at least so far as the industrial countries are concerned. The neo-classical economics of the nineteenth century developed, in part, as a reaction against this excess of pessimism. Economics is now in a much more optimistic mood, leaving it to other disciplines to identify potential 'limits to growth' resulting from the exhaustion of essential raw materials or damage to a sensitive ecological balance.[114] The market system itself is seen as generating growth, and the poorer nations are being encouraged to benefit from fuller participation in it.

114 See the report of the Club of Rome's famous project on the 'Predicament of Mankind', Meadows, D. L. et al, *The Limits to Growth*, Earth Island, 1972. For an economist's critique of that study, see Beckermann, W., 'Economists, Scientists and Environmental Catastrophe', *Oxford Economic Papers*, 24, 1972.

Section Two: Christian Belief

Creation and blessing

The process of transformation in the productive process described by modern economists is very different from the biblical account which eventually gave rise to the Christian understanding of divine creation. Economic theory is concerned with constrained optimisation, in which output is maximised subject to the constraints of resources and of technology. What is the productive process in which the Trinitarian God created the world? 'In the beginning God created the heavens and the earth' (Genesis 1:1). The theologian Jurgen Moltmann argues that the text makes a clear distinction between creation (Hebrew *bara'*) in the first verse and the various Hebrew verbs for making, building and other activities in subsequent chapters. The Hebrew for creation is *Bara'*, the Hebrew for making is '*asah.* Creation refers to the creation as a whole, and is absolutely new.

There can be no accusative in the grammatical structure of a sentence when the word *bara'* is used. In other words, God does not make (Hebrew *bara'*) wood into a table. Equally a person building a house out of clay which had been baked into bricks is described in Hebrew as making (Hebrew '*asah*) the bricks into a house using mortar. However the creation of the world does not make anything into anything else. This means that any Christian or Jewish discussion of production has to distinguish the divine production from everyday reality. Divine creation is not inherent in anything else. Creation refers to the bringing of existence out of nothing: ex nihilo. Indeed in the Priestly writing in the Old Testament which makes up the first chapter of Genesis as well as other writing such as Leviticus in the Old Testament, *Bara'* is only used for God's bringing forth. *Bara'* creates what did not exist previously.

Divine creation cannot be compared to human production. If we are to talk about the biblical view of human production, the search for an analogy must turn to God's making or '*asah.* Therefore it is with '*asah* that the study begins. Making refers to the purposeful manufacture by God of an object. It is because God made the works of heaven and earth in six days such as at Exodus 20 and 31:17 that the seventh day, the Sabbath, is a day of rest. The works of heaven and earth include animals, plants and the contours of the land. Each can be shaped, and given a character and distinctive nature. It is a forming and producing. There can be no comparison between creation and human work, but only between divine and human making. Human work shapes, produces and forms.

Nevertheless, while it is salutary to be reminded that the divine creation of the world is not the same as the productive process in modern economic theory, human beings can engage in production in ways that do correspond to the divine making. Genesis 2:15 speaks of God placing Adam in the garden to till it and keep it. Production is therefore embedded in the biblical narrative. Work is not defined on its own, nor apart from the Sabbath, but is defined and limited by the word of God. Moltmann summarises his analysis as follows:[115]

> Workday and Sabbath lie also on the same temporal level. They concern the same people. They are not divided between human beings and the gods, or between enslaved and free.

It follows that God can create out of nothing, make covenants where there were none, and bring about miracles. Humanity is seen in a different light. It is finite with finite powers and must engage in productive activity. Deliverance from sin is no release from work. The only change of work is from being under a curse to being in a blessing.

It is this view of production and work as having a dual moral and theological nature which distinguishes the biblical understanding of production from a contemporary secular one. For a modern day economics textbook the question is whether there is an efficient relationship in the productive process. The concern of scripture is not at all to do with this, but with the quality of divine blessing (or not) which inheres in it. That makes a fundamental point about the productive process. It is always seen in scripture as embodying

115 Moltmann, J., *God in Creation*, SCM, 1985 and *On Human Dignity*, SCM, 1984.

relationships. There is the relationship of humanity to each other, to nature and to God. Productivity is never seen as a separate category. What is blessing or cursing in a productive process will be related to other aspects of life. So in Genesis Chapter Three the relationship between the man and the woman is one of enmity even as the work process is seen as one of struggle. Hardy and Ford describe blessing and cursing as fundamental biblical terms for the interaction of God and the world.[116] The Jewish Rabbis at the time of Jesus spoke of God ruling the world by blessing it and this concept is worth exploring further.

Blessing is neither a magical concept, nor simply a metaphor of speech. It is related to the way that God is active in the world and especially to the causality of God in creation. The blessing of the disciples by Jesus (Luke 24:50–53) leads into the return of the disciples to Jerusalem where they bless God in the temple. Blessing affirms what a thing, person, animal, or situation is in the way most appropriate to its future and nature. At the time of Jesus it was thought that if one used anything of creation without blessing God then this was to deny the authority of God and so to rob God of what was his. In the life of Jesus God blessed humanity and in turn this blessing is returned to God. So Acts 3:25 speaks of the children of Abraham being blessed by God through the covenant, by which all the families of the earth received blessing. Now in the ministry of Jesus, who here is called the Servant, the blessing is fulfilled and the covenant is brought to its proper goal.

The question must be how this theological concept relates to the economic one of production. Given that the creation of the world is not to be compared to the productive process and that what is produced is also to be blessed, and so set in the context of divine and human relationships, what can be said about the nature of production as it is seen in modern economic theory? *Bara'* takes place in what Moltmann calls 'the sphere of history, nature and spirit, through which something comes into existence which was not there previously'.[117] The miracles in the biblical narrative are part of this world of history,

116 Hardy, D. W. and Ford, D. F., *Jubilate*, Darton, Longman and Todd, 1982.
117 Moltmann, J., *God in Creation*, SCM, 1985.

rather than nature. The turning of water into wine and the story of the loaves and fishes are designed to elicit faith, and the stories are deeply symbolic of the new messianic age. They are intended as signs in the story of the coming of the Messiah. Indeed even the reference in 1 Corinthians 3:7 to God making things grow is again a reference to the way in which the act of creation in the world of faith is neither to be dissected into different processes nor is it to be compared to anything else. It is a unified action, unique and outside time.

Where the biblical picture turns to inputs and outputs there is the sense of living in an agricultural world where the constraints are very great. This is not simply the constraint of the agriculture of the time, with limited technology, but also of the lack of any biblical analysis in terms of inputs and outputs at all, any sense that the technology might be improved. The Old Testament scholar Friedemann Golka shows how the Wisdom tradition is not concerned with general theories but with countless empirical observations.[118] There is no Aristotelian tradition in which the laws that govern the universe, or even the farming of a field, can be worked out and codified. Hebrew Wisdom is compared by Golka to African tribal folklore, as researched by anthropologists. Science is there to trace the path of the Creator in creation. And it is seen as part of the praise of God: doxology, or the adoration of the source of all life. In the Book of Proverbs the world of nature and human nature is explored so that a relationship is established between plants, animals and humans. There is surprise at the correspondence between the world of, say, ants and people. It is an inductive method, in which the ways of farmers, workers and animals are united. There is simply no attempt to build up a theory of optimisation but only of stewardship which we will come to in the next section. The description of work in Job 28, where the mining of precious metals is described, is again made up of observations contrasted with the ways of God. It is striking that commentaries point out that there were no mines in Israel, then or now, although copper was found in Edom and smelted at Elath. Gold, silver, and lapis lazuli were all found far away. The description is one of 'general

118 Golka, F., *The Leopard's Spots: Biblical and African Wisdom in Proverbs*, T and T Clark, 1993.

knowledge' unrelated to economic reality. The purpose of the description is simply to draw a parallel between Wisdom and the search for gold, but then to negate this parallel by arguing that the search for Wisdom is beyond comparison even with such difficult pursuits as underground excavation.

We are left with the realisation that the biblical understanding of production yields no relationship with the contemporary one. It is not that the economic reality was more primitive, and of course agricultural, but rather that this is a theocratic world view where everything is related to the nature of divine activity, and how this can be encountered and respected on its own terms. Blessing is the central term here. Work certainly has meaning but it is not seen in a productive way.

Stewardship in the Bible

There is a much closer relationship with efficiency and stewardship in the biblical tradition. If one returns to the Wisdom tradition then it is clear that the question of poverty is related to idleness and bad stewardship, in a highly moral way. Golka points out that the early capitalism of the Israelite and Judean monarchy worsened class divisions and increased inequality. In the tribal society that preceded the monarchy there were divisions, but they were exacerbated in the succeeding centuries. The Wisdom literature on the creation of humanity functions as part of a social criticism in which social conflict was defused. Wealth does not last forever and must be kept in good shape, as Proverbs 27:23–24 makes clear: 'Know well the condition of your flocks, and give attention to your herds, for riches do not last for ever and does a crown endure to all generations?'

Much of the stewardship of wealth is seen as to do with avoiding idleness, as in Proverbs 10, 15, 20 and 22. Indeed some parts of Proverbs directly relate poverty to idleness, or the pursuit of pleasure. It can also be caused by the failure to follow instructions. Golka compares this negative view of poverty with the African understanding of poverty in some tribal societies. Here there is a largely negative view of poverty which is not matched by the biblical understanding of the poor person as close to God and made by God. The biblical notion of stewardship is largely based on the idea of preserving what one has inherited for one's children (Proverbs 20:21) or else is tied to the care of property: 'House and wealth are inherited from the fathers [...]' There should be care for this inheritance or it will fail. 'An inheritance got hastily in the beginning will in the end not be blessed' warns Proverbs 28:8. Golka quotes the English scholar Norman Whybray:[119]

> Such evidence as is to be found here suggests that their settings are predominantly those of the life of the small farmers farming their own land (and, perhaps, to some extent, of an urban proletariat). It is strongly implied that only constant hard work allied with common sense and a resistance to temptation to fritter away one's substance on inessentials and self-indulgence can stave off the threat of poverty. While some of the warnings would no doubt constitute sound advice if offered to members of any social class, they would undoubtedly be far more relevant to the circumstances of the manual worker than of the relatively secure upper class.

It is however not simply the avoidance of poverty which concerns the farmer in the Wisdom tradition but also the doctrine of the right time. Here the farmer knows the right time to sow and reap at harvest. This is elaborated in the Book of Ecclesiastes, although it sees the life and destiny of humanity as being worth no more than those of the beasts. They have no moral superiority and their destiny is the dust of the earth. This is an unusual biblical viewpoint, but the idea of the right time permeates the Wisdom tradition. As Golka says:[120]

> The species (human, animal and plant) which proverbial Wisdom observes are a product of God's blessing. Wisdom looks at human beings in their natural communities (family, neighbourhood, clan, and village), at old and young, generation after generation. Hence the need to make provision for oneself, for one's descendants, and ultimately for the whole planet earth.

The stewardship of work and time is also picked up in the New Testament epistles where in Thessalonians 1 and 2 there is a stress on

119 Whybray, N., *Wealth and Poverty in the Book of Proverbs*, JSOT Press, Sheffield, 1990.
120 Golka, F., op.cit. p. 120.

working cheerfully and well. Indeed Paul speaks of his own ministry in terms of hard work, and in ten places he refers to the most menial tasks of slavery *(kopos)* as being the same as missionary work. In Galatians 4:11 he speaks of labouring in vain, and in 2 Corinthians 11:23–28 Paul's defence is that he has worked harder than his opponents. The work is however metaphorical, for it refers to beatings, hunger and persecution which Paul has endured more than others. There is little developed account in the New Testament of the literal stewardship of economic resources or of the importance of actual physical work, as compared with the Wisdom tradition in the Old Testament.

In an agricultural economy stewardship requires, above all, the preservation of the quality of the land. The appreciation of the gift of the land to the people of Israel is one of the themes of recent biblical scholarship, and the keeping of the law is seen as a response to this gift. The gift of the land to Israel is part of the deliverance of Israel from slavery in Egypt.[121] It is also the case that this land was highly productive. Here the blessing of Israel, referred to in the first section as a distinct biblical category, becomes part of God's care for his people. Deuteronomy 8 links 'the ability to produce wealth' with the confirmation of the covenant in the past with their forefathers. This materialist interpretation of the covenant's benefits, or fruits, is not typical of the biblical narrative, but it is certainly true that the appreciation of the land given in the exodus story remained a potent factor in Israel's beliefs and values. The Gospels tend to be silent on the theme of wealth, and place much more value on the healings and exorcisms which accompany the message of deliverance and salvation. There is then a bodily and physical aspect of the ministry of Jesus, but it is not related to the gift of material things, still less to their growth and increase. The language of Jesus about the Kingdom of God is metaphorical, although it does involve the imagery of plenty.

121 Brueggemann, W., *The Land*, Fortress Press, 1977; Evans, B. F. and Cusack, G. D. (eds.), *Theology of the Land*, The Liturgical Press, 1987; Habel, N. C., *The Land is Mine*, Fortress Press, 1995.

Section Three: Summary and Discussion

To understand human beings one must observe them in their natural environment. In this chapter we move on from the description of human choice and evaluation to consideration of the resources available to satisfy human wants and needs – from the demand to the supply side of the economy. Economic theory is about the efficient use of scarce resources, saying that there is no such thing as a free lunch; Christian belief, responding to the same natural world, says rather that the best things cost nothing and rejoices in their abundance.

The production process as described in economic theory seems most appropriate to the world since the industrial and economic revolutions. The entrepreneur selects from a range of technologies combining labour, land and capital in different proportions. One imagines an improving landowner contemplating the purchase of a combine harvester, or an industrialist replacing half his workforce with a new machine driven by steam. In pre-modern times these possibilities did not exist. In recent years the nature of technology is changing, making the standard model less relevant. The key input now may be information, and the output may be no more tangible than that.

In the beginning, the world was created out of nothing, but the bounty of God, as recorded in the Bible, involves a process rather like human production, in that it transforms some input into an output, shapes material and gives it a new form. Yet the process is not predictable like that of a mathematical production function: the same quantity of seed (with the same quantity of labour) may produce an increase of a hundred-fold or nothing at all. One must ask God's blessing on the land, but piety is not a factor of production with effects that can be known in advance. The New Testament in particular recognises that rain and sunshine may fall on the just and the unjust alike.

The miracles of the Bible demonstrate that God is not constrained by the scarcity of resources. He can provide food and drink to excess. This may be understood literally, but it is also intended as a kind of metaphor. The things that are of most real value in life, that may be love or spiritual blessings, come as free gifts to those who seek them, with nothing demanded in return.

The modern world is not comfortable with miracles of any kind. They cannot be verified by science, and moreover they distract attention from the effort required to make tangible improvements in human well-being, and to allocate the limited resources which we know that we do have to their best use. Such careful stewardship is what most people nowadays would regard as a good Christian attitude to the natural world. Economic theory shows how this can come about through the profit incentive and the market mechanism.

Economic theory takes it for granted that natural resources are there to be used, even on occasion to be used up. This is generally the assumption in the Bible as well. The wisdom literature of the Old Testament is especially concerned that resources should be used with care, so as to provide for the future, in accordance with the conventional views to be found in any stable society living close to the margin of subsistence. But nature is not itself an object of worship or reverence: trees and rivers are not sacred in the Bible, any more than they are in an economic cost-benefit analysis. The more mystical attitude to nature adopted by some contemporary Christians is borrowed from other kinds of religious belief.

The ideal of faithful stewardship might seem to bring economic theory and Christian belief close together. But this is to forget much of what the Bible itself has to say on the subject. In the Old Testament the best of the flock and the harvest is to be sacrificed, burnt on the altar and totally destroyed. After the conquest of the Promised Land whole cities were treated in this way which must seem to us wasteful as well as barbaric. In other parts of the Bible generosity is praised even when it seems rash or irresponsible. We are told to respond to God's bountiful over-provision by an equally lavish dedication of resources to his worship. Jesus himself in the New Testament praises what seemed to his disciples (and may seem to us) to be nothing better than conspicuous waste.

To summarise, and to simplify, the Bible has a pre-modern view of production. It takes as normal what we would see as poverty and relies on God's providence rather than human endeavour to escape from destitution. Its visions of abundance belie experience like mirages in the desert. Economic theory is modern in its assumption that care and calculation can increase output. Much of the present-day world is still very poor or in the early stages of modernisation, but some of the richest countries have entered an age of post-modern affluence. They have little appreciation of scarcity because they have come to take abundance for granted.

Chapter Six

The Supply and Demand of Labour

Introduction

Contrasting attitudes to 'the work of human hands' illustrate well the different views of anthropology implicit in neo-classical economics and in Christian teaching. The popular perception may be that economics simply treats labour as a commodity to be bought and sold like any other, whilst Christianity supports a work ethic, or even a 'theology of work'. Both these characterisations are subject to important qualification, as this chapter aims to show.

Labour is a factor of production, combining with land and capital to produce goods and services, as we saw in the last chapter. The supply of labour is obviously motivated, at least in part, by the wish or need of human beings to earn a living. This is true, not only in the marketplace, but also in the household, and even of Robinson Crusoe on his desert island. The cost of supplying labour is the leisure time that is lost. That time could have been devoted to rest and recreation which are necessary to health and enjoyable in their own right.

This strictly economic view of work must be contrasted with the views of psychologists and sociologists. They point to the sense of participation and self-fulfilment which most people claim to find in their working lives. Certainly those deprived of the opportunity to work do not suffer only from the resulting loss of income.

It has been suggested that the propensity to work is part of our genetic inheritance. According to Michael Argyle in *The Social Psychology of Work*:[122]

> Forms of work and social behaviour similar to those of humans are found in higher mammals and birds. Work among apes and monkeys is in fact

122 Argyle, M., *The Social Psychology of Work*, Penguin, 1989.

remarkably similar to work in the most primitive human societies, suggesting that there may be innate factors in human work-patterns also.

Christian teaching about work may have something in common with this view, but it is not just psychology, or common sense, retold in religious language. It is part of a distinctively Christian understanding of human nature in relation to God, to one another and to creation.[123] The motive for work is not just self-interest, or even self-fulfilment, but especially service. It is offered out of gratitude, not seeking a reward. Yet, it is recognised, at the same time, that hard work is a necessity, to preserve life and civilisation. Christian belief was first expressed by people who lived very close to these harsh economic realities.

Section One, as usual, begins with some standard theory. This is followed by some thoughts on unemployment and the future of work from the point of view of neo-classical economics. Section Two reviews the attitudes to work to be found in the Bible. This includes material on slavery which we find important to contrast with a modern view of what is required by human rights or the dignity of labour.

Section One: Economic Theory

Labour supply and demand

The demand for labour is a derived demand; it is not wanted for its own sake but for its contribution to production. Different kinds of labour can be classified according to their role in production-skilled or unskilled, with or without experience, possessing strength, dexterity, perseverance, honesty, imagination, loyalty and so on. To some extent

123 Peter Sedgwick gives a brief survey of Christian teaching on work in Annex A to *Unemployment and the Future of Work – An Enquiry for the Churches*, Council of Churches For Britain and Ireland, 1997. This chapter draws on that enquiry. Andrew Britton was the executive secretary of the working party that prepared it.

one kind of labour can substitute for another, some capabilities can be learnt. One of the advantages of human beings is their adaptability.

It is much too simple to describe the demand for labour in terms of an undifferentiated demand for hours of work. Economists nowadays use the concept of 'human capital'.[124] Education and training increase productivity, but they are costly to acquire. In this respect they are analogous to the process of investment in fixed assets. They may be of general application, like basic literacy and numeracy, enhancing productivity in a wide variety of tasks, or they may be specific to just one occupation, or even to a single employer, as might be the case with coal mining or public administration. (If there is no suggestion that education is anything more than a means to the end of higher earnings or profits, then there is less point in education the older one becomes.)

With a relatively simple technology, the productivity of labour depends on physical strength which in turn depends on the state of health and the intake of food. The economics of labour supply under conditions of poverty are not often included in an elementary economics course, but they are very relevant to the living conditions of the majority of the world's population even today. Partha Dasgupta sets them out in his study of the economics of poverty already cited above. He writes:[125]

> The link between consumption and production is at its most vivid when we think of the transformation of calorie intake into work. It highlights our sense of the circularity of living. [...] Humans, like all animals, obtain their energy from their food in a chemical form, derived directly or indirectly from plants.

It is generally true that we work in order to consume. In poor communities it is also true that we consume in order to work. Diet affects productivity in many subtle ways, including its effect on resistance to disease. Chronic malnutrition may not kill, but it prevents those affected from achieving their potential ability to work. The state

124 The classic reference for this concept is Becker, G. S., *Human Capital: A Theoretical and Empirical Analysis with special Reference to Education*, Univ. of Chicago Press, 1975.

125 Dasgupta, P., op. cit., Chapter 14.

of health is like a stock of capital which can be built up or run down progressively over many years.

The supply of labour, like everything else in economic theory depends on its price. It is suggested, however, that the supply of labour may be unusual in that higher wages may reduce rather than increase the hours worked by those who are relatively affluent. As people get richer it is suggested that they will value leisure more, and that will be enough to outweigh the extra incentive to work provided by a better rate of pay per hour. The supply of labour is an exercise in the efficient allocation of limited resources of time.

Economists have become increasingly interested in the division of labour within the household, typically as between the parents of young children. The household has its time budget to allocate to work in the home and outside it, paid or unpaid. The assumption once was that nearly all men worked a standard week and most mothers stayed at home to look after the children and the housework. That made the labour supply very inflexible and the subject uninteresting to the economic theorist. Now it is recognised that this was just one historical phase, corresponding to a particular technology of mechanisation and mass production. The issue has now become a very interesting one again.

The relationship between household members can be seen as the result of an optimisation exercise choosing the most efficient use of all the time, and indeed the food input, available to it. Sometimes the best solution really is to give the husband the sole responsibility for earning a money income, and providing him with the diet which that requires. But another way of looking at the same issue is to see it as a bargain struck between household members in which one may have more bargaining power than the other. A mother who does not feel able to leave her children may be in a weak position relative to her husband, and end up doing more than her fair share of the work.

In the industrialised countries, the last fifty years have seen a marked increase in the proportion of women in paid employment. Studies of time use show that this is partly at the expense of unpaid work in the household, but it is also true that women work more hours in total than men. Perversely it seems as if women are choosing to work harder even though living standards are rising, as if they did not value leisure time as the theory assumes. Unless work itself is attractive, this does not look like rational behaviour.

One explanation could be that women have always wanted to be able to earn their own income, but were prevented from doing so until recently by restrictive rules devised to protect male monopolies. Another explanation would be that women no longer feel able to rely on the stability of marriage and therefore need to acquire skills and work experience as a kind of insurance. Yet another view would be that new technology has made the old gender division of labour obsolete, so that women may actually be better employees than men. Logically this would result in a more symmetrical household, perhaps a reversal of traditional roles.

The usual assumption is that work itself is not a source of enjoyment. Nevertheless, some jobs do have 'non-pecuniary advantages' which mean that they might provide more utility per hour than some kinds of rest. It might not require too fundamental a revision of the standard theory to recognise that some people actually want to work and would do so if necessary even if they were not paid. What the neo-classical model does require is that work should become less enjoyable the more time it takes up. At the margin the worker has to be paid to work more. The theory would only break down if workers are actually addicted to work and never want to stop.

Pay and conditions of work

In the simplest version of neo-classical economics, labour is bought and sold in a competitive labour market. Its price, or wage, is at the level where supply is equal to demand. When there is excess demand for labour the wage rises, and when there is excess supply it falls. If we distinguish many grades or types of labour, then relative wages will respond to relative supply and relative demand. In general equilibrium with a competitive market, it is as simple as that.

The theory is a little different in markets where there is monopoly power, of buyers, or of sellers, or both. A large firm may provide so much of the employment in one place or one occupation that it can effectively set the wage rate itself. Individual workers will have no choice but to accept it. However, trades unions, guilds and professional associations may be able to organise their members so as to create monopoly power on the other side of the market. In economic theory this is all explicable by self-interest. The workers may see themselves as heroic and the bosses as greedy; economic theory makes no use of such emotive terms.

Labour can be hired by the hour, by the day, by the year, or for an indefinite period. The rate of pay may be set for the duration of the contract or be renegotiated periodically. It may be a set wage per hour or depend on output and other indicators. At one extreme the worker is self-employed, selling an output of services rather than units of labour input; at the other extreme would be an indenture, requiring the worker to serve in whatever capacity is required in return for living expenses or payment in kind.

So far it would appear that the labour market is being treated much like any other. But economists are well aware of its special character. A more advanced treatment of the subject can take this into account without abandoning such key neo-classical assumptions as rationality and individualism.[126] Employment under any form of contract short of slavery is a co-operative relationship requiring an element of mutual trust. Employers cannot monitor in detail the effort which every worker puts into every task. For some purposes an arm's-length agreement is good enough, provided the terms of the contract are clear and enforceable. The workers employed on such terms are sometimes called 'outsiders'. The 'insiders' do not need such detailed monitoring; they can be left to get on with the job.[127] Perhaps they are family members, or craftsmen whose ability and application is guaranteed by their union; perhaps they are long-term employees who have built up a stake in the business.

An employment contract is a means of allocating risk. A casual worker, employed by the day, has plenty of freedom, but no security. There is a risk of unemployment when demand is slack. Conversely a

126 For example see Akerlof, G. A., 'Gift Exchange and Efficiency Work Theory', *American Economic Review*, 74:2, 1984.

127 Lindbeck, A and Snower, D., *The Insider-Outsider Theory of Employment and Unemployment*, MIT Press, 1988.

long-term contract throws some of the risk onto the employer, who may have to pay wages to workers who are surplus to requirements. On the other hand continuity of employment reduces the hiring and firing costs of the firm.

When contracts are long-lasting employees can be seen as assets of the firm. Indeed the human capital, that is the skill and experience, embodied in the core of the workforce can be one of the key determinants of competitive success. Human resource management – significant terminology – is about preserving and enhancing the value of that precious asset. It will be worth paying for the training of staff if they are expected to stay in post, not if they are expected to move to a competitor. If workers are free to move then they may have to pay for their own training in the expectation that they will earn more as a result in the future.

Whatever the form of contract, the worker is always in the last resort free to quit, subject perhaps to some financial penalty. Even if a contract were voluntarily entered into which made this impossible, it would not be enforceable at law. This is one fundamental difference between human capital and capital of other kinds.

The end of work?

The high levels of unemployment in America and Europe in the 1980s prompted much concern that the demand for labour might be inadequate to provide work for all those who wanted it. In the standard neo-classical model persistent unemployment can arise only if wages fail to clear the labour market. This may be because of minimum wage laws, trades union monopoly power or the provisions of the social security system. (Keynesian economics, by contrast, attributes unemployment to failure in markets generally, not just the market for labour but the markets for savings and investment as well – but that is beyond the scope of this book.) If the demand for labour is reduced, real wages can be expected to fall, in so far as the institutional constraints will allow.

The demand for labour, especially unskilled labour, might be reduced for a variety of reasons, but in particular by competition from low-wage countries abroad or by the development of new labour-saving technologies. Globalisation certainly encourages firms to locate production where it is cheapest, and standard trade theory suggests that wages, and the returns to other factors of production, will tend to be equalised by the exchange of goods and services. The extent to which this happens in practice is a matter of dispute amongst economists.[128]

The nature of work is undoubtedly changing as a result of new technologies. Some writers, not generally economists, would argue that we are approaching the end of work, when there will be nothing useful for most of us to do. The only workers will be a small elite of experts and managers. Could almost all human work go the way of the ox-cart and the pit pony? One popular American book about this possibility begins like this:[129]

> From the beginning, civilisation has been structured, in large part, around the concept of work. From the palaeolithic hunter-gatherer and the neolithic farmer to the medieval craftsman and assembly line worker of the current century, work has been an integral part of daily existence. Now, for the first time, human labour is being systematically eliminated from the production process.

If this does not appear an attractive prospect, then a small amount of standard economic theory may be somewhat reassuring. The literature on 'the end of work' has not taken sufficient account of market reactions. The choice of factor inputs must depend on their relative prices. If capital is being used in preference to labour that may be because labour is relatively expensive to employ. Indeed the new technology itself may have been developed, in part, as a response to the high level of wages in the industrial countries. The problem, from the point of view of economic theory, must be that wages, in the industrial countries at least, cannot fall to the level that would clear the market. The answer might be to subsidise wages so as to encourage firms to adopt more labour-intensive technologies, and consumers to buy more labour-intensive products.

128 Wood, A., *North–South Trade, Inequality and Unemployment*, OUP, 1994.

129 Rifkin, J., *The End of Work – The Decline of the Global Labor Force and the Dawn of the Post-Market Era*, Putnam, 1995.

It is also possible, however, to question the basic assumption that the demand for labour is decreasing and must continue to do so. We have to ask what it is that human labour actually contributes to production, to open up the production function and look inside. Capital may be a substitute for labour of some kinds and a complement for others. In design, for example, a computer can do the calculations better than a human being, but it lacks the capacity for aesthetic judgement. The technologies now in use depend on the interaction of human minds with artificial intelligence. It would need a substantial further change before machines could be regarded as creative in the same sense as we regard ourselves.

Another argument suggests that human labour can never be altogether obsolete. Human work is undertaken to satisfy human wants and needs. It is not just a matter of producing products with given design capabilities; new products are being invented all the time. This involves a close relationship between the producers and the consumers, who are beings of the same kind. It requires insight, imagination and empathy. Often a human relationship is part of the product itself: a teacher must relate as a person to engage the interest of a pupil; an entertainer projects a personality which the audience enjoys observing; a financial advisor is there in part to reassure and to build up the confidence of the client. This kind of work is becoming more important as the service sector increases as a share of total production.

Work in the service sector, using human relationships, does not always require analytical skills or sophistication. It need never be confined to an educated elite. Moreover it has often to be undertaken locally, thus escaping the threat of competition from abroad. In the rich countries service workers like nurses, receptionists, advertising executives and so on should be able to earn a living from the custom of the beneficiaries of new technology, or from the taxes that they pay to finance public expenditure. The problem is not that there is no more work to be done; rather it one of finding the right means to pay for it.

It is possible to imagine a society in which all citizens receive an income as of right, which is deemed adequate to meet their basic needs. Thus income and work could be separated, for some at least of the community. Those who worked without pay would not go hungry.

People would be free to work, or not to work, as they chose. In *The Future of Work*, for example, Charles Handy asks:[130]

> In most modern states today the state provides, as a universal right, access to education and health care. Why not then access to the basic necessities of life such as food, clothing, shelter and heat, by means of a straight cash payment?

Many distinguished economists have written in support of such a proposal.[131] If there is no pleasure to be derived from work as such, it may be an attractive idea. Admittedly it would involve high rates of taxation on the incomes of those who did chose to work, but it preserves the freedom of individuals to decide what use they will make of the resources they are given.

Against these considerations, however, must be set the social significance of work, and also the social significance of wages. We define our social roles by the work that we do. It gives us status and identity. These factors are not easily incorporated into economic theory. Pay itself is highly symbolic. Whatever its economic significance, a wage is understood as the value which society puts on a person's contribution. An economy of reward is still perceived as just, however much we might prefer to see an economy of grace established.[132] For the present, and indeed for the foreseeable future, paid work remains the norm.

Writing in 1944 and recalling the mass unemployment of the thirties, William Beveridge wrote:[133]

> Idleness is not the same as want, but a separate evil which men do not escape by having an income. They must also have the chance of rendering useful service and of feeling that they are doing so.

130 Handy, C., *The Future of Work*, Blackwell, 1984.

131 A useful survey of the arguments is given a sympathetic point of view in, Brittan, S., *Capitalism with a Human Face*, Edward Elgar, 1995; Chapter 13, 'Basic Income and the Welfare State'.

132 See the related discussion of the economies of gift and of exchange, in Selby, P., *Grace and Mortgage*, Darton, Longman and Todd, 1997, Chapter 8.

133 Beveridge, W. H., *Full Employment in a Free Society*, Allen and Unwin, 1944.

Such sentiments have in fact motivated many economists to seek a cure for unemployment. Yet they do not accord well with the assumptions of neo-classical theory. In the standard model of labour supply 'idleness' would count as leisure, being a good rather than an evil. If the unemployed want to render useful service there are many opportunities for them to do so on a voluntary basis (if the benefit regime permits). Surely we should leave them to make their own choices as to how they spend their time. There are value judgements implicit in the Beveridge quotation which neo-classical economic theory invites us to 'unwrap', and quite possibly to reject.

Section Two: Christian Belief

The biblical understanding of work

Work is central to the Genesis account of creation, as we have already discussed in Chapter Five. There is an extensive account of how God creates, and in what way this reflects his sovereign power. This is not the same however as a work ethic. The praise of the mighty acts of God cannot be reduced to a set of precepts for employers or a moral example for workers. Indeed in much of scripture there is no work ethic. Only in a few passages, such as the one often quoted from Proverbs Six where the hard working ant is praised, is there really any work ethic as we would know it.[134]

But the biblical understanding of work is very different from Egyptian wisdom literature, where the sages deprecated manual labour. In the Egyptian *Instruction of Dwauf* it was regarded as demeaning. The expectation that poverty and misfortune are avoidable in the tribal society of Israel rests on a strong belief in industry and forethought. This is a very individualistic ethic which contrasts with the outlook of the Old Testament Prophets. In the Wisdom literature, poverty is due to sloth (Proverbs 10:4, 13:18, 20:13, 23:21, 24:34,

134 Volf, M., *Work in the Spirit: Towards a Theology of Work*, OUP, 1991.

28:19). This forms part of a tight ethical code where the preservation of wealth is all-important in Israelite society.

What there is in the Old Testament is an assumption that human beings will work. This work is however always morally subordinate to the demands of worship, of keeping the obligations of a tribal society and of caring for one's family. It is difficult to argue that work as such was praised in the way in which it came to be seen in the early stages of the Industrial Revolution in England and the American colonies by those Puritans who interpreted scripture for their purposes. It would be going too far to deny that there was any work ethic at all, but it was certainly highly qualified.

One of the clearest restrictions on economic life in the Old Testament was the Sabbath law, found in Exodus 13, where extremely harsh penalties were imposed on anyone who worked on this day. It expressed forcibly the priority of worship over material wants and needs. At the same time the Sabbath is for rest as part of the natural ordering of the creation, and worship is then interwoven into this day of rest. This principle is not contradicted in the New Testament – indeed the story of Mary and Martha (Luke 10:38–42) supports it – but the law itself was not upheld. It was the strict interpretation of this law which Jesus challenged in Mark 2, since he believed that the law had become restrictive in its effect. Behind this challenge rests a struggle between different parts of the reform movement in Judaism, as to how God was to be served. Jesus argued that a law which prevented his healing a sick man was not serving the purposes of God.

There has been much controversy about the Hebrew words used for dominion in Genesis. Dominion is a relevant concept since the task of exercising responsibility over nature on behalf of God is a task which involves manual labour. The Hebrew words for dominion are *Rah* and *kbs* which have been described as being aggressive terms, and certainly the nuance of these verbs are those of mastery and control. On the other hand the discussion mentioned above in Chapter Five of God's work of creation, or *Bara'*, is not simply an account of creation from nothing. Although it is true that creation is ex nihilo, or in other words a creation out of no pre-existing matter, there is also the struggle in mythological terms in Genesis which describes the emergence of the earth to be a cosmos known as shaped and ordered.

This involves in mythological terms a struggle to subdue the forces of chaos, where the imagery is that of the Lord enthroned over the floods, as in Psalm 29:10. When the Genesis account in Chapter One moves onto the relationship of human beings and the creation, some of this harshness is still there. It is a relationship which sets human beings in charge of nature, although the end of dominion is to glorify God in the care of creation.

The early Christian writers made much of the way in which Adam was set to till the garden. Indeed Augustine contrasted the work of the farmers in his native North Africa with the reluctance to work manually shown by the monastic orders which he was in charge of.[135] Only by Augustine's time, around the period 390–430, do we find the development of an ethic of work, although even here it would take centuries for this to be fully developed:[136]

> The need which compelled me to write the book on the work of monks was this: when there had begun to be monasteries at Carthage, some maintained themselves by their own hands, obeying the Apostle; but others wished to live on the gifts of the faithful, and did no work to supply the necessities of life. They boasted that they fulfilled the words of the Gospel, where the Lord said, Behold the fowls of heaven, and the lilies of the field, (Matthew 6:26).

Indeed most of the New Testament references to toil, labour and work (*ergazomai* in Greek) are not to physical labour. There are the odd few references to the thief doing 'honest work with his hands' (Ephesians 4:28) but the context is that of 'giving to those in need'. It was certainly the case that Paul knew the experience of manual labour directly (1 Corinthians 4:12), yet the controlling ethic was that of being self-reliant. In 2 Thessalonians 3:10 there is an appeal to those who do not work. If they persist, they cannot expect to be supported by the Christian community. Instead the early Christian congregations were expected to 'work in quietness' and to 'earn their own living'. Paul suggests that all should provide for themselves through work if

135 Sedgwick, P. 'Wealth Creation and the Early Church', *Epworth Review*, 1993.

136 Augustine, *Retractions*, 2. 2. 1. The reference is to his text 'On the Work of Monks'. Translation in *Nicene and Post-Nicene Fathers*, Series 1, Volume 3, Eerdmans, 1999.

they can. Some commentators have therefore argued that Paul was interested in work as a productive activity. This is a difficult argument to sustain, even on the basis of these verses.

The reason why this is a problematic argument is because of the context in which Paul writes which is that of the expectation of the end of the world. Instead there is a different issue in view which a simplistic application of this verse would obscure. Paul was faced with the problem of ethical conduct in a pagan city. On the one hand there was the transition from a sexual ethic which was far more permissive in pagan cults than in Christianity. On the other hand there was the irresponsible behaviour of those Christians who had come to believe that the imminent end of the world meant that work was no longer necessary. Both in this chapter and in 1 Thessalonians 4:1–11 Paul strives to disabuse them of this idea. Paul's teaching on widespread rebellion against God, and the references to the 'Man of Sin' who will appear before the end time, show that it is not possible to take the command to 'earn one's own living' as anything but a rebuke to feverish apocalyptic speculation.

It is not therefore from the New Testament that a work ethic is to be found directly. The parable of the talents (Matthew 25:14–30) is about using the gifts which Christ has given his followers as a response to the judgement which is to come.[137] This certainly includes the examples of trading and investing in verse 16. But the most that this parable can show us is that Jesus did not deny the validity of such economic activity. The primary focus of this parable is on a responsible use of the master's goods before the end of this world. It therefore shares Paul's 'interim ethic' which lays down guidelines for the life of discipleship before the final judgement of the Son of Man. The emphasis in the parable of the talents is on the failure to act. The parable leads into a famous discussion of those who did not feed the hungry, clothe the naked and visit those sick or in prison. Action is illustrated by the act of investing in the parable; it is a choice as to whether one invests or not, for economic activity does not just happen.

137 Brown, R. E., Fitzmyer, J. A. and Murphy, R. E. (eds.), *New Jerome Biblical Commentary*, Geoffrey Chapman, 1989 on Matthew 25, 'The Parable of the Talents'.

But the act of investing is what matters, not the investing itself. As Senior and Stuhlmueller put it in a standard commentary on biblical understandings of mission:[138]

> This emphasis on action as the expression of faith is something Matthew derives from the whole spirit of Judaism, a spirit the evangelist finds strongly ratified in the teaching and ministry of Jesus.

Economists who are Christian have argued that the Bible is interested in work as a productive activity but the context of Paul's writings undermines this claim. As mentioned above, it is later theologians such as Augustine who begin to construct a distinctively Christian ethic of work, centred around manual labour. Rather what is distinctive in the Gospels is the attitude of service, where Jesus portrays himself as one that serves at table. This attitude has come to characterise much Christian reflection on the nature of work, especially in the twentieth century in the writings of William Temple. He wrote in his classic work *Christianity and Social Order* that the choice of a career must be determined 'because in that field he can give his own best service'.[139]

Nevertheless, for a long time Christian ethics implicitly (and sometimes explicitly) accepted conditions of work that were far from this ideal of voluntary service. Such conditions included serfdom in feudal times, and until the nineteenth century in Russia. Equally there was an acceptance of slavery in England throughout the eighteenth century and the abolitionist campaign of a Christian like William Wilberforce caused great anger among church people. A similar story could be told of the crusade by Abraham Lincoln to abolish slavery in the United States of America. Christians took a long time to be convinced of the moral force of the campaign against degrading and dehumanising work. There was a class of rich and privileged people who lived off both the work and enslavement of others. Intellectuals and academics prior to the Industrial Revolution either belonged to this class or were funded by it. Few Christian writers, with the

138 Senior, D. and Stuhlmueller, C., *The Biblical Foundations for Mission*, SCM, 1983, Chapter 10 on Matthew.

139 Temple, W., *Christianity and Social Order*, Penguin, 1942.

exception of some at the Reformation and the English Civil War such as the Levellers and the Diggers, were able to identify with the labouring poor.

As Temple pointed out, one of the objections to harsh work was not simply the conditions under which people worked but the fact that such conditions brutalised people, making it impossible to preach an ethic of service. In the next section we will examine in detail the attitude of the Old and New Testament to slavery, before moving on to the idea of work as service.

Slavery in the Old and New Testaments

There are constant criticisms in the Old Testament of slavery, and of harsh economic conditions. Slavery is defined as 'the form of human servitude in which persons become the property of others'.[140] In Deuteronomy 26:6–8 the Lord is praised for bringing Israel out of Egypt, where 'hard labour' was laid on them. This recitation of the evils of slavery in a foreign land not only formed part of the central act of ritual commemoration at the Passover, it also acted as a reminder to Israel that such practices were abhorrent to the Lord himself. The Holiness Code in Leviticus 25:39ff makes this point quite clear.

> If your brother becomes poor beside you, and sells himself to you, you shall not make him serve as a slave. [...] For they are my servants whom I brought forth out of the land of Egypt. [...] You shall not rule over him with harshness, but shall fear your God.

Israel recognised moral responsibility to the slave, sharing in the Sabbath rest (Exodus 20:10), religious feasts (Deuteronomy 12:12), and at times being entitled to freedom. This was however because the slave had been assaulted, and freedom was a form of compensation for the hurt caused (Exodus 21:26–27). There could be an awareness of the needs of the slave (Job 31:13), but non-Israelites continued to be

140 Maquarrie, J. and Childress, J. (eds.), *A New Dictionary of Christian Ethics*, Articles on 'Slavery' and 'Mosaic Law', SCM, 1986.

imprisoned in the Old Testament period in Israel. Slavery was regulated to check the mistreatment of slaves by their owners. And if the regulations in Leviticus 25 were enforced then slaves were freed after six years, and after forty-nine years there was a release from indebtedness as well. The Jubilee ethic is discussed in a later chapter.

In spite of these regulations the exploitation of the worker was a common feature of Israel. Jeremiah 22:13 speaks of those 'who makes his neighbour serve him for nothing, and does not give him wages'. Instead Isaiah 65:21 and 23 speak of a vision of a new earth, where 'they shall not labour in vain'. At the same time Amos 9:13 foresees an enormous increase in productivity for the ploughman and the vinedresser.

The New Testament wrestles with the problem of slavery which it was of course far beyond the power of early Christian individuals or communities to abolish. Jesus speaks of a ministry to 'those who are oppressed' in Luke 4:18, quoting Isaiah 58:6. This at the very least can imply the liberation of the poor and exploited, but the issue is not followed up in any thorough going way. Instead after the death and resurrection of Jesus the early church spreads out into the Greek and Roman world, and encounters the vexed problem of slavery.[141]

This caused one letter in the New Testament entirely on this difficult moral problem. The Letter to Philemon was written, almost certainly by Paul himself, to resolve the issue of a runaway slave called Onesimus. Paul gave him refuge, and converted him to Christianity. Paul wanted to keep him as a colleague in the task of evangelism, but in the end he relented and sent Onesimus back to Philemon. Philemon was also converted by Paul, and was a young well-respected Christian in a town in Asia Minor, probably Colossae. Paul echoes the pagan philosopher Pliny the Younger, when he begs Philemon to take back his slave as a brother. It is clear that Philemon had incurred expenses from the escape of Onesimus. Paul offers to repay these, and in effect asks Philemon not to inflict the severe penalties which a runaway slave would incur by law.

141 Moltmann, J., *On Human Dignity*, SCM, 1984, reflects on the significance of this for the issue of slavery in America.

It is unclear whether Paul wants the emancipation of this slave, and it is certain that Paul is not attempting to change the social structure of slavery and wealthy owners. In Galatians 3:27–28 Paul argues that distinctions of male, female, Jew, Greek, slave or free cease to apply to those who have accepted Christ. This means that baptism and the gift of the Spirit override such categories within the Christian church. In 1 Corinthians 7:19–24 Paul addresses the same problem, advising Christians to 'remain in the state in which you were called' to follow Christ. Slaves should not refuse manumission, through which their master could set them free, but the prior claim is one of love for those who are fellow Christians, whatever state they are in. This has been described as an inner transformation of social structures, where all are brothers in Christ. This principle became central in Christian teaching in subsequent centuries, but it meant that a sharp dichotomy existed between the inner relationship of love between Christians, and the existing social and economic status.

Christians continued to justify slavery until the nineteenth century on the basis of quotations from the Letter to Philemon, and other New Testament passages. It is only recently that Christians have become aware just how much the use of scriptural texts has allowed, and even given support to, the continuing existence of slavery. The use of texts in a particular way after they have been written does not of course mean that the original authors were themselves wanting to act as apologists for slavery. But it does imply that Christianity has been complicit in this social evil long after the original conditions of its existence in the Ancient Near East had ceased to exist.

Work as service

What remains of permanent value in the scriptures is the idea that work, whether paid or not, is for a purpose. The way in which this aspiration can be embedded in social structures has been of constant fascination to modern theologians and economists. Mention can be made of Christian Schumacher and Miroslav Volf as two contrasting styles in Christian social ethics.

Schumacher is a theologian and management consultant, who in a series of books and in a long career in management has promoted the idea of 'whole work'. He means by this that all work can be broken down into a series of tasks, with a transformation of the product occurring in this task. This may be as varied as transforming a set of ideas into another paper, or the stages of production which turn iron ore into finished steel. Whatever the task, there are actions which a group or individual can perform, and through which they can give service to another worker, consumer or participant. In an imaginative analogy, Schumacher compares this process to that of the sacraments which also transform matter and individuals. The deformation of work occurs when there is no clear set of tasks for a group or person to perform, and no way of assessing the value of the changes which their effort has brought about. His writings and consultancy aim to restore the meaning of work to the workers themselves, even if the ownership of the production process is a conventional joint-stock company.[142]

Volf is from the former Yugoslavia, and trained as a theologian under the leading German systematic theologian Jurgen Moltmann. He now teaches in America, but his ideas remain influential in Europe. In his book *Work in the Spirit* he examines how work may be humanised. He notes that 'there is a strong tendency today to treat alienation in work not as an objective discrepancy between the nature of the worker and the character of his work, but as an overall negative affective response to a particular work role'.[143] The problem of alienation becomes the problem of job satisfaction. The sense of being powerless and the need to restore control become all important. Volf accepts this argument so far as it goes, citing Ecclesiastes 6:19 as one text where a person should 'find enjoyment in his toil'. However he argues that alienation goes beyond individual or group feelings and preferences.

Work for Volf should correspond to the intention of God for humanity. He argues from Exodus that the Israelite tradition relives each year their deliverance from forced labour and slavery in Egypt

142 Schumacher, C., *God in Work*, Lion, 1999. Peter Sedgwick is grateful to this author for many illuminating conversations.

143 Volf, op. cit.

(Exodus 1:13–14). This leads him to discuss what the modern equivalent of slavery might be today. He takes a strong line on participation in management decisions, and also argues that technology must not be developed in a way that dehumanises people. There are strongly Marxist echoes in this account, but whatever the judgement on his conclusions it remains a powerful account of a contemporary theology of work.

How Christianity will contribute to the question of relationships at work remains an open question. Some theologians have been very critical of modern management practices, seeing them as a form of pseudo-religion with their talk of mission statements and the importance of vision. In their view it represents a corruption of religious language into commercial exploitation.[144] The report entitled *Unemployment and the Future of Work* in 1997, to which both the present authors contributed, spelled out what a proper concern for relationships at work might be.

Section Three: Summary and Discussion

In standard economic theory the purpose of work is to produce something of value to use or to sell. Its cost is the leisure time that has to be given up. This should be uncontroversial enough, but something important is missed out. There is no recognition that work, of itself, can be good or bad, a pleasure or a pain. It is left to other disciplines, sociology or industrial relations, to explore the subjective meaning of work and how people actually feel about it.

The distinction is well illustrated in the way that unemployment gets discussed. In the neo-classical model of the labour market, with a simple utilitarian system of values, the problem is presented purely as one of poverty: wages are so low that it is not worthwhile to work, or if the labour market fails to clear then some would-be workers can earn nothing at all. If society were willing and able to provide an

144 Pattison, S., *The Faith of the Managers*, Chapman, 1997.

adequate level of social benefit to the unemployed, then the problem would go away. But this is to ignore the psychological costs of unemployment, the loss of social participation, of self-esteem and the quality of life.

A quite different philosophy of work has developed in modern times, with no direct influence on mainstream economics. According to this tradition there is an inherent dignity in work itself, hard physical labour as well as craftsmanship and professional skill. Work is not only productive, but also fulfilling, giving a purpose to life and the satisfaction of a job well done. It is often a team activity, reinforcing social solidarity amongst fellow-workers, either in support of the company or in opposition to the boss.

Christians in modern times have often been very sympathetic to this secular work ethic. It accords with their belief in co-operation and mutual support. It echoes the language of calling which originated as a mission to prophesy or to preach. It is easily combined with the more distinctively Christian ethic of service and self-sacrifice. For some it is backed by a Marxist belief in the destiny of the working class and the conviction that all value is derived from the input of labour.

In the Bible itself work is often seen quite differently from this, as a distraction from things which matter more. Thus the Old Testament law is concerned mainly to stop people working on the Sabbath when they should be at rest and be at prayer. In the New Testament it is wrong to rely on one's own labour instead of trusting in God to provide what is needed. It is better to listen to the preaching of the Gospel than to do the housework. The early church did recognise that work was a necessity if its members were to be fed, but that is a long way from the Christian work ethic of modern times.

Between the two comes the life of a monastic community, in which work and prayer were combined. The work was done for God, not for a wage. It could be seen as co-operation with God as well as with the whole community. God's creative work goes on, and his people should work with him – not because he needs their help, but because they need to give it. It teaches them discipline and humility, saving them from the temptations of idleness.

The nature of work is changing as new technology takes over the more mechanical tasks. What remains may be a more creative activity and also a more human one. The demand may be more for personal service, less for strength or dexterity. This would be in keeping with a modern Christian belief about the inherent value of work, as well as offering greater satisfaction and wider opportunity for the fulfilment of potential. Work is becoming less of a commodity, more of an expression of a unique personality. In some shape and form, work goes on. The question to be asked is not how much work there will be, but whether it will be work that is worth doing.

Chapter Seven

Capital and the Accumulation of Wealth

Introduction

The history of economic development in modern times is, in part, the history of capital accumulation. Each generation spends a little less than it produces, passing on to its successors an enlarged inheritance. Gradually the stock gets bigger. There are more buildings, more machines, and more pieces of productive equipment; there are better roads and bridges, better schools and hospitals; households acquire more furniture and consumer durables. Even if technology did not progress at all, merely adding to the stockpile of existing types of capital would make the economy more productive in the future.

The purpose of saving, we naturally assume, is to make a higher standard of living possible in the future. We expect to get a return on our investments, whether as rent, or interest or dividends. To save is to delay consumption, and we expect our patience to be rewarded. We may regard such thrift as virtuous, or at least as requiring admirable self-control. Such behaviour has made possible the rapid economic growth which has continued ever since the industrial revolution. It is the behaviour described in neo-classical economic theory.

One might question, however, whether the motive for acquisition is always as rational as that. Thrift can surely become a passion. There is an instinct to collect and to hoard up which often seems to go beyond any sober calculation. People like to own things, for a variety of reasons, not all of them to do with the enjoyment of a higher standard of living. Ownership means security, or status, or power, as well as comfort and the leisure to enjoy it. It means a lot to have a place of one's own to live in. It means, above all, independence. Even little children feel the need to have possessions of their own.

Economic theory barely touches the surface of the psychology of ownership.

If we were simply to set the classical theory of capital accumulation alongside Christian teaching about the vanity of riches, the two systems of thought would hardly make contact at all. We have to take into account all the rest of the personal and social significance of wealth and its ownership. Otherwise, why can we not have both treasure on earth and treasure in Heaven? Why can we not serve both God and Mammon?

It is not just a question of inequality. Certainly it matters how much of the capital stock is owned collectively and how much by individual households. Certainly it matters if the process of accumulation results in a few vast fortunes amongst a mass of destitution. But Christian teaching in fact questions the whole process of acquisition, irrespective of how the proceeds are divided up. It is as if accumulation were a rival religion, a strange god before whom we are tempted to bow down. Most other religions and moral philosophies do not see so much danger in riches. What is it that makes Christians, in principle if not in practice, so suspicious of the whole business of saving and investment?

After the treatment of capital in a standard model of production, we move, in Section One of this chapter to the determination of interest rates as a reward for delaying consumption. There is then a digression about the concept of 'capitalism' derived from Marxist economics and criticised by orthodox economics. This is followed by some material on debt and usury intended as a response to possible criticisms of orthodox economics in its turn. Section Two describes the Jubilee ethic. It then considers how wealth, and the process of accumulation, is to be regarded and the very ambivalent attitudes expressed by Christians up to the present day.

Section One: Economic Theory

Capital as a factor of production

In economic theory capital is a factor of production. It is an input into the production function, alongside labour and land.[145] Each increment of capital makes possible an increment of output. But, as with the other factors of production, successive increments of the same size to the capital stock earn diminishing returns. When production is already capital intensive, then it becomes less effective to substitute further capital for labour or land. There comes a point when the return to further investment is so low that it is not worthwhile. Thus, economic growth due only to the accumulation of capital, with no change in available technology, eventually comes to a halt. It is not rational to save and invest beyond that point, except to offset the depreciation of the capital stock already in place.

In economic theory capital is distinguished from land by the fact that it is reproducible. Capital is itself produced. The size of the capital stock, unlike the quantity of land, is a decision variable. A distinction is made between the short term, in which the stock of capital is fixed, and the long term, in which it is itself subject to choice. Thus in the short term a firm must make the best use of the buildings and equipment it has, whilst in the long run it can decide to have more or less. These are examples of 'fixed' capital, that is capital which has been invested in tangible assets that cannot readily change their function or form. Money in the bank, by contrast, is liquid capital that can be put to any use, or allowed to circulate, in effect lubricating the works. One well-known theory of investment is called the 'putty-clay' model, because most capital is no longer malleable once it has been put to use.

145 See Kregel, J. A., 'Capital Theory', in Kuper, A. and J., op. cit. For an empirical study of the contribution of capital to growth in the UK, see Oulton, N. and O'Mahony, M., *Productivity and Growth – A Study of British Industry 1954–86*, CUP, 1994.

In the very long run all capital is malleable, because old machines have to be replaced with new ones, and at that point fresh decisions have to be made about their design and the technology embodied in them. For that reason the implementation of technical progress and the process of capital formation cannot really be treated as separate contributions to economic growth. Nevertheless it is often useful to think of capital simply as accumulated and undifferentiated product which is itself productive, rather like the seed-corn which is not made into bread and eaten, but is instead sown to produce the next crop.

This suggests another way of thinking about capital altogether. In the long run capital can be regarded as an intermediate product, just a step in the production process. It is made, not for its own sake, but so as to facilitate the next stage in the production process. Machines are manufactured in order to produce more and better goods and services for final consumption. In the long run the only extraneous inputs to the production function are labour and land.

If production is viewed in this way, however, one needs to add a less tangible factor of production, the time that it takes to complete the process. More capital-intensive methods take longer to produce the end result. That delay is what enables them to be more productive. If a man takes time off from digging his field to build a new irrigation system, then he will have a less abundant harvest for some years, but in the end his patience will be repaid.

For the economy as a whole the process of capital accumulation takes time, but for the individual it can be instantaneous. There is no need to own the equipment you use if there is a rental market. Existing assets, like land itself, can provide an income for their owners derived from their scarcity in the short term. The value of an asset can be calculated by discounting the stream of income which it can earn over its lifetime. Although productive assets are often used by their owners, there is no need for this to be the case. Ownership involves a different set of risks from the management of production and the two may not always go well together.

A firm, deciding whether to build a new factory, or buy a new machine, will go through a process of investment appraisal.[146] This involves estimating the additional cash outlays and cash receipts to be expected in the future as a result of the project. This is obviously a very uncertain calculation in most cases, but it makes efficient use of what information is to be had. These estimates of cash flow are then discounted to calculate their present value. A benefit in the future is worth less than a benefit today, because in the market for capital time itself is valuable.

The discounting factor in the calculation of present value is the opportunity cost of capital, that is the return which could have been earned from that capital if it had been invested in another project with similar risk. The higher the rate of discount, the lower the present value of any project that involves spending money now in return for net revenue in the future. In principle any project which has a positive net present value is worth undertaking, and the firm should be prepared to borrow the funds it needs to finance it. But there remains the consideration that the higher the rate of discount, the fewer the projects that will pass that test.

For the economy as a whole the desired rate of investment will depend on the market rate of interest. The higher that rate, the less investment will be planned in physical assets. It is the price of time itself that matters, and how it compares with the marginal product of delay through a more 'roundabout' capital-intensive method of production. Of course there are many other factors, which influence investment decisions as well, some of them quite intangible like the state of confidence in the business community.[147] Neo-classical economic theory, as ever, concentrates on the rational elements in choice, on the factors which can be specified precisely and made subject to rigorous analysis. Aggregate investment in the classical

146 See for example Brearley, R. and Mayers, S., *Principles of Corporate Finance*, McGraw-Hill, 1996.

147 For a formal analysis of aggregate investment, see for example Sargent, T. J., *Macroeconomic Theory*, Academic Press, 1979, Chapters 6 and 14. For a less formal, and more Keynesian account, see for example, Ackley, G., *Macro-economic Theory*, Macmillan, 1961.

model is a function of the market rate of interest. In total investment must equal savings, and it is by variation in the market rate of interest that equilibrium is maintained.

Time preference

All other things being equal, economic theory commonly assumes that we prefer enjoyment now to the prospect of the same enjoyment in the future. That is a characteristic of the consumption functions used by economists and the utility functions that underlie them. There are several different ways to justify this assumption.[148]

People may simply be myopic, lacking the imagination to foresee how they will feel in the future if they use up their resources now. Perhaps human beings are instinctively prodigal. But this does not accord at all well with the rationality which is assumed to guide the other choices made by 'economic man'. We are not supposed to be like greedy children, who eat the whole bar of chocolate and then cry because there is none left! There are other, more respectable, reasons for some degree of time preference.

Human life is finite, and the further ahead one looks the greater the risk of being dead. If consumption is delayed indefinitely then it will never happen at all. Wealth can be passed on to one's heirs who will then benefit from one's present abstinence. But not everyone identifies their own interests completely with those to whom they leave their estates. Rational individuals will take this into account in deciding the profile of their consumption and saving in different stages of their lifetime.

Another reason for discounting the future might be that the typical individual or family can reasonably expect to benefit from the growth of the economy as a whole. There is less urgency about saving if one expects one's earnings to increase over time, less incentive

148 There is an interesting formal discussion of time preference in consumption in Blanchard, O. J. and Fischer, S., *Lectures on Macroeconomics*, MIT Press, 1989.

to provide for one's children if they can expect to live in a more affluent age.

Yet another motive for time preference is to do with uncertainty of a different kind. If we make plans to consume our wealth in the future, all kinds of accidents could make that difficult or impossible. No store of value is absolutely safe. The value of money can be eroded by inflation; governments can renege on their debts, even insurance companies can fail; there can be revolutions and wars. The return on a so-called 'risk-free' asset may actually include compensation for uncertainty of this kind. Against this, of course, must be set the risk that those who do not save may find themselves short of the income that they anticipated and unable to borrow the funds that they need for immediate consumption.

The higher the rate of interest the more willing people will be (at any level of income) to delay their consumption, and the higher will be the incentive to save. Thus the rate of interest, through its influence on both savings and investment, can bring the two into balance. It is determined by productivity on the one hand and thrift on the other. It is the price of time itself. It is usually positive, but it is not impossible to imagine an economy in which the rate of interest was negative, at least for a period. Faced with the prospect of famine in the future individuals might be prepared to save even if they knew that there was no way of conserving the value of their wealth entire. In fact the ex post real rate of interest, after allowing for inflation, has often been negative for several years in succession.

Strictly speaking, of course, there is not one rate of interest but many: the one-period rate, the two-period rate and so on, where the periods could be years, or months, or even days. Time in economics is almost a continuous variable. The shape of the yield curve, as it is called, will reflect expectations of relative supply and demand for funds in the future. Typically long-term interest rates are higher than shorts, but this is certainly not always the case. Contracts to borrow and to lend can take a great variety of forms, designed to attract investors with many different financial risks and prospects.[149] Pension funds for example want to be confident that they will have flows of

149 See for example Brearley, R. and Mayers, S., op. cit.

income extending far into the future to match their liabilities. Households need to borrow for decades to finance house purchase. Financial markets are certainly not all obsessed by the need to make gains in the short term.

Most rates of interest quoted in the market are nominal rather than real, that is to say they take no account of the rate of inflation. It is now possible, however, to deal in index-linked bonds which compensate the holder for movements in the retail prices index. It is, of course, real rates which are relevant both to savings and investment. Another hedge against inflation is the holding of equity, since its value is tied to the value of the real assets which are owned by the firm.

The risks involved in shareholding are not the same as those involved in holding debt. But for most individuals the relationship they have with the firms to which they entrust their savings is not of a fundamentally different kind; they do not own enough of the equity to be able to exercise influence on how that money is used. They may well choose to have small holdings in many different firms so as to diversify away the risk attached to any one. The institution of limited liability has created a class of financial asset well suited to the needs of vast numbers of individuals with relatively moderate means. The willingness of millions of shareholders to take clearly-defined and limited risks has contributed very significantly to economic growth throughout modern times.

'Capitalism'

It is important to distinguish the role played by capital in neo-classical economics from the role of 'capitalism' in the Marxist 'heresy'. The term 'capitalism' is often used loosely to mean any market system, as opposed to socialist economic planning. More precisely used, it means a particular organisation of society which is taken to typify the industrial market economies of modern times. Phyllis Deane sums it up clearly in an encyclopaedia entry:[150]

150 Deane, P., 'Capitalism', in Kuper, A. and J., op. cit.

> For Marx, capitalism was a 'mode of production' in which there are basically two classes of producer: the capitalists, who own the means of production (capital and land), make the strategic day-to-day decisions on technology, output and marketing, and appropriate the profits of production and distribution; and the labourers, who own no property but are free to dispose of their labour on terms which depend on the numbers seeking work and the demand for their services.

Neo-classical economics does not assume that the organisation of economic life is 'capitalistic' in this sense. Indeed the word 'capitalism' does not really have any part to play in mainstream economics. The market system is compatible with a wide variety of different patterns of ownership and control. For example private pensions schemes give millions of small savers a stake in the ownership of firms. Banks, who lend funds for investment, have different interests from the owners and managers of corporations, although both are 'capitalists'. Some employees are wealthier than the owners of the firms they work for; some are so vital to the success of those firms that they can virtually dictate decisions about the running of the business. Self-employment unites capital and labour in a single person. Workers may have bargaining power through membership of a trades union. Capitalism, as described by Marx, is just one possible variant of the market economy amongst many.

As a matter of economic history, rather than economic theory, one might say that the organisation of certain economies, particularly in the nineteenth century, did approximate to capitalism as described by Marx. The key distinguishing feature of capitalism is that workers own no assets. It is also important that they have no access to credit, because they cannot sell or pledge their 'human capital', that is their earning capacity in the future. This is what produces the imbalance of power in the capitalist system. The workers need to work more urgently than the capitalists need to employ them. If they withdraw their labour they can be starved into submission. This is a relationship which could be analysed within mainstream economics, using the theory of games.

Does this relationship amount to 'exploitation'? This is, of course, an emotive or evaluative term. It implies that the distribution of power is not only unequal, but also unjust. It suggests that there is a different organisation of society which would be more natural, or fairer. In Marxist economics the labour theory of value is used to imply that workers have a right to the whole product of their labour; capitalists deny them that right when they pay them only what the market requires. In neo-classical economics, which treats the factors of production symmetrically, this language is either meaningless or wrong. Neo-classical economics would naturally assume that whatever result the market produces will generally be fair, unless good reasons can be found to doubt it.

What judgement is passed on the capitalist system as such will depend on the alternative with which it is compared. The systems that preceded it often concentrated wealth and power in the hands of aristocratic regimes which were both oppressive and resistant to change. The transfer of power to the newly rich entrepreneurs, which initiated the capitalist system described by Marx, also made possible technical innovations which ultimately raised the living standards of the whole population. If only the capitalists save, then the higher the rate of profit, the higher the rate of investment and growth. A more equal society would stagnate. A purely utilitarian calculation, taking a long-term view, might judge that the organisation of the economy in the nineteenth century was of benefit to the poor as well as the rich, at least to future generations in the countries concerned.

It would be very different if one could realistically compare capitalism with an idealised version of socialism, in which all economic exploitation and conflict had been abolished. That is the comparison that inspires Marxist analysis and the call to action which follows from it. Twentieth-century history, however, is full of examples that must make one question the realism of this alternative. In practice the lack of private incentives results in economic stagnation.[151] What many supporters of the market economy would like to see is a society in which capital is privately owned but equally distributed. This organisation of society may also be difficult to achieve or to sustain, but perhaps it is not quite so unrealistic an ideal.

151 Fukuyama, F., *The End of History and the Last Man*, Hamish Hamilton, 1992.

The market for debt and the rate of interest

The existence of markets for debt greatly increases the opportunities open to the individual consumer or producer. One can borrow in bad times and repay in good times. An adequate standard of living can then be maintained throughout. Those who do not have access to credit are often at a great disadvantage. Without access to credit small firms could not so readily grow. The market for credit, like other markets, exists because there is mutual advantage in exchange. From the point of view of mainstream economics all this is so obvious as hardly to need saying. Nevertheless the advice, 'neither a borrower nor a lender be' is widely regarded as common sense even by some people today. Economic theory can help to explain why that might be so.

The simple theory of time preference outlined so far assumes that debts will always be paid in full. But the very fact of an exchange between a payment today and a repayment tomorrow must raise the possibility that one party will not keep to the bargain. Economic theory recognises this difficulty and considers how market behaviour is affected by it. Borrowing creates a moral and a legal obligation to repay, but the borrower may still be unwilling, or indeed unable, to meet it. That possibility must influence the terms on which loan contracts are drawn up.

Lenders may try to cover the costs of possible defaults by charging a higher rate of interest to more risky customers. The problem is that the risk of default may be very difficult to assess. The risky customer has no incentive to reveal his or her intentions, and the lender will find it difficult either to screen applicants for loans or to monitor the behaviour of those that they accept. Higher rates of interest will deter the good borrowers who really do mean to repay. They will not deter those who are in greatest need, or those who are prepared to face the penalties of default. A lender who charges a very high rate of interest will end up lending only to borrowers who are over-optimistic, irresponsible or desperate for a loan. Usury of this kind is not in fact good business.

If raising the price of credit is not a solution to the problem of default risk, lenders can instead ration the quantity available to each individual, require security for the loan, or attach conditions to it, giving them some control over how the money is spent. Since there is a public interest in the stability of financial markets and institutions, governments and central banks make regulations designed to make their business less risky. The ultimate lenders are typically people who place deposits in institutions which they believe to be safe, like High Street banks and building societies. Governments feel some responsibility towards them.

One means of increasing the access to credit is to increase the penalties for default. The borrower has to make a credible commitment to repay. The more severe the consequences of breaking that commitment, the more likely it is to be believed. The lender will want the threat of these penalties to be a real deterrent to irresponsible borrowers. After default has in fact occurred, however, the enforcement of the penalties will not help anyone. They may well seem unreasonable, since the proximate cause of the default will typically be bad luck rather than dishonesty. By invoking the penalties the lender may loose all hope of an ultimate repayment. That may have implications for the lender's own credit rating, or even solvency. Often the lender will feel obliged to extend the loan, possibly tightening the conditions, even if this is really to 'throw good money after bad'.

Anyone who borrows is obviously restricting their own freedom, at least to the extent that they are agreeing to repay by the due date. But there may be other conditions attached to the loan. If the loan is made to start up or expand a business, the borrower may insist on sharing in the management of it. In a rather similar fashion the IMF attaches 'conditionality' to many of its loans to member governments, requiring them to put in place economic policies which will increase the chances that they will be able to repay. This may be burdensome, but it also means that credit is available to firms and governments which would not otherwise be able to borrow at all.

Sometimes the balance of power is heavily weighted in favour of the lender. The lender can afford to refuse a loan, whilst the borrower cannot survive without one. In a one-to-one bargaining situation, the lender can then dictate the terms. One of the advantages of a competitive capital market is that it puts such borrowers in a rather better position. If there are many potential lenders then the borrower can seek out the best terms available and need pay nothing more than the market rate, however urgent the need may be. One may be able to borrow from many sources at once, thus evading the attempt of any one lender to ration the availability of funds. One may borrow from one source in order to repay another. One may attempt to conceal from one lender the extent of debt outstanding elsewhere. It is not surprising therefore that lenders sometimes exchange information about borrowers, or make use of rating agencies.

A borrower who defaults on one loan, or obliges the lender to renegotiate, will not find it easy to secure another. This is as significant a deterrent as the formal penalties of the law. Borrowers who are known to be reliable have access to funds with less trouble, delay and expense. Business needs the law as a safeguard but it is conducted from day to day on the basis of trust. Economists in recent times have become fascinated by the problems of building and maintaining a good reputation. Is this always compatible with enlightened self-interest? Is honesty always the best policy? It seems that it often is so, but not always. What is the value of a good reputation if you never intend to borrow again?

The rate of interest can be viewed as the rental price of capital or the relative price of consumption today and tomorrow. It is a price like any other, determined by supply and demand in the market. There is, nevertheless, something in economic theory which might more properly be described as usury, that is to say the charging of a very high rate of interest to borrowers with limited access to credit whose need to borrow is urgent.

In Medieval times the church forbade the charging of any interest on loans at all. In modern times that position is not taken by many Christians, although it is still the teaching of Islam.[152] There is one school of thought, going back to the ancient Greek philosophers, which says that it is in some way unjust or unnatural to put a price on time. That view would find little support today. Goods or services delivered tomorrow are not the same commodities as goods and services delivered today. There seems no reason why they should have

152 Mills, P. and Presley, J., *Islamic Finance*, Macmillan, 1999.

the same price. The ratio between the price of something delivered today and the same thing delivered tomorrow is in fact the rate of discount or the value of time. It is just one of many price ratios one might calculate. There is nothing more unnatural about it than about any other price ratio.

If both borrowers and lenders accept the rate of interest ruling in the market that does not strike us today as unjust. There are also situations in which the borrowers are strong and the lenders are weak. A large firm, or a government, takes the small savings on which poor widows depend. It could exploit their ignorance or trust by allowing the capital value to be eroded or lost in risky ventures. Surely the lenders, who may depend on their few assets for security and a few comforts in old age, should at least be compensated for inflation and for the risks that they take, and for their patience in not spending their savings too soon. A prohibition on all interest payments would make that impossible. Most people would say that the scandal of government borrowing for much of the past half-century has not been that it paid interest, but that the interest rates were so low.

Usury laws, as commonly interpreted, do not prohibit the payment of dividends to shareholders. Yet, with limited liability, the distinction between equity and debt is not as sharp as their legal status seems to imply. The risks on individual company shares can be diversified away. It is hard to believe that some vital moral, let alone religious, principle separates fixed interest securities like Consols or debentures from blue-chip equities which pay regular dividends year after year.

As we have seen, a serious discussion of usury needs to begin with consumer credit especially in poor countries. The Old Testament prohibition of usury arose in a poor agricultural community. The very high rates of interest charged by money-lenders in such communities today are well described and explained by Partha Dasgupta in his study of 'well-being and destitution'. He uses the orthodox assumptions of modern neo-classical economics.

Interest rates in poor communities have to be high to make up for the proportion of loans which are never repaid. But the higher the rate charged the greater the probability of default. Borrowers who know that they are unlikely ever to repay will accept credit on rates which they know are unrealistic, thus driving up the rate which must be paid by those who do hope to repay as well. There is 'moral hazard' in the market, because borrowers are tempted to enter into contracts which they know they cannot expect to keep. There is also 'adverse selection' in the market, because the poor risk borrowers will accept the most stringent terms. Dasgupta concludes:[153]

> It can be shown that, in the market we are considering here, there is in the aggregate too little credit on offer, relative to what there would have been had lenders been able to distinguish the various projects in terms of their riskiness.

What he recommends is a public subsidy to the supply of credit. This might take the form of a government small loan scheme. It would clearly help if one could introduce some competition into the supply of credit, in the hope that this would bring down its cost. The alternative of prohibiting rates of interest above some ceiling is not so attractive. The effect could well be to exclude some borrowers from access to any credit at all. It might also result in other terms being made more stringent, for example the provision of collateral security, which would also militate against the very poor.

Section Two: Christian Belief

Modern economics assumes the existence of property rights which are questioned in the Bible. Without such rights the whole process of capital accumulation described in Section One above is in doubt. As we shall see in Chapter 8 below, this has a profound effect in biblical attitudes to the land and to the institutions of the market. In this chapter, we shall concentrate on Christian attitudes to debt and its repayment, with related questions about the use of money to discharge any legal obligation.

153 Dasgupta, P., op. cit., Chapter 9.

The Jubilee ethic and usury

It is helpful to indicate the response to the treatment of debt given above, since at this point the divergence is great between the world of modern economic theory and the world of the Bible. We begin with the issue of usury and the question of the Jubilee.

The Jubilee ethic stems from the particular relationship which Israel had to its God. God had called Israel to be his people and redeemed its failures by his constant love. One sign of this was the concrete and tangible gift of the land. The main discussion of the land is left to Chapter Eight, for it is an alternative to the market system.

As they dwelled in this rich and fertile land which is Palestine, there are many references to the generosity of God in placing them there. If this land were lost, then the covenant between God and his people would be in doubt. The performance which Israel enacted in ritual worship and in keeping the moral law (the Torah), was an expression of gratitude for the blessings given by God. The Judaic ethic is therefore based on what is in fact a theocratic society. Israel believed that divine revelation had showed its people what the nature of land distribution and economic relationships were. This meant that charity to the poor was a foreign concept, since *tsedequah* is not to be translated compassion, or charity, but justice. It is the restoration of the original, divinely given, set of relationships which Naboth defended at the cost of his life. Deuteronomy 4:24 and Proverbs 10:2 make this clear.

One of the consequences of justice to the poor is the concept of the Jubilee year. It is not at all certain whether this was ever applied in law, or whether this is an ideal vision of what might one day be the case.[154]

> Although we cannot exclude the possibility of its being observed in the early years of the land's occupation, its presence here is best explained as a social blueprint, founded on the deeply religious concepts of justice and equality which strove to apply the simple sabbatical principle to a society that had

154 Brown, R. E., Fitzmyer, J. A. and Murphy, R. E. (eds.), *The New Jerome Biblical Commentary*, Geoffrey Chapman, 1991 on 'Leviticus 25' and 'The Jubilee'.

> become more economically complex. It was drawn up and added to the Holiness Code in the period after the exile. Although not realised in the letter, its spirit of appreciation for personal rights and human dignity synthesises much of Old Testament teaching.

This suggests that the reference to the Jubilee in Ezekiel 46:17 and perhaps in Isaiah 61:1–2 is to a future ideal. Some have seen this law as a theological construction from the time of the exile, while others regard it as a supplement to the legislation on the release of Hebrew slaves. The practical result was that it gave those who had been given their freedom the chance of an autonomous social life. Again the relationship to the land received in common on the entry into Canaan cannot be alienated for ever.[155] Whatever the status of this concept, Deuteronomy 15 argues that there was a law which remitted debts every seventh year and all slaves were to be freed. In every fiftieth year, according to Leviticus 25:8, all land alienated for any reason was to be restored to the family which lived there before its alienation. Such a law would ensure 'that there will be no poor among you' (Deuteronomy 15:4). It is important to realise however that 'of a foreigner you may exact it' (Deuteronomy 15:3), since this was a tribal ethic for the people of Israel alone. It was, as Brueggemann argues, a Sabbath ethic which sets limits to the existence of debts.[156]

> Debt Sabbath is a dramatic affirmation that human society does not rest finally on buying and selling, owing and collecting. Landed people are accustomed to managing things. And as we manage things we would manage people. We manage them by taxation and interest rates, by debts and mortgages and soon everyone is either owner of others or part of the owned. [...] Sabbath in Israel is the affirmation that people, like land, cannot be finally owned or managed.

155 Epsztein, L., *Social Justice in the Ancient Near East*, SCM, 1986.
156 Brueggemann, W., op. cit.

The teaching of Jesus about property stands in this tradition. Indeed, a number of theologians have pointed out that the land crisis in Jewish society was deep. John Riches writes in his study of the relationship of Jesus and Judaism:[157]

> Economic pressure, resulting from heavy taxes and rents, from shortages of employment, etc, coupled with shortage of land and the demands of the terrain will have affected the main mass of the Jewish peasantry more immediately and continually. Families could be faced at almost any time with disaster – loss of land tenancies and ultimately with slavery – as a result of poor harvests or adverse market conditions. Many Jews found they were no longer able to conform to the norms which were set in their society and were forced to adopt forms of deviant, anomic behaviour.

Jesus preached a message of good news to the poor:[158]

> He identifies himself with the poor, the persecuted, those who hunger and thirst after righteousness. His call to men to leave all and follow him stresses his poverty, marks out his identification with the poor and uprooted among the Galilean peasantry.

His message is one of healing, forgiveness, and a vision of fulfilment. His attitude to property was therefore critical, telling his followers to forget about economic security (Matthew 6:33) and condemning the pursuit of wealth. Riches could lead to idolatry, and may lead to the practice of injustice – Luke 16:19; Mark 10:25 and other references.[159] Above all the expectation of the end of history led to indifference about the things of this world.[160]

The generosity practised inside the Christian community was not constrained by the concern which its members might have for their own future. The teaching of Jesus on the way in which God clothed the fields, and looked after the birds, stood as a rebuke to any finely

157 Riches, J., *Jesus and the Transformation of Judaism*, Darton, Longman and Todd, 1980.

158 ibid.

159 Gorringe, op. cit.

160 Hengel, M., *Property and Riches in the Early Church*, SCM, 1974.

calculated ethic of how much could be afforded. Equally it will be clear by now that biblical ethics did not encompass the exchanges which the market facilitates. This means that the issue of debt is not central to the New Testament.

In Romans 13:7–8 Paul discusses what is owed by the Christians to the civil authorities. He mentions taxes, tolls, respect and honour. In verse 8 he continues that Christians are to owe no debt to anyone, except mutual love. The letter to Philemon equally sees Paul offering to remit anything which is owed by Philemon. In both these cases Paul avoids entering into the world of exchange, and the debts of the market. Instead Jesus continually sought to establish community, especially for those who were excluded from the community of the time.[161]

It is true that several of the parables of Jesus deal graphically with the issue of debt. This shows that the early followers of Jesus were well aware of the reality of debt which is a necessary institution in a market economy. In the parable of the unjust steward in Matthew 18, and in Luke 7 and 16, the issue of debt is well to the fore. Jesus says to Simon the Pharisee in Luke 7 that the person who loves most is the one who is forgiven most, using the example of a creditor who forgave two debtors who owed different amounts of money. In Luke 16 the parable is ironic. A steward who is about to be dismissed makes friends with his master's debtors by reducing their debts before his dismissal. 'The master commended the dishonest steward for his prudence; for the sons of this world are wiser in their own generation than the sons of light' (Luke 16:8). The interpretation of the parable has been disputed, but at least one interpretation is that even if the brotherhood of Israel does not persuade the Jewish leaders to follow a more forgiving attitude, prudence should do so. The irony of the parable mocks the Pharisees. Debt and exchange is not seen as part of the kingdom which is coming with the ministry of Jesus, but those who can handle financial affairs do at least recognise the seriousness of the hour. The Pharisees do not even do that.

In Matthew 18 the need for genuine forgiveness of one's neighbours is related to the forgiveness given in the ministry of Jesus.

161 Lohfink, G., *Jesus and Community*, SPCK, 1985.

Again the illustration is by way of an unjust servant, who was forgiven by his king for the debts which he owed, but who oppressed his fellow servants in turn. The result of his double standard was that the king took his revenge on his servant, and imprisoned him until he paid his debt. Paul in Romans uses the term debtor three times, in 1:14; 8:12; and 15:27 using the Greek word *opheiletes* as opposed to the term *xreofeilets* or creditor. This is the term in Luke 7 and 16. However the notion of debt is not emphasised, for the debt is seen as a duty, and this duty will take him to Rome.[162]

Current interpretations of the biblical ethic

One writer who has produced a very influential study of this topic is Peter Selby, in his recent study of debt. His book *Grace and Mortgage* takes a particular interpretation of the *Nunc Dimittis* as a paradigm account of how God deals with debt. Simeon is a person who goes into the Temple in Luke 2. He believes that the Spirit has revealed to him that he will see the Messiah before he dies. He meets the parents of Jesus in the temple, and takes the child into his arms, saying the words known in Anglican worship as the *Nunc Dimittis*. These announce that today God is 'releasing his slave', according to his word in peace. At the same time an elderly woman called Anna was also in the temple with Simeon. She was expecting 'the liberation of Israel' (Luke 2:38). Together these two people put the story of Jesus in the context of the hope of liberation. Selby argues that the market economy devalues Christianity, and that the original meaning of the Lord's Prayer was that it could deliver us from this slavery to the past.

Selby reads the New Testament story of Jesus as being about personal and social liberation. He finds it impossible to imagine that the impact of Christ as redeemer upon his audience was not drawn:[163]

162 Barrett, C. K., *Commentary on Romans*, A and C Black, 1962.
163 Selby, P., op. cit.

> From the deepest memories and contemporary experience of a people who knew what debt could accomplish and saw it as the reverse of the freedom which new life in Christ was intended to be.

He feels that the power of debt in the Old and New Testament is so great that it closes down the possibility of the future, and that if Jesus came with a message of hope for the future, then this must address the problem of debt. He also turns to the story of Joseph, who was sold into slavery in Egypt, and finds a confirmation of his theme there. Therefore the message of the Bible for Selby is one of a deep hostility to the market world, even in its primitive form at the time of scripture, for the market involves debt which destroys the message of Christ.

The question is how the biblical account of wealth can be related to a contemporary understanding of capital. An answer is attempted in *The Enterprise Culture*, written by one of the present authors in 1992. The theological methodology is analogous to that of Rowan Williams in his recent collection of essays, *On Christian Theology*. Williams considers the demand that 'Theology redescribes reality within the scriptural framework rather than translating scripture into extra-scriptural categories'.[164] This would mean that the fundamental activity of the Christian theologian is to enable a Christian to view the world through the perspective of scripture, thus allowing the values and beliefs of contemporary culture to be challenged by Christianity. There is little doubt that such a method, aided and abetted by his commitment to Marxism, underlies Gorringe's attack on contemporary methods of wealth-creation. However there are problems with such a simple acceptance of the use of scripture. Williams replies that the world of scripture is a historical world, in which meanings:[165]

> Are discovered and recovered in action and encounter. To challenge the Church to immerse itself in 'text' is to encourage it to engage with a history of such actions and encounters.

164 Williams, R. D., op. cit., citing Lindbeck, G., *The Nature of Doctrine; Religion and Theology in a Postliberal Age*, Philadelphia, 1984.

165 ibid.

Even the action of interpreting can change the way in which the narrative can be seen. The text of scripture has generated an enormous variety of variations and interpretations.[166]

> All of which means that we are dealing not with the insertion of definable blocks of material into a well-mapped territory, where homes may be found for them, but with events of re-telling or re-working traditional narrative patterns in specific human interactions; an activity in which the Christian community is itself enlarged in understanding and even in some sense evangelised. Its integrity is bound up in encounters of this kind, and so in the unavoidable elements of exploratory fluidity and provisionality that enters into these encounters.

In a similar way it was argued in *The Enterprise Culture* that there was no one theme to the relationship of Christianity and the nature of wealth. There are in fact three stories. One is the story of the moral demands of God, and the inherent nature of wealth to corrupt those who seek spiritual renewal. In this story there is the appeal to Jubilee, and the obligations which the occupation of the land brings. This is in fact not a story about economics at all, but about the faithfulness (or lack of it) of the people of God, whether in Israel or as the followers of Jesus. Secondly there is the story of the use of wealth to praise God in the use of the land, and its benefits. It is the enjoyment of riches as a blessing of God to his people. This is also the story told by Brueggemann, of the gift of the land, and the blessings which this brings. Thirdly, there is the strand found so prominently in Gorringe which is the story of poverty caused by exploitation.

What matters is that the Christian churches have continued to encounter the texts of scripture in many different ways. One of the most challenging aspects of this encounter is to examine the transformation of nature into material which embodies the intelligence of the society which makes this possible.[167] The Christian understanding of creation is that it is to be respected, but also used in a way that enables the purposes of God to be fulfilled through it. We are therefore returned to the overall dialogue of this book, between the

166 Williams, op. cit.
167 Sedgwick, op. cit.

understanding of human nature implicit in neoclassical economics and the Christian viewpoint. The next two chapters on market forces and on strategic interaction, will enable this dialogue to be outlined in a way which shows clearly the contradictions between them.

The price of a life

It is not simply material debt which the New Testament is concerned with. There is also the intertwining of religion and commerce in the issue of redemption. The early church was well aware that the death of Jesus involved 'thirty pieces of silver' paid to Judas by the high priests. The symbolic description of this silver alludes in Matthew 26:15 to passages in Zechariah (11:12–13) and Exodus (21:32), where the price of the life of a slave gored by an ox is put at thirty silver schekels. Jesus is sold by his friend. This is the same Judas as protested against the waste when a woman poured fragrant oil over Jesus' head. He wanted a price to be put on that as well! Jesus himself on the contrary celebrates the wasteful gift as a proper way of preparing his body for death and burial.

These passages can be read simply as condemnation of greed, or (more speculatively) of financial value, but they should also be seen in a wider context. This includes the role of money in the ethical and religious life of the Jewish community. The Hebrew term *koper* in Exodus 21:32 refers to the price of a life which is taken by violence, either through the murder or manslaughter of one person by another, or by an accident, such as the goring of a slave by an ox. In Exodus 30:12 and in Psalm 49:7 the issue of redemption is raised in financial terms. The provisions are like those of the law in medieval times, like the *wergild* offered for the life of a murdered person to appease the kinsmen. Redemption is literally the buying back of what has been lost, by death or by enslavement. It is a monetary transaction. It might seem appropriate enough therefore that the chief priests were paying in advance for the life of the 'servant' that they were about to kill.

Redemption is one of the central themes of the Old Testament. It is also closely linked to the sacrificial system where animals, and agricultural produce of value, were sacrificed to God in religious acts.

Some of these sacrificial acts were sin offerings, where the anger of God was expiated, or propitiated, and the sacrifice was itself redemptive. The inter-penetration of religious and materially symbolic worlds is all-important.

In the breakdown of personal and social ties, redemption was also applicable. Individuals who had become slaves were bought back from another person, or from a conquering tribe. They were exchanged for money; in other words they were ransomed or redeemed. This language of exchange was felt by the early church to be also appropriate when applied to the salvation won by Jesus on the cross.

There were limits, however, to the commutation of legal or religious duties, cases where money could not take the place of personal service or redress. A foetus has a price (Exodus 21:22), but harm to the mother is measured, not in money but by the famous *lex talionis,* in which harm is extracted in retaliation. This implies two things. First there was a limit to vengeance which stopped short of taking another life. The law was brutal, but at least the 'eye for an eye' philosophy put a stop to the cycle of violence and vengeance. It was designed to restrain and limit violence to a single deliberate act of retaliation. Secondly, and this is significant, there were even in the period of ancient Israel some cases where a financial transaction or penalty was insufficient. The harm to a foetus was one thing, but the harm to a mother went beyond a financial penalty. In Psalm 49 a similar point is made.

> Alas! No man can ransom himself, nor pay God the price of that release; his ransom would cost too much, for ever beyond his power to pay, the ransom that would let him live on always and never see the pit of death.

Here the financial aspects of redemption reach their limit, for money cannot bring a person back from death. Yet, these words anticipate precisely the language used much later to describe what Jesus was able to do for those who believed in him.

The 'price of the life of Jesus' is a literary and theological construct, which therefore signifies two things. It is about the base financial motives in the character of Judas, which are corrupting, and which contrast so starkly with the unknown woman who gives oil to anoint Jesus. Secondly, however, it makes a symbolic link, which is a deliberate choice made by Matthew, with the Old Testament theology of redemption and the price of a person's life. The death of Judas in Matthew 27 picks up all the Old Testament references, with an explicit mention of Jeremiah's prophecies of 18:2–3 and 32:6–15. The death of Jesus is redemptive, but it also uses the financial measure (of thirty pieces of silver) as a symbolic echo of the past.

From this moment on Christian theology will explore the significance of the death of Jesus in terms of a theology of redemption and atonement, but the financial aspects of his death will be no more than illustrations or metaphorical language. The system of financial or material redemption, which was so prominent in the Old Testament, ceases to be applicable. Jesus explicitly repealed the *lex talionis,* saying that his disciples should seek no recompense for harm at all. One might see the expulsion of the traders from the temple as a related episode in his life. Money had a part to play in the temple cult, but it would have no part to play in the worship of the new community. The death and resurrection of Jesus superseded the old sacrificial system because it was a sacrifice that transcended the previous religious order.

Section Three: Summary and Discussion

Capital, like labour and land, is a factor of production. The more machines, buildings and roads there are, the more output the economy can produce. Capital accumulates as people save some fraction of each year's income. The returns to investment are diminishing – that is to say, the more capital there is already in place, and the less will be the effect on output of adding a little more. The supply and the demand for capital are brought into balance by the rate of interest which is a price like any other.

Economic theory does not regard thrift as virtuous. The purpose of all economic activity is to consume, now or in the future. The optimum life-cycle for most people would be to borrow when still young, to repay in maturity and then save for one's old age, leaving behind at death only such legacies as altruism inspires. This would be consistent with a steady state economy with a constant stock of capital overall. The incentive to save would not of itself result in persistent economic growth.

As with the theory of labour supply, so in the case of capital, economic theory seems to tell only part of the story. The motives for saving are not quite as straightforward as that, or quite so benign. Wealth does not just confer a higher standard of living at some time in the future: it also enhances independence, security, status and power. It would do all this even if it was not productive and did not earn any return. Wealth is most potent in some ways when it is kept liquid, as gold stored under the mattress or as money in the bank.

What the Bible does understand very well is the imbalance of power between the rich and the poor. For example, the poor need to borrow, whilst the rich do not need to lend. Hence the need for laws prohibiting usury; hence the pleas for debt remission. Economic theory never talks about power as such, although it does recognise problems of credit worthiness when borrowers can offer no security for a loan. The Bible never mentions the possibility of competition between lenders; economic theory takes perfect competition as the norm.

In the New Testament wealth is seen as dangerous to the owner. It is a false god, seeming to offer security, but providing no protection against disaster and death. It is better to rely on God, or on the generosity of one's neighbours. The rich themselves cannot be truly generous or they would have given all their wealth away. This teaching has not, of course, stopped some Christians through the ages becoming very rich indeed.

In modern times it has been the Marxists rather than the Christians who have been most vocal in denouncing the rich. Their beliefs are explicitly opposed to orthodox economic theory which they regard as capitalist ideology. They do recognise that capital is productive, but they argue that all of the increment to output will be appropriated by a small class of wealth owners, whilst the lot of the workers will get worse rather than better, until they revolt. This has not in fact been the general experience of the last hundred years. Indeed one must now recognise that many of the owners of capital may be poorer than some employees. 'Capitalism' is just one kind of market economy, typical of one stage of development.

The accumulation of wealth depends on the existence of property rights, including the right to collect debts that are legally due. There are passages in the Bible which appear to challenge these rights, thus undermining the market system. There would be little incentive to improve the land by investment if ownership lasted only until the Jubilee. There would be no incentive to lend, either for the finance or investment or to relieve a temporary necessity, if debts were not collectable. In modern times, most Christians have defended property rights while at the same time, perhaps, urging that they should be enforced with clemency.

In modern times most Christians have come to recognise the productivity of capital and have dropped their opposition to the payment of interest on loans. They have even learnt to preach about the virtue of thrift and to bless the creators of wealth. It is still true, however, that Christian teaching understands better than economic theory some of the less attractive motives for acquisition and its damaging effects on rich and poor alike.

Chapter Eight

The Market and Perfect Competition

In previous chapters we have examined aspects of choice and of the factors which constrain it. We have looked at consumption and production, at demand and at supply. In this chapter, and the next, we turn to the relationships which bring people together, and to the ways in which social interactions can be organised. This is all part of what we have characterised as the 'anthropology' implicit in neo-classical economic theory and also in Christian belief. In this chapter we are concerned with the market, taking the extreme case of perfect competition, under which relationships are entirely impersonal. The following chapter will consider imperfect competition and the strategic interaction which that involves. Markets can be seen as an efficient means of disseminating information, more efficient for example than centralised economic planning.

Markets convey information about the preferences of multitudes of individual consumers, and the technological possibilities of multitudes of individual producers. There is no need for a plan, because the system is self-organising. Each individual seeks his or her own advantage, yet the common interest is served. The 'mechanism' requires that certain legal forms, and norms of behaviour, are observed – respect for property rights, for example. It is therefore a political, even a moral, institution, as well as economic.

The resulting allocation of resources can be shown to be, on certain criteria, the best, or one of the best that can be achieved. The moral claims that are made on behalf of the market system are not confined to its efficiency in the allocation of scarce resources. The real enthusiasts for the market believe that it is the only economic system fully compatible with political freedom and human rights. It requires the rule of law. If national governments seek to manage the national economy then, inevitably it is claimed, they will move, step by step, to managing the lives of individual citizens as well. This must be, in the words of Hayek, 'The Road to Serfdom'.[168] By contrast the market is flexible, open to change, encouraging not only efficiency but enterprise as well. It promotes the qualities of self-reliance, thrift, diligence, trustworthiness and so on.

Yet few Christians have been altogether comfortable with the market. It seems to undermine all that they would preach about the need for self-sacrifice, altruism, fellowship and compassion. It is impersonal: human contact is kept to the minimum necessary for exchange; we deal with one another as if we were strangers. And yet it seems to usurp the functions of Providence, distributing the gifts of nature according to rules of its own which have little respect for concepts of justice or equality. Christian assessments of the market have varied greatly, and still do today.[169] Some see it as an order of creation, like the state or the family, ordained by God for the benefit of humanity. At the other extreme, others regard it as, at least potentially, demonic, corrupting human nature, destroying communities, encouraging greed and the love of luxury, enabling the rich to enslave the poor. In between are the many Christians who see the market as a necessary institution, neither good nor evil in itself, but inevitable. They talk of making the market the servant and not the master, using it to promote social and political aims, such as the conservation of the environment or the maintenance of full employment. They also want to keep the market in its proper place, limiting the range of goods and services that can be bought and sold. Whatever its merits in this present age, most Christians would say that the market has no place in the kingdom of God.

Section One of this chapter describes the theory of perfect competition. It also shows how neo-classical economics anticipates some of the criticisms of the market economy which might be made,

168 Hayek, F. A., op. cit. For much more recent advocacy, in a much more triumphalist tone, see Fukuyama, F., *The End of History and the Last Man*, op. cit.

169 For a very useful and balanced account see Atherton, J., *Christianity and the Market – Christian Social Thought for our Times*, SPCK, 1992. A collection of papers on the subject was published as Davies, J. (ed.), *God and the Marketplace*, Institute of Economic Affairs, 1993.

not least by Christians. Is it fair? Does it impoverish human relationships? Does it enslave, rather than liberate? Is it a form of idolatry?

Section Two draws together some of the themes of the Bible which seem to state, or at least to imply, strong opposition to the market as it existed in the ancient world. It examines the two central pillars of a non-market system which are the land and the household. The second part then moves on to look at Jesus' warnings on money. If the love of money is the root of evil (as when Jesus himself was 'sold' at his betrayal), is that because buying and selling are wrong in principle, or just that they may lead to temptation? What becomes clear in the study of the New Testament is how much Jesus was concerned to preserve the transcendence of God, rather than directly attacking an unfair economic system. Certainly he was deeply moved by the poverty of his people, but the message of the kingdom must be seen in the context of the land and the households of his day.

Section One: Economic Theory

The market system

> A system of perfect markets provides a mechanism to co-ordinate the activities of individuals who pursue their own self-interest, and thus embodies the essential social and political institutional framework that allows economists' assumptions about human behaviour to result in optimal efficiency and welfare outcomes.[170]

This one sentence from an encyclopaedia entry by B. R. Tomlinson describes very succinctly the model of perfect competition which is at the centre of neo-classical economic theory. The first lesson in an introductory course of economics is likely to be about the determination of prices.[171] Two intersecting lines are drawn on a chart;

170 Tomlinson, B. R., 'Markets', in Kuper, A. and J., op. cit.
171 Pindyck, R. S. and Rubinfeld, D. L., op. cit., Chapter 2.

one slopes downwards to the right, showing how the demand for a commodity falls as its price rises; the other slopes upwards, showing how supply increases. Where the two lines cross we will find the equilibrium price and the quantity of the commodity that is traded. At that price, the market clears, with no queues, no rationing and no goods left unsold. We are asked to imagine an auctioneer calling prices and observing the offers and bids. When there are too many offers the price is reduced; too many bids and the price goes up. Crucially, we are asked to imagine many buyers and many sellers, none of them large enough to be able on their own to influence the price one way or the other. By a relatively simple extension, this partial equilibrium, determining just one price, becomes general equilibrium in which *n* commodities are traded, determining *n -1* price ratios.

To understand how markets work in practice, it is necessary also to study transactions costs – a more advanced field of economics.[172] Goods have to be brought to market, in a literal or a metaphorical sense. First the commodities being traded have to be defined to the satisfaction of all parties. Property rights have to be established. Some means has to be found of testing the quality of the goods offered for sale. Provision has to be made for subsequent litigation and redress. There has to be some guarantee of the honesty of buyers and sellers. 'Caveat emptor' is not acceptable in most markets. There are often specialist dealers who buy in order to resell, and a variety of brokers and middlemen who may save the final purchasers and sellers the costs of searching out their trading partners. There are often arbitrageurs that keep prices for the same product in line in different marketplaces. There are often also speculators who take a view of where prices will move in the future, reducing (or on some assumptions perversely increasing) the fluctuations in prices over time.

The first theorem of welfare economics,[173] as it is called, proves that the allocation of resources resulting from perfect competition is optimal in the sense defined by Vilfredo Pareto. This means that it is

172 Ciborra, C., 'Transaction Costs', in Kuper, A. and J., op. cit.

173 Sen, A., *On Ethics and Economics*, Chapter 2.

impossible to make anyone better off without at the same time making someone else worse off. In this statement, 'better off' is assessed in terms of the individual's own preferences, that is using the same utility or preference ordering as is assumed to motivate that individual's trading behaviour. It amounts to saying that all the gains from trade that can be mutually beneficial have already been achieved. The theorem is not a truism. When competition is not perfect, for example because some traders exercise monopoly power, then all parties could benefit from a move to the perfectly competitive equilibrium, provided that those who gained from that move were willing to compensate those who lost.

Competition can only be perfect when each buyer and seller takes the market price as given. Indeed, all each trader needs to know is that one item of information. It is an entirely arm's-length interaction, with no elements of strategy involved at all. It is not really a competitive situation at all, as that word is used in everyday speech. All individuals react to the same market forces, and can blame their success or failure only on them. The market is as indifferent as the physical environment. There is no conscious rivalry, just as there is no altruism or co-operation.

The contrast is with 'imperfect' competition which is what seems to characterise most markets that we actually observe. But markets may be closer to 'perfection' than at first sight they appear. Even if there are few actual participants involved, the threat of entry may cause them to behave as if entry had already occurred. Some economists would defend the theory of perfect competition, not just as an interesting limiting case, but as a useful approximation to how the market system actually does behave.

In an often-quoted passage, Adam Smith described how self-interest could achieve the advantage of all, 'It is not from the benevolence of the butcher, the brewer or the baker, that we expect our dinner, but from their regard for their own interest. We address ourselves, not to their humanity but to their self-love.'[174] The individual is,[175] 'led by an invisible hand to promote an end which has

174 Smith, A., *The Wealth of Nations*, 1828 edition, Book 1, Chapter 2.
175 ibid., Book 4, Chapter 2.

no part of his intention'. The point has never been made more eloquently since then.

Beneath the rhetoric we need to distinguish two different issues. The first is about the motive for exchange. Very often, in all spheres of life, people can interact so as to benefit each other. This is so obvious that it hardly needs saying. It is not to deny that, in other situations, we may indeed owe our lives to the benevolence or even self-sacrifice of others. The second issue is more interesting. The economy in general equilibrium is a very complex and highly ordered system. Yet it has emerged spontaneously, without the need for anyone to design it. It does not have a purpose or plan. The whole point, really, is that there need be no 'invisible hand' to guide it. No wonder then that many Christians have found Adam Smith's well-chosen words disquieting. They were like a foretaste of the debate about biological evolution and the origin of species.

Trade, then, is in the interest of society, but it may be costly to organise. Hence the need for a medium of exchange. A market system of multilateral exchange using money is vastly more efficient than one which requires the barter of commodities. In a barter economy each participant has to find a partner who wishes to exchange the same pair of goods, what is called a 'double coincidence of wants'. The provision of some generally accepted exchange medium eliminates what would otherwise be prohibitive costs of transaction. The fact that money can be stored is another great advantage since it means that receipts do not need to balance payments at every point in time. Money, as such, has no value – it is just a piece of paper or an entry in a ledger – but it may be useful as a store of value from one time period to another. (The idea of 'loving' money, as such, is simply ridiculous from the point of view of economic theory.)

A market requires a framework of law. In particular it requires some means of enforcing contracts. Thus when debts are incurred there must be some way of making sure that they are paid. As we have suggested in the previous chapter, the more severe the penalties for default, the more willing lenders will be to extend credit. There will, of course, be situations in which the enforcement of contracts will inflict severe hardship on one party. Such misfortune may be entirely undeserved, due to circumstances which could not have been anticipated when the contract was drawn up. But it does not follow that the market system itself is in any way to blame.

Fair trade

There are many ways in which trade can be unfair. Goods can be wrongly described, weights and measures can be inaccurate, bargains can be struck under duress, and so on. There are certain minimum standards of ethical behaviour on which anyone would insist. The more that these standards can be taken for granted the lower the costs of transactions and the wider the scope for trade. Mutual trust between dealers ('my word is my bond') is part of the social infrastructure of the market.

A competitive market should also be fair in another sense. Everyone ought to have equal access. The market can then help to break down prejudice, of race, caste, religion, sex or age. It can set free oppressed minorities and reduce the inequality of wealth and power. Gary Becker, one of the most famous economists of the neo-classical Chicago school, showed in his study of *The Economics of Discrimination*[176] that perfect competition should eliminate wage differentials that are based on prejudice and not on real differences in productivity or skill. Employers who practice discrimination will find their prices undercut by those who do not. They will eventually be driven out of business. The market itself will ensure fair play, it is argued, so there is no need for any special legislation. Unfortunately, the same result does not hold when competition is imperfect.

A move towards more perfect competition can in some circumstances be a move towards justice. In a bilateral bargain the outcome cannot be predicted by the economic theory of competition. There is a range of possible prices, along what is called the 'contract curve'.[177] At each end one participant enjoys the whole of the benefit

176 Becker, G. S., *The Economics of Discrimination*, Univ. of Chicago Press, 1957 and 1971. See also Chiswick, B. R., 'The Economics of Discrimination – A Primer', in Tommasi, M. and Ierulli, K. (eds.), op. cit.

177 Pindyck, R. S. and Rubinfeld, D. L., op. cit., Chapter 16.

from trade, whilst the other is hardly any better off than if no trade had taken place at all. Sometimes one partner has no real 'outside option' at all, since a refusal to trade would leave them with an income below subsistence. In that case a subsistence income may be all that they can get. The partner who does not need to trade may be able to exploit the weakness of the other. That does seem unfair. The introduction of competition into the market, with many buyers and many sellers, puts an end to such unequal bargaining. One might still question the justice of the outcome, but at least the procedure seems more acceptable.

The opening up of trade should in principle result in net economic gain. There will however be some losers as well as those who are better off. The winners should in principle be able to compensate the losers, and still be better off, but that does not often happen in fact. Sometimes the winners will be rich, sometimes they will be poor; there is no general presumption one way or the other. Suppose for example that trade in textiles is liberalised between India and Europe. The winners will probably include relatively poor workers in textiles in India, whilst relatively well-paid workers in textiles in Europe will probably lose. But the winners may include relatively rich consumers of textiles in Europe, not to mention the shareholders in Indian textile firms.

No one has ever claimed that a competitive market will produce an optimal distribution of income. If that is the criterion of fairness then it will fail the test. There is a suggestion, nevertheless, that those who do well in a competitive market do in some sense deserve their success. In competitive sports the best players are said to deserve to win, although they do not always do so. In a competitive market the most productive workers may in the same sense deserve to get rich, although they too will often be unlucky. Some people would make a distinction between success which is earned by hard work, and success which comes from innate ability. This is certainly relevant to incentives, which may justify inequality, although not necessarily to the acceptability of the outcome itself. In general the distribution of income resulting from competition is best regarded as arbitrary; those who care about equality need to look for means of changing the structure of the market so as to move the distribution in the direction they seek. This calls for policies that are actively redistributive.

The term 'fair trade', as opposed to free trade, is used in the debate about relations between rich and poor countries.[178] Under free trade the price of goods produced in poor countries will reflect low wages and inferior conditions of employment. The same goods produced in rich countries will cost more. Is this fair? Should not rich consumers be prepared to pay the same price for the imported goods so that wages and conditions abroad can be improved?

Trade theory says it is efficient to pay the lower price because it encourages production where labour is relatively abundant. The switch of demand to poor countries should help to bid their wages up. There is, however, another consideration, which trade theory recognises, but which does not always get a mention. One reason for the difference in wage levels is the restriction of migration; one reason why migration is restricted is to keep the wage difference intact. That is surely an important part of the unfairness. A free market can only be as fair as the society in which it operates. It is then a matter of judgement whether trying to distort the market for goods in favour of the poor is actually an appropriate way of compensating for the absence of a free market in labour itself. This is what economists call the 'theory of the second best'. It has very little practical guidance to offer.

Reductions in the cost of transport, and the lifting of restraints on trade, have made possible the integration of markets across the world, often called 'globalisation'. This is sometimes seen as a threat to the economies of relatively poor countries. Against this, mainstream economics would stress that the advantage of free exchange is usually mutual – no one is being forced to buy something that they do not want to have. Part of the task of neo-classical economics has always been to point out the benefits of free trade against sectional interests which have supported the protection of particular industries. Nevertheless the theory can readily be extended to include some of the less attractive side effects of globalisation, such as environmental depletion, and to suggest remedies for them.

178 Jacobs, M., *The Politics of the Real World*, Earthscan, 1996.

Whenever there is supply and demand, economics naturally expects there to be a market. There is no distinction made between commodities which it is right to trade, and those which it is not. If the transaction technology permits it, then there will be welfare benefits from trade. The issue is raised in one introductory economics textbook in relation to trade in human kidneys:[179]

> Should people have the right to sell parts of their bodies? Congress believes that the answer is no. In 1984 it passed the National Organ Transplantation Act, which prohibits the sale of organs for transplantation. Organs may only be donated. Although the law prohibits their sale, it does not make organs valueless. Instead, it prevents those who supply organs (living persons or the families of the deceased) from reaping their economic values. [...] Some potential recipients die as a result. [...] Many complex ethical and economic issues are involved in the sale of organs. These issues are important, and this example is not intended to sweep them away. Economics, the dismal science, simply shows us that human organs have economic value that cannot be ignored, and that prohibiting their sale imposes a cost on society that must be weighed against the benefits.

Not everybody would agree with this. A famous study by Richard Titmuss called 'The Gift Relationship' made an ethical and economic case against the sale of human blood:[180]

> From our study of the private market in blood in the United States we have concluded that the commercialisation of blood and donor relationships represses the expression of altruism, erodes the sense of community, lowers scientific standards, limits both personal and professional freedoms, sanctions the making of profits in hospitals and clinical laboratories, legalises hostility between doctor and patient, subjects critical areas of medicine to the laws of the marketplace, places immense social costs on those least able to bear them – the poor, the sick and the inept – increases the danger of unethical behaviour in various sectors of medical science and practice, and results in situations in which proportionately more and more blood is supplied by the poor, the

179 Pindyck, R. S. and Rubinfeld D. L., op. cit.

180 Titmuss, R. M., *The Gift Relationship – From Human Blood to Social Policy*, George Allen and Unwin, 1970.

> unskilled, the unemployed, Negroes and other low income groups and categories of exploited human populations of high blood yielders.

Despite that long list of arguments, and despite what the economics textbook says, the issue here is surely not only the economic and social costs and benefits to be expected from trade in human blood or kidneys. Many people would object even if it could be shown unambiguously to raise the living standards and life expectancy of all groups in the population. They would object on grounds which are not related to the consequences at all. They would say that it is a kind of sacrilege, an insult to the dignity of the human body. As we have seen welfare economics is most at home with a purely utilitarian ethic, and that keeps creating tensions when other kinds of evaluation are proposed.

A similar debate could take place about prostitution. It would be easy to put forward an economic argument in support of legitimising and regulating the trade (and perhaps taxing it for the benefit of the community as a whole). It has after all been well-established throughout history all over the world. A case could be made that the most unsavoury aspects of the business are the result of moral stigmatisation, rather than its cause.

What we are seeing here is a sort of boundary dispute. (It is related to, but different from, the dispute over the boundaries of economics as a subject.) Nearly all economists would recognise that the scope of the market cannot and should not be universal. But economic theory has little to say as to where the line should be drawn. Economic analysis will not help to identify where exactly the ethical objection to prostitution is based. It could be expressed in terms of human rights, but that might be a reason to regulate the trade rather than to ban it.

Again it is may be more appropriate to use the word 'sacrilege'. The commercialisation of this part of human relationships just seems to most people to be wrong in itself. These ethical or religious objections to trade are not irrational or arbitrary. What is being maintained is that there are spheres of life to which the impersonal, self-interested mode of behaviour characteristic of the market is totally inappropriate. There are relationships which demand a commitment of body, mind and spirit. There can be no 'limited liability'. If the medium of money were to be introduced the relationship would be changed and corrupted. It would become something different, much less significant, a parody of the real thing. As always, the sacred needs to be protected from such contamination by vigorous condemnations.

If it is agreed that the scope of the market is subject to limits of this kind, then it is possible to address in a similar fashion some very different questions of social ethics and policy. Is it right for doctors and teachers, for example, to be motivated by private gain? (Should hospitals be renamed as 'health enterprises', as they were in New Zealand?) Should prisons be privatised? What is at stake here is not so much the efficiency of the market system as its appropriateness to different kinds of service. Economic theory does find these questions difficult to address.

Gifts and exchanges

Goods and services, which cannot properly be bought or sold, can always be given and received. The market is not the only place of exchange. The model of neo-classical economics has occasionally been applied to non-market transactions, as well as to its more usual subject matter. It may be useful, in the present context, to elaborate a little on how this might be done,

Amongst family and friends the normal relationship is one of sharing in both production and consumption – although it is not unknown for parents to give their children money as a reward for helping with the housework. The essence of a gift is that one person transfers ownership or enjoyment to another without explicitly receiving anything in return. There is no contractual obligation to give in the first place, and no contractual right to expect reciprocation. There is not, strictly speaking, an exchange at all. But, of course, social custom creates expectations which few people would wish to disappoint. Economists talk of contracts that are 'implicit', even if they are never overtly made.

At Christmas each year, parents buy presents for their children. They will be something which they hope that their children will want, but also something which the parents want them to have. Two sets of preferences have to be reconciled, the children's wishes and the wishes of the parents as to what the children's wishes should be. It is not always easy to choose. Economic theory suggests that it would be best to give money, leaving the children to choose how they spend it.

Adults sometimes have great difficulty choosing gifts to give to one another. The ideal present would be useful, without being utilitarian; it would appear generous, without actually being too expensive. The existence of specialist gift shops makes the choice easier and the objects chosen more predictable. Colleagues at work or business associates send one another cards or small presents to convey the message that their relationship is not merely a commercial one. These customs, which might seem quaint from the perspective of economics, are not some vestige left over from a pre-market organisation of society; they are a very important part of social life today.

The practice of tipping for service, on the other hand, does now seem archaic, justified if at all only by long tradition. It speaks of an age of masters and servants, when the reward for labour was at the discretion of the employer. That was one way of ensuring that the work was well done, also giving the servant an incentive to be pleasant and to try to be liked, to go beyond the minimum that could actually be required. What was originally an expression of gratitude became an expectation although never quite a right. Judging the correct size of the tip has become an embarrassment; to be dependent on tips for an adequate wage is seen as demeaning. The institution is no longer pleasing to many in a society of social equals, a society where most people prefer to know where they stand.

Before the development of an efficient market system, economic relationships were formed largely around reciprocal obligations. The instinct to give, in the expectation of return, seems to be at the foundation of much human interchange – indeed it can be seen in the behaviour of social animals as well.[181] The requirement to give is

181 Ridley, M., *The Origins of Virtue*, Viking, 1996.

enforced by the threat of contempt, ostracism or neglect. The rules governing exchange can be very complex indeed. It should not be imagined that this informal exchange of favours exists only in primitive societies. On the contrary it continues alongside the market in the most sophisticated of professions, and modern society could not function without it.

Adam Smith famously said that we do not rely on the benevolence of the butcher and the others for our food. That it true, but there is a minimum level of co-operation and courtesy necessary for the economy to work well. It is impossible to say where self-interest ends and altruism begins. The butcher may well feel some special obligation to regular customers, making sure that they get a good turkey for Christmas. How much is that calculation and how much a gesture of real goodwill?

In every society there are those who, for one reason or another, are dependent on gifts. If we insist on seeing self-interest behind every transaction, then giving to the destitute can be seen as a kind of insurance. The fortunate give to the unfortunate, not in the hope of a direct return, but because they want the safety net to stay in place, just in case they ever need to rely on it themselves.

There are however two problems with charitable giving, if it is understood this way. Both are very familiar to economists from many different contexts. The first is the problem of moral hazard. It is not easy to tell who really needs help and who is just pretending. Few people are prepared to allow their generosity to be exploited. There are therefore specialist organisations, of which the churches may be examples, which sort out the deserving from the undeserving poor. Particular groups, like orphan children, are identified as being unambiguously needy. Charitable organisations compete with one another for the donations of the kind-hearted, each offering an especially worthy class of recipient, as well as an efficient distribution of the aid. Thus the individual donor is spared the task of assessing the credentials of the poor.

The second problem is that of a public good. No one wants the poor to starve, but why should the burden of supporting them fall on some of us and not on the rest? Few people want a disproportionate share in giving. Hence the welfare state: voluntary giving is largely replaced by a system of taxes and benefits. The system enjoys popular support – up to a point – because everyone has to pay their share whether they personally feel charitable or not. Those who want to give more can, of course, still do so.

The economics of charitable giving and welfare payments make the transactions impersonal. The ultimate giver and the ultimate receiver never meet each other face to face. It is remote as a transaction in a perfectly competitive market. This is very different from the giving of presents, for example at Christmas. The point of Christmas presents is largely to express and affirm a personal relationship. But those who cannot reciprocate may not wish to enter into a personal relationship at all. If they have nothing to contribute then they may feel inferior and resent the patronising attitudes of those on whose generosity they depend. If there was a personal relationship often neither party would know how to handle it The very word 'charity' can get a bad name, because these attitudes of compassion and gratitude can so easily be corrupted.

Section Two: Christian Belief

The market and Christian belief

Economic development did not exist in biblical times. Yet the relationship between the existence of the market and Christian belief can be drawn out of scripture in various ways. First there is the method of liberation theology which engages with the meaning of the text at a deep level, beyond the apparent surface presentation of the text. For these writers Christianity is essentially redemptive, and the true understanding of redemption is that it frees human beings from what binds them and oppresses them. That is why, in their view capital is at its core a fundamentally unchristian institution, and why Christianity has to be far more aware that the opposite of graced relationships are indebted ones.

Hence the title of Peter Selby's book is *Grace and Mortgage*. His engagement with the texts in this way is why he feels that the most valid interpretation of scripture is this materialist one which shows how the grace of Christ can redeem such enslavements – can redeem indeed the mortgages which some present-day home-owners sometimes find burdensome and oppressive.

The second thing which this encounter with the biblical world does is to show the precursor of the market as we know it today. In the New Testament there is nothing that approximates to the impersonal transaction of the market as described above. In different periods of history religion and finance have been interwoven in many different ways, for example under the feudal system of the Middle Ages. In the New Testament the Kingdom of God, as taught by Jesus, can be seen as a challenge to all aspects of society, economic as well as religious. But it can also be seen as separated off from society, enabling its 'citizens' to escape the evil of the world, rather than enabling them to reform it.

That is why the biblical world is not so foreign from our own day. It can be read as limiting the scope of the market, protecting some areas of life from it, rather than seeking alternative institutions which would do away with the market altogether. There is a clear sense in the New Testament that certain matters are off-limits to the place of trade, and the issue of simony epitomises this. So too does Paul's teaching on prostitution.

So does the New Testament stand at one remove from the world of the market?

Jesus said that it is impossible to serve two masters, God and Mammon. This text has been taken as a prohibition of the worship of money, of turning money into a god. In its original context it does not necessarily have quite this religious connotation. To 'serve' money does not necessarily involve idolatry. It may be rather a warning against putting one's trust in wealth, whatever form it may take, instead of trusting in God. But, in any case, it is clear enough that Jesus and his followers saw money as dangerous, if not positively evil.

In Acts 8, the great magician Simon Magus attempts to buy the power to deliver the Holy Spirit, and Peter roundly rebukes him for his actions. The term 'simony' is taken from this account. It led to a long campaign in the early and medieval church, against the sale of ecclesiastical office or preferment. The story is not just about the danger of money as such, it is about the proper limits of the exchange economy, and about the radical 'gift' nature of the Holy Spirit, and this is emphasised in several parts of Acts (10:44–45 and 11:17). For some purposes Jesus himself was prepared to use money, for example when paying his taxes. But the general sense of the New Testament is that gifts are better than exchanges. There will be no buying or selling in the kingdom of God.

This leaves a number of issues, or problems to be resolved. The most prominent one is the place of compassion, and of the nature of personal gifts in an impersonal market. The danger with the market, apart from the issue of injustice, is that it renders all transactions impersonal. Indeed it might go further than this. Theologians today are aware of what can be called 'commodification', where an object is bought in place of a personal relationship. This is fine if it does not happen too often: the flowers which apologise for a moment of rudeness are a material gift that represents something else. However where objects replace relationships altogether, then something serious is happening. In the worldview of the Old Testament, these objects become idols, and displace the relationship that should be there. The market is an efficient servant, but a heartless master. Christians, amongst others, will want to keep it in its place.

If the Bible is not about the market, then it may be asked what is it about? The answer is that there were two pillars of biblical society which have been much studied by scholars in recent years. One is the land, and the other is that of the household. In the response to the description of the market, we shall look at these two in turn, before finally discussing Jesus' attitude to wealth. The gift of the land falls into two parts. First there is the journey of Abraham, followed by the exodus from Egypt into the Promised Land, and secondly the settlement. Only in the settlement is the land actually enjoyed. Both the land and the household can be contrasted with the market and trade.

The biblical account, presented of course in narrative form, is a story of trust in the future, and the giving of future benefits from a God who remains inscrutable. The trust which is demanded in the future is one in which there will be future benefits, because of the nature of God's trustworthiness. Yet the process of evaluating this promise is not one within our control.

It is significant that the book of Genesis swiftly moves into the story of Abraham, who moves towards having land which is promised to him by God. Abraham is asked to trust in God, for he will be given an heir, and through him there will be great blessings. The response of Abraham is one of uncertainty, but the promises of God must be accepted as they stand. There is no bargaining at this point. Epsztein points out that nomadism is of importance for two reasons. First, this is where the covenant promises made by God to Israel were first given. Secondly, these pastoral figures living in tents represent the absolute antithesis of a structured society. We shall see that in time the land, and later in addition to the land also the household, represent a structured hierarchical society which opposes the impersonal transactions of the market. But the time of the patriarchs represents a time of no structure at all.[182]

> There are no hierarchical relationships [...] this egalitarian structure explains one of the main foundations of the Old Testament laws, according to which, contrary to what we find elsewhere (for example in the Code of Hammurabi) compensation and penalties do not vary with membership of a particular social class: the principle of an eye for an eye and a tooth for a tooth is applied to everyone (Exodus 21:23–25; Deuteronomy 19:21) except for the slave – though he is not treated as a simple object but benefits from numerous favours.

It is here that Israel is given the promise of the gift of the land which is to be so important in the succeeding centuries. The biblical accounts in Genesis 15–18 are full of heavy symbolism which indicate the non-rational nature of the faith in the future which Abraham is being asked to have. These include such things as a dread and great darkness; a

182 Epsztein, L., op. cit.

deep sleep; smoking fire pot and a flaming torch; the appearance of three men at the oaks of Mamre. From this series of encounters the covenant is also brought into being. This is one way in which the memory of landlessness was remembered. Landlessness was not to be overcome by trade, or market transactions. It could only be overcome by God's gift.

The other memory of landlessness was the experience of the wilderness. In the story of Abraham and the patriarchs there was eventually an intense trust in the promises of God, after the initial scepticism. In the wilderness journeys there was again a duality of doubt and disobedience, set against the prayer of Moses in Numbers 14:14. 'They have heard that you, Lord, are in the middle of this people'. The test in verse 16 is whether the 'Lord was not able to bring this people into the land which he swore to give to them'. Moses is very aware that the people are furious, and wish that they had never been brought out of slavery in Egypt to die miserably in the wilderness.

The response of God is remarkable. Those who doubted will not reach the land but in time future descendants will inherit the Promised Land. Hence it is clear that the correlation of the absence of wealth and the existence of trusting faith is by no means simple for Israel. In the wilderness the absence of wealth nearly destroys Israel, for the wilderness shows the reality of vulnerability in the experience of Israel. Israel is fed by manna, so even though landlessness is not the destiny of Israel, it can look back on these events with gratitude. Over against this are stories of those who quarrelled with the leaders of Israel, as in Exodus 16:3. Here the people protest that 'you have brought us out of this wilderness to kill this whole assembly with hunger'. It is clear that Moses did not convince some of the Israelites, and the struggle to carry through the decision to remain in the wilderness was never an easy one.

Finally Israel is given land, where the promise is delivered, and the wanderings in the wilderness cease. As Brueggemann says, this is 'the moment of the most radical transformation of any historical person or group, the moment of empowerment or enlandment'.[183]

183 Brueggemann, W., op. cit.

What is important however is that once Israel enters into the possession of the land, then there are reciprocal obligations.

The promised gift of the land

The discussion of the land brings together both the description of what the Bible says and how theologians like Peter Selby have interpreted the biblical material for today. Another theologian who has written a great deal in this area is Tim Gorringe.

He has written several books on contemporary economic debates which incorporate a detailed study of the biblical texts from a particular standpoint. Gorringe is helpful in showing how much support there is in the scriptures for a critical attitude to wealth.[184] At the period of the Judges in the Old Testament, which may have lasted for two centuries as the Jewish people organised themselves, the tribes of Israel struggled with the kings already living in Canaan. This was the entry into the Promised Land. There are great tensions within the biblical account, especially in the book of Joshua, as to how the Israelites entered into the land. As well as the description of the entry in to the land, there are also stories of conquest and forced occupation of the land belonging to the tribes and city dwellers already there. These small city-states were eventually overcome, and the tribes formed themselves into a peasant economy.[185] Politically they were a tribal federation, with a tribal council. The early years of the entry into the Promised Land are the years before the institution of kingship. These are the years of the judges, when Israel was a tribal society.

This was later seen as a golden age in the history of Israel, where differences of wealth were not marked. There are many passages of scripture from this period which enshrine the common memory of Israel. Some of the psalms are difficult to date, but the themes are constant and repetitious: ‘The earth is the Lord’s and the fullness thereof, the world and they that dwell therein’ (Psalm 24:11). ‘For every beast of the forest is mine, the cattle on a thousand hills [...] the

184 Gorringe, T. J., op. cit.
185 Habel, N., op. cit.

world and all that moves in the field is mine', echoes this in Psalm 50:9-11. More pointedly there is Psalm 37:11 where 'the meek shall possess the land and delight themselves in abundant prosperity'.

The fundamental economic philosophy of this semi-egalitarian peasant economy is a combination of stewardship allied to the demands of a subsistence way of life. There is a denial of the absolute rights of private property, since the land belonged to the God who had brought them into Canaan. It was he who had created it, and given it to his people.

We have already discussed in a previous chapter the view that Paul in Thessalonians was not expounding a contemporary work ethic. Instead he was responding to the problems caused by those who would not work because they believed that the end of the world was about to happen through the action of God's judgement. In a similar way in Leviticus the emphasis is not on social and economic equality in itself. Rather it is an attempt to have a theocratic economy, where everything is subordinated to the will of God who 'owns' the land. This is clearly expressed in Leviticus 25:23, where it commands: 'The land shall not be sold in perpetuity, for the land is mine; for you are strangers and sojourners with me'. Private property, in the sense of capital accumulation which is inalienable from the owner because it is legally protected, is not a concept which makes sense in this world.

Israel however ceases to be a peasant and tribal economy. It becomes a monarchy, with growing trade and wealthy cities. This leads to social and economic inequality. The words of the prophets are a reaction to this wealth, and their denunciations hark back to the earlier periods of Israelite history. In the great story of Naboth's vineyard, the king, who is Ahab of Samaria, offers Naboth another vineyard in exchange for his which was near the king's palace. Alternatively he offers Naboth the value of the vineyard in cash. This was not an exploitative transaction, but Naboth refuses because he will not give up the land which was given by God to the peasants of Israel. This land was called the *nachalah.* In 1 Kings 21:3 Naboth puts his case: 'The Lord forbid that I should give you the inheritance of my fathers'. When Ahab's wife arranges for Naboth to be killed on a false charge, the prophet Elijah denounces them both not only for murder, but also for 'taking possession'. It is this latter crime which violates the inalienability of land from the people of Israel, who hold it in trust from the Lord, as much as murder violates the equally God given right to life.

Other prophets who attack the growing power of the wealthy in Israel are Isaiah, Amos and Jeremiah. Again and again the fundamental charge is that the rights of those who lived in the property, or who used the land to farm, are denied. 'Woe to him who builds his house by unrighteousness, and his upper rooms by injustice.' (Jeremiah 22:13). In similar vein Isaiah attacks those who join up fields by expropriating the existing fields of the peasantry (Isaiah 5:8). Such rights are grounded in the idea of the land as being held in stewardship, where outright ownership was an illicit development. The memory of the tribal confederation lived on long after its demise, much as the ideals of nineteenth century Socialism outlived the demise of late nineteenth century society.

The main concern of the Bible is undoubtedly with the use and ownership of the land, rather than with the institution of the market. This enables both Judaism and Christianity to present themselves as material, physical religions. It is however also the additional factor of the transcendent presence of God which must be taken into account. That is, the land in the Bible is never just land, but is also land as promise; gift; a land to be anticipated as the gift of God.

This giver stands outside history, and yet religious faith claims that he has been faithful in history. This means that there are two distinct, but interwoven, elements of the discussion of wealth in the biblical account. One is that we are considering land as the pre-modern form of wealth, and not (as we would now) wealth in contemporary economic theory which includes money, buildings, equipment, as well as land. As in modern economic theory, so also in the Bible, land is given, not man-made. The second factor, therefore, is that we are considering land as gift of God to his people, which implies the deliverance of this gift in history, and therefore over future periods of time. The gift is therefore personal, and cannot be seen as separate from the giver.

How then do we evaluate the enjoyment of the land which was eventually given to Israel? It is clear that, as Deuteronomy says, this was a land flowing with riches. What is even more crucial is that this is a personal gift. The land is not simply an object to be conquered, but rather the land is the expression of the promises of God. Deuteronomy 6:10-11 says: 'And when the Lord your God brings you into the land which he swore to your fathers, to Abraham, to Isaac, and to Jacob, to give you.' The land redeems the oath sworn by God to the patriarchs. It is also a land to be enjoyed which will satiate its inhabitants, for it is fertile beyond their comprehension. This land brings temptation, and responsibility, for Israel had to be faithful to the God who had brought Israel into the Promised Land. Much of the succeeding criticism of wealth, by the prophets, and of course by John the Baptist and Jesus of Nazareth, is centred on this failure to live up to the obligations which the gift of the land implies.[186]

The household at the time of Jesus

Land remained central to the community in which Jesus lived. Jesus preached in the villages of Galilee, proclaiming the kingdom of God, and his stories are full of references to the land. But as well as this there was the household. This had always been vital to Israelite life, but with the Roman occupation the household was now reinforced in two ways. First there was the use which the Roman civilisation made of the household, as can be seen from a visit to Pompeii. It was a centre of culture, social relationships and commerce. Secondly, Roman law strengthened the obligations of the household, to the point of death for disobedience. The basic economic unit of society at the time of Jesus was the household. Wealth was usually fixed by inheritance within families, and household economics was fixed by kinship. There are many references to buying and selling in the New Testament, yet most economic functions were determined by kinship, and not by the market, nor (as in the previous chapter) by considerations of capital accumulation. This included production, consumption, the employment of labour and the cultivation of crops.

186 There is a helpful summary of Brueggemann's views on this point in his article 'Land: Fertility and Justice', in Evans, B. (ed.) and Cusack, G., *Theology of The Land*, The Liturgical Press, 1987.

The only other factors than kinship would be political ones which would cover power and honour.[187]

Reciprocity, redistribution and householding were the ways in which economies were organised. Reciprocity involved implicit, often non-legal, obligations of rank. They were enforced by codes of honour and shame. Such obligations are a direct alternative to the market, for they were, at least implicitly, contractual, although they did not involve monetary exchange. Redistribution included the collection and storage of goods which were then reallocated to other individuals and bodies. Tax and rent in excess of economic value were the most common forms of redistribution.

Householding underpinned both the relations of redistribution and reciprocity. Large quantities of goods and services were produced for the use of the family. Households made up villages according to lineage, and so ensured basic reciprocal relations. Gradually these households became attached to cities for administration. Equally cities were ordered into households.

Households were deeply patriarchal, and the family *(oikos)* lived in a house, which could be large, and was called an *oikia.* The *oikos*, or household, was defined not only by kinship but also by relationships of subordination and dependence. The head of a household was responsible for his family, which could be extensive. In addition to this there would be slaves and former slaves, hired servants, and even tenants and business partners. Roman law reinforced the obligations of reciprocity. There was *potestas* which was power over children, slaves and servants; *dominium,* over goods; and *manus* which was over wives and his son's wives. At the heart of the household was a system of patronage, where a person who had skills and expertise would put himself under the patronage of a household. If a person was lucky, he would be born into a household which would provide such assets. Then influential connections, administrative expertise and skills would be part of inherited relationships. If a person was clever, but born into a poor household, he would have to find the right patronage. So society was made up of

187 Crosby, M. H., *House of Disciples: Church, Economics and Justice in Matthew*, Orbis, 1988.

thousands of households, some of enormous size. Households could be understood both socially, in terms of relationships of honour and obligation, and economically. Each reinforced the other. Each presupposed order, authority, and a fixed set of relationships. Overall there was security, and a sense of belonging. In the midst of it all were the household gods, and wives trained children in the worship of these gods. These gods provided protection and blessings, not only for the children, but also for the slaves and hired servants. Religion and economics were organised through the household.

This is why the New Testament pays relatively little attention to the market system. The section in Section One on Economic Theory and the Market discussed gifts and exchanges. It referred to the way in which reciprocal obligations continue alongside the market today. However in biblical society there was often no alternative to reciprocal obligations. This solves some of problems of charitable giving mentioned in the same section. The problem of moral hazard is reduced, for those in need will be subject to close observation and discipline within the household. There were also wider associations, called *ekklesiai* (or in Latin *collegia),* which could carry out voluntary works of charity. These were often far more egalitarian. Secondly there is the issue of the public good. Again the public good is replaced in the main by the good of the household. Charity began at home, as the saying goes, although the Roman Empire at the time of Jesus would organise some charity (bread and circuses) in cities like Rome.

The New Testament begins with the ministry of Jesus which is itinerant and rural. This is the background for Mark's Gospel which uses the term *kome* for village seven times. By Matthew's Gospel village is used only four times. The terms which Matthew uses are house and household. As mentioned above, these are *oikos* and *oikia*: the household and the building, or house. Indeed, in the New Testament, *oikos* is used 112 times, and *oikia* 94 times. What has happened is that the early Church has moved from a rural Galilean society into a Greco-Roman culture, from the Aramaic language to the Greek, and from a homogeneous, deeply impoverished way of life to a diverse, urban community, where rich and poor live near each other. In brief, Christianity very soon became urban.[188]

Matthew is much concerned with justice, but not with the market. For Matthew the household is where the faithful community who follow Jesus gather. It is the entry into the Kingdom of God, just as the Roman Empire also rested on the loyalty of the householders. In Chapter 12:25, he argues that kingdoms fall through divisions: so too do households. Obedience is again a central theme, but the obedience is to the Father, who is in heaven. Indeed, in 12:46–50 Jesus is depicted by Matthew as contrasting his family with his disciples, who are the true household.

The concern with justice in Matthew is spelled out in Chapters 6 (charity) and 18 (the forgiveness of debts). This of course relates to the Jubilee ethic discussed in the previous chapter of this book on capital and debt. Jesus announces the Jubilee in Chapter 11 of Matthew's Gospel, and in 19:21 he calls on his followers to 'sell what you possess and give to the poor'. All this is part of a strategy in Matthew to reorder the household in a way that is still obedient, and indeed at times patriarchal, but which includes the dispossessed in a new, and inclusive, household.

It is clear that the market does not figure in this account at all. Matthew ignores the trade in grain, which was carried on in the Empire, and prefers to build up the followers of Jesus in a new way. This is fundamentally different from the impersonal, market based system of modern economic life. Matthew's vision is not one of fair trade, nor of welfare economics. It is a vision of households which encompass transformed relationships.

Finally it is worth referring back to chapter Four, where we found Paul reworking the understanding of well-being in the house churches in Corinth. In Chapter Four the argument of Paul on the new creation was contrasted with the understanding of needs and wants in modern economic theory. Now we look at the social context of Paul's writings which as in Matthew turns out to be a household. It is no surprise that if the context is different, so will be the arguments on well-being stemming from this context. Stephen Joubert's article on

188 ibid., page 39.

the Pauline household illustrates how patriarchal Paul could be. Paul sees himself as brokering the patronage of God, thus embodying the social and ethical honour of the Corinthian household group. It is this understanding of honour which means that the market is seen as fundamentally irrelevant to the beliefs and values of the early Christians.[189]

Criticisms of wealth in the biblical tradition

When we move into considering the attacks of Jesus on the dangers of wealth it should not be forgotten that they stand against the Judaic acceptance of land as God's gift. This offers a redefinition of the meaning of wealth. Therefore it is not a rejection of wealth per se that Jesus offers, but rather of wealth which is divorced from the gifts of God and which perverts the purposes of God. The nature of the gift of land to the people of Israel then is the means by which a dialogue with economic theory can be developed, rather than simply presenting Jesus (or the prophets) as proto-Marxists ahead of their time. The argument changes and the blessings of possession are what matters.

The ambiguity in the teaching of Jesus about wealth has often been noted, and it remains a continuing corrective to a society which places a high regard on the pursuit of material gain. The argument for accepting the value of wealth is that material things come from God, and are gifts to the people he has created. In another interpretation, they are the products of the talents which God has given to humanity. If it is acceptable for music or art, which are themselves the products of God-given talents, to be used to glorify God in worship and in sacred buildings, why may not the material goods created by human beings be similarly enjoyed as a gift from God? Some theologians have noted that Jesus was supported by women in Luke 8:3 'out of their means' which implies an acceptance of wealth, so long as it was

189 Joubert, S. J., 'Paul as Paterfamilias of the Christian Household Group in Corinth', in Esler, P. F. (ed.), *Modelling Early Christianity: Social scientific studies of the New Testament in its context*, Routledge, 1995.

properly used.[190] However this argument is in constant tension with the teaching of Jesus that riches can, and do, ensnare those who possess them. It blinds people to the needs of others, and above all it obscures the need which even the richest person has of the love of God. The love of money is indeed the root of all evil.

We have seen so far that it is far too simple to deny that the Bible has a positive attitude to wealth. This positive attitude to wealth, in the shape of the gift of the land, and the blessings of the land, is however in constant tension with the failure to live up to the obligations which this will carry with it. The story of the exile, and the song of Mary ('the rich he has sent empty away') are the biblical attempts to redress the balance in favour of the obligations which the gift of the land carries with it.

Section Three: Summary and Discussion

It is a mistake to describe the market as either good or evil in itself. It is neutral, impersonal, and sterile. If it is compared with relationships of gift exchange in which the powerful dominate the weak, as is often the case, then it is a liberating institution, as well as an efficient one. If, however, it is compared with personal relationships of real fellowship and generosity, then by contrast it is inhuman and legalistic.

The Bible is set in a pre-modern economy, mainly agricultural. There is no expectation of growth or development. Wealth consists mainly of land, flocks and herds or grain stored in barns. When productive land is in fixed supply it is easy to conclude that the rich can acquire wealth only at the expense of the poor. This makes it objectionable, even when it is honestly earned. There is no suggestion that the rich can be of service to the poor by making labour more productive.

190 Meeks, W., *The First Urban Christians*, Yale University Press, 1983, and Sedgwick, P., op. cit. on positive attitudes to wealth in Scripture.

What is almost completely lacking in the Bible is any expectation that the land could be traded and the profits of the land sold in a market system. There was trade, but it was very limited. There is an intense discussion among biblical archaeologists about how much trade actually went on in Galilee at the time of Jesus, but the land as such was not traded.[191] The rich who owned the land lived off a rental income, and were not using their wealth productively. The landowner in Matthew 21, however, does undertake investment, planting a vineyard, putting a wall round it, and building a winepress and a watchtower. Then he finds some tenant farmers and expects them to share the produce with him. The tenants are condemned for refusing to recognise the claim of the landlord to his just share in the enterprise. No doubt those hearing this parable are invited to reflect on the failure of the Jewish religious leaders to recognise the just claims of God. The fact that God can be likened to an improving landlord does not amount to support for the private ownership of capital! On the other hand it does not suggest outright opposition either.

The attitude of the Bible to the market, in so far as it existed in ancient times, is one of suspicion or outright hostility. Sometimes it seems to be defending a pattern of customary reciprocal obligations against the encroachment of impersonal market relationships. Sometimes it is defining a religious sphere from which the 'traders' must be expelled. But sometimes, especially in the New Testament, it is portraying an ideal society in which community ties are so strong that there is no need for the market – or indeed for the state either. All these adverse assessments of the market have been carried over into Christian teaching in modern times.

In practical terms, however, Christians are not much better placed than anyone else to design a working alternative to the market mechanism. The market is one of the defining institutions of modern society. It is very difficult to imagine an alternative which would be compatible with the individual choice, and economic progress, which is now taken for granted. In judging the market one is judging the

191 Horsley, R. A., *Archaeology History and Society in Galilee: The Social Context of Jesus and the Rabbis*, Trinity Press International, 1996. Chapter 3 discusses Galilee as a market economy.

modern way of life, and it is not easy to stand back far enough to get it in perspective.

Clearly the market is not the answer to all of society's needs. It cannot, for example secure the rapid deployment of resources, and the social cohesion, needed in wartime, or in other times of national emergency. Its boundaries are, and must remain, a matter of dispute. It overlaps in different directions with the state, the family and the informal community. In some spheres the market is, by common consent, inappropriate, for ethical or religious, rather than for economic reasons. In recent times, the boundaries of the market may have expanded on all sides, but they have often contracted in the past, and may do so again.

Market institutions might be made more just, although they can never be made compassionate. Justice is defined in many different ways, in terms of process and in terms of outcome. Different definitions are not in general compatible. The enforcement of the necessary rules of the game produces a minimum kind of fairness, but few people will be satisfied with that alone. Some will rely on opening up more competition to make the market fairer, but others will think it necessary for the state to intervene so as to achieve fairness more directly. If justice is assessed in terms of outcomes, equality of income for example rather than equality of opportunity, then the market is not the best means of achieving that end. The political sphere will need to expand at the expense of the economic.

Compassion is expressed in the giving of gifts, not in the market. Giving and receiving are essentially reciprocal and usually set in the context of a close community. There will always be disputes as to who deserves to receive, and how the burden will be shared amongst those who give. Christian teaching about gifts is theological as well as ethical in character. The donor can make the recipient feel very small unless both feel proper gratitude towards God. Failing that, charity itself can become impersonal; the marketing of good causes can be just another sector of an efficient economy.

Chapter Nine

Strategy, Emotions and the Theory of Games

Introduction

In this chapter we continue our examination of how relationships are represented in economic theory and in Christian belief. In the previous chapter we concentrated on behaviour in competitive markets, relationships which, for better or for worse, were entirely impersonal in character. We now turn to relationships which could be described as 'face to face', that is between identifiable individuals who take account of one another's reactions in deciding what to do.

Economic theory retains its commitment to methodological individualism. Thus there are no joint decisions, even if individuals act together, and even if they 'care' for one another. Each individual calculates his or her optimal strategy, even if that strategy is intended to benefit other people. This may, or may not, involve a process of bargaining; it may or may not, require an element of mutual trust. It might be described as 'friendly' or as 'hostile'. The mathematical tools of analysis are provided by the theory of games.

The approach remains strictly rational, and devoid of emotion. Each 'player' seeks to achieve his or her own objectives in a logical and dispassionate manner. It is like chess as it is played by computers. Personal relationships are reduced to mathematics. We are thus in a very different world from that of most psychology, whether popular or academic. There is nothing mysterious about the way that people relate to one another, no need for empathy or intuition in order to understand it. In game theory relationships are never good or bad in themselves, neither healthy nor sick.

The contrast between the two 'anthropologies' compared in this book is perhaps sharper in this chapter than in any of the others. In the Bible, and especially in the New Testament, the quality of relationships is of paramount importance. They are of value in their own right, not just as a means to an end. The emotions involved, love and hatred, trust and suspicion, are of the essence of relationships, not mere by-products. This does not mean, however, that the mathematics is of no significance at all. It is, on the contrary, inescapable. It tells us something about the structure of relationships which are valid irrespective of the ethical or religious importance that is attached to them. It may well assist a better understanding of the aspects of human nature and experience which Christians and others believe to be most important.

In Section One below, we begin with a brief account of simple game theory as applied in economics. We then offer some comments on it, designed to highlight its limitations and its profound difference from the account of relationships one finds in Christian belief. Yet the attempt to categorise the possible meanings of the word 'love' within a utility framework does not seem altogether without value for Christian anthropology. Section Two, as usual, seems to make a sharp change of direction, as it turns from merely human relationships to the relationship of the chosen people to God. Yet one can see that some of the same problems, both intellectual and emotional, are involved.

Section One: Economic Theory

The theory of games is a branch of mathematics developed for the analysis of any strategic behaviour. Two or more 'players' plan their 'moves', calculating how their decisions will influence the decisions of the others. It is the interaction that is interesting; each calculation must be based on the assumption that the other participants will be calculating too, in the same rational and strategic way. In the last twenty or thirty years the theory of games has been used by economists in a variety of contexts and some fruitful theoretical innovations have resulted from it. It has, for example, been the main stimulus for new developments in the theory of oligopoly and imperfect competition.[192]

When competition is imperfect, firms know that their decisions will have a significant effect on market prices. When there are just a few buyers or sellers in the market, then they will all study the behaviour of the others with great care, knowing that their own behaviour will be observed with the same attention. For example, a monopolist may sink more capital into a business, knowing that a show of strength is one way of frightening off potential rivals. But equally two firms may agree to divide the market between them as a duopoly, knowing that both would suffer if they competed too aggressively for market share.

The choice of strategy

Games, or any situations which require strategic behaviour, can be defined by a set of 'pay-offs' available to the various participants. In 'zero-sum games', the gain of one player is necessarily the loss of the rest, but not all the games analysed are of this kind. Some games allow only one move to each player; others require a sequence of moves, responding to one another. Some games are predetermined; others introduce an element of chance, represented by the throwing of dice.

In analysing a game the theory identifies any positions of equilibrium. This is analogous to the position in a competitive market when the price exactly balances supply and demand. It is a position in which no participant has any incentive to alter his or her behaviour. In game theory it is a position in which no player has the incentive to make another move. The establishment of a duopoly might be such an equilibrium, or the uncontested control of the market by a single firm. Not all games contain such solutions. In some cases the game will go on for ever, repeating the same sequence of moves over and over

192 There is an introduction to the use of game theory in Pindyck, R. S. and Rubinfeld D. L., op. cit., Chapter 13. See also Kreps, D. M., *Game Theory and Economic Modelling*, OUP, 1990.

again. Different definitions of equilibrium are possible. The one most commonly used is called a Nash equilibrium; in such a position each player is maximising his or her own pay-off, given the supposed actions of all the others.

Two points can be made about such solutions. First, they may not be unique: the game may contain two or more situations in which no player would have the incentive to make another move. The outcome of such a game will be indeterminate unless some other information can be provided about methods of play. This is a serious problem for economic theory, which seeks to provide a full explanation of events. It could not occur under perfect competition. Economists are reluctant to introduce arbitrary elements into their models.

The other point to be made about Nash equilibria is that they may not be robust. A player might choose a very different strategy if he or she were uncertain about the choices that the other players will make. For such an equilibrium to be sustainable each player must be certain that all the others will calculate their moves in the same rational fashion. If they are doubtful about that, then they may well seek safety by adopting quite a different approach to play.

One of the attractions of game theory as a research area for economists is the fact that it is possible to conduct experiments. These do not, of course, involve competition between firms in real life situations. Typically they are games played between student volunteers in which the prizes are modest and the rules straightforward. In practice the students do not always follow the strategies which their professors would predict. There is a tendency, for example, for the players to co-operate in situations where game theory would maintain that such behaviour was irrational. It is then an open question whether the experimental subjects are not clever enough to see where their interest lies, or too clever to define their interest in such narrow terms.

One of the most famous of theoretical games is called 'The Prisoners' Dilemma'. Two captives are each told that they will be set free and also rewarded if they give evidence against the other. If just one of the captives refuses to give evidence, then that captive will suffer a severe penalty. If both give evidence then both will be moderately punished; if neither gives evidence then both will be set free. There is no way for them to communicate with each other and they must make their decisions independently.

The first prisoner will logically reason thus: suppose the other prisoner decides to give evidence against me, then I shall be better off giving evidence against him as well, since I shall only be moderately punished; suppose he decides not to give evidence against me, then I can be even better off if I decide to give evidence against him, since I shall not only be set free but rewarded as well. Therefore the first prisoner does give evidence against the second; and the second prisoner, following independently the same line of reasoning, also gives evidence against him. Both are moderately punished; and both are worse off than they would have been had they agreed to support one another. Self-interest in this case does not serve the common good.

In some real-world situations not unlike this game, we do in fact observe mutual support and co-operation between individuals who would gain individually by defecting. It is a challenge to game theory to explain how such behaviour can be reconciled with the assumption of rational self-interested calculation. One important difference to be recognised is between games which are played just once, and games which are repeated. In a repeated game one prisoner might try out a strategy of not giving evidence to see how the other prisoner would react. If the other prisoner did the same then the basis for co-operation might be established. It is not so simple, however, to establish exactly what conditions must hold for such a solution to be an equilibrium position.

Co-operation between the prisoners would not be possible if there were a finite and predetermined number of repetitions. In the last repetition there would be no incentive to co-operate at all, so both players would certainly defect. That being established, both have an incentive to defect in the next-to-last repetition as well – and so on. The prisoners can only create incentives for one another to co-operate if the number of repetitions is infinite, or at least unknown. The answer is for each prisoner to make his responses predictable, in other words to make a commitment in advance. One of the most effective strategies is called 'tit-for-tat'. When either player defects in one repetition of the game, the other player defects in the next. Provided that the rule of behaviour is mutually understood, and the commitment to it is believed, co-operation can then be sustained between people who are motivated by self-interest alone.

It seems that we have uncovered the mathematical foundations of trust. It can be seen developing, not only in experiments with human subjects, to whom an instinctive trust of one another might come naturally, but also in computer simulations of games where the motivation of each 'virtual' player can be specified precisely as self-interested, using a simple mathematical formula. It has been shown that it can pay to make your behaviour predictable, and to use it as a signal to others as to how you will respond to the moves that they might make. You can invent rules which are robust in an environment of uncertainty. For example, the punishment strategy of 'tit-for-tat' may be made a little more forgiving to allow for the possibility that the other player did not really mean to defect.

The importance of games like the Prisoners' Dilemma to economic theory is obvious. In a market exchange, both parties can gain if the exchange is honest; but either may be able to gain more by cheating. In a one-off situation, each will logically expect the other to cheat, so no deal can take place unless cheating can actually be made impossible. The ability to make promises and keep them is a gift of great economic value. Game theory shows how it is possible, although not easy, to have that gift whilst remaining entirely motivated by self-interest. This is not, however, the only possible explanation of its existence.

Rationality and the emotions

The theory of games is a very useful tool for economics, but it can be extended in ways which may conflict with the definition of rationality commonly used in neo-classical theory. There are circumstances in which the pursuit of advantage by rational choice can prove self-defeating. It sometimes pays not to be too rational.

Economic man is not devoid of all feelings. He has preferences, based ultimately, it must be assumed, on consciousness of what makes him happy or miserable. He must be able to feel hunger and thirst, fatigue, excessive heat and cold. To account for the more sophisticated tastes of an affluent society, a wide range of feeling must be attributed to him, like aesthetic pleasure, pride of possession, ambition, fear of shame or insecurity. He seems to care what others think of his lifestyle. Yet he is often assumed to feel neither love nor hatred towards the other members of his species, except perhaps in the sense of including their well-being in his utility function.

In real life, following the method of introspection on which all economic theory ultimately stands, we know that happiness and misery both depend in large part on the quality of relationships. The paradox is that the happiest people are not necessarily those who seek such happiness most single-mindedly. The good opinion of those people we admire is a great source of self-satisfaction. Yet the more consciously we seek such esteem, the less likely we are to earn it. Those who try hard to be loved will go about it in the wrong way. They would do better to concentrate on loving other people. All this familiar folk wisdom, or popular psychology, seems totally alien to the theory of rational choice.

But the theory of games itself identifies another nice paradox. In a strategic interaction, the best outcome may be secured by individuals whose behaviour is not motivated by self-interest.[193] The person with a trusting nature who earns the trust of others would be one example. But it is not only benevolent feelings that can be of economic value. The most frightening adversary in a fight is the one who does not care how much he, or she, gets hurt. Such a person can win many conflicts unopposed. It may actually pay a firm to engage in competition in a ruthlessly vindictive and self-destructive fashion, thus deterring more rational competitors from behaviour that might be seen as provocative. The passions, of both love and hatred, are powerful weapons in economic competition, provided that they are not consciously deployed. If the emotion is contrived and not sincerely felt then any other logical player in the game will simply call your bluff.

At another level of explanation the link between the emotions and competitive success may be established, not by economics but by

193 This paradox is discussed in Ridley, M., op. cit., Chapter 7 and in Frank, R. H., *Passions within Reason*, Norton, 1988.

biology. Emotions which are not self-seeking, may nevertheless favour the survival of individuals and their genetic inheritance. The distinction always needs to be made between the conscious calculation of advantage, which is the normal assumption of economic theory, and natural selection, which is the basis of biological evolution. The fact that both fields of study make use of some of the same mathematical models does not mean that they are offering explanations of exactly the same kind.

The theory of games helps to identify situations in which co-operation can be sustained on the basis of self-interest. It also shows how apparently irrational emotions can serve the interests of the individual, either by encouraging trust or inspiring fear. The point should also be made, however, that emotion can often work against the interests of the individual. Some behaviour really is self-destructive. That needs some explanation too.

Varieties of hatred and of love

The same word 'love' is used to denote a wide range of different feelings and motives for action. The standard representation of individual behaviour in economic theory can be used as the basis for a typology or categorisation. Economists often use the word 'altruism' to describe behaviour which is not self-interested. In distinguishing different types of altruism they have already marked out some of the ground.[194] The starting point is the standard case of the individual whose utility or happiness depends only on his or her own consumption or enjoyment of a set of goods and services. The individual makes choices subject to the constraints imposed by the environment, in particular a budget limit, and maximises his or her own utility according to a ranking order or index.

One kind of love treats other people as if they were goods or services to be consumed, or possessions to be treasured. The

194 Sen, A., 'Rational Fools – A Critique of the Behavioural Foundations of Economic Theory', reprinted in Sen, A., *Choice, Welfare and Measurement*, Blackwell, 1982.

behaviour of one person then enters directly into the utility of another. It would be easy to find a thousand quotations to illustrate the point, but one from the Bible seems particularly appropriate. In the Song of Songs 4, we read: 'How delightful is your love, my sister, my bride! How much more pleasing is your love than wine'. Here it seems that we actually have a hint as to the shape of a utility function in which both love and wine enter as arguments! But negative emotions can fit into the same categorisation. The presence of another person can cause acute pain or misery rather than pleasure. Either way, this is to treat other people as objects, to value them for what they do to one's own state of mind. They are being used, being regarded as means to an end.

A second kind of love would be represented by the inclusion of the well-being of one person within the utility function of another. This might be ascribed to benevolence. I gain happiness from your enjoyment. In fact two sub-categories can be further distinguished within benevolence: in one case I gain happiness from your happiness as you assess it yourself; in the other case I gain happiness from your consuming goods or services which I value myself. I may identify particular 'merit goods', for example like classical music, to which I would want you to have access, even if you do not give them a high priority yourself. This distinction is important to the choice of gifts, and also to the design of social policies. Either of these sub-categories would count as altruism or benevolence. It must be possible, however, for the sign on one person's well-being in the utility function of another to be negative instead of positive. The opposite of benevolence is malevolence, rather than just indifference.

A third kind of love is associated with commitment. For all sorts of reasons, people make promises which they then feel obliged to keep. The relationship may or may not be reciprocal. The appropriate treatment of such commitments in the theory of individual behaviour would be to include them in the set of constraints subject to which all choices are made. Although originally undertaken voluntarily, they subsequently become conditions which have to be met. As we have seen, in the theory of games, such promises – and of course also threats – are essential elements in the strategic interactions, which characterise human relationships. More generally we could include tacit commitments made only to oneself and designed to influence one's subsequent behaviour. The point is that a commitment makes subsequent behaviour independent of subsequent emotions. It requires one, for example, to express love or hatred in action, even if one does not actually feel those emotions strongly at the time.

The fourth category attempts to transcend the utility function and place it within a higher-level preference ordering or index of value. The individual may adopt a system of values in which his or her well-being has to be set alongside the well-being of others. This is not quite the same thing as benevolence because I do not feel that my well-being depends on the well-being of others. Instead I am trying to stand back a little and weigh the merits of my own well-being against the well-being of other people. I may be impartial, giving the same weight to everyone, like a good utilitarian. More commonly I have a preference for myself and for those closest to me.

A recent article in the *Economic Journal*[195] illustrates very well some of the issues discussed in this chapter. It derives a mathematical model of decision making by families. It is intended primarily to provide 'a rigorous theoretical foundation for empirical work on transfers within the household', for example studies of the effects of targeting welfare benefits to women rather than to men. It is described as 'a straightforward extension of the theory of rational choice'.

Two people live together, both benefiting from shared consumption, for example of housing, as well as from goods enjoyed separately. They each make their own decisions as to how they will spend their own income, but each cares about the happiness of the other. One partner may make a transfer of income to the other. The process of decision making is first analysed as a 'non-co-operative game' in which each partner takes the decisions of the other as given. The possibility of a 'co-operative game' with bargaining between the partners is then considered, such that the size of any transfer from one to the other will reflect their relative bargaining power.

Two interesting results emerge. Firstly, the allocation of resources within the household will not in general be efficient. Joint

195 Chen, Z. and Woolley, T., 'A Cournot-Nash Model of Family Decision Making', *Economic Journal*, October 2001.

consumption of, say, housing means that each partner can have a 'free ride' benefiting from expenditure by the other. There is therefore the likelihood of under-expenditure on such goods. Secondly, the expenditure pattern of the household will depend, not only on its total income, but also on its distribution – resources are not generally pooled. Therefore the decision making process of the household cannot in general be modelled as if it were the same as the maximisation of a joint household utility function.

Thus individualism is strictly preserved even in a model which includes mutual 'caring'. It is assumed that each partner cares more about his/her own welfare than about that of the partner. Moreover, a footnote rules out the possibility that one partner might enjoy a 'warm glow' from the act of giving itself. What follows is in effect a social contract. Indeed it is suggested that a written agreement might help to make the bargain enforceable, although it is recognised that it is not easy to draw up such a document, or to give it the force of law. The article is typical of a growing literature that models personal relationships in this way. One is left wondering whether this really is an adequate treatment of love, and exactly what it is that may have been left out. Perhaps the two individuals have to become one – thus denying the assumption of individualism fundamental to neoclassical economic theory.

Section Two: Christian Belief

Altruism and the theory of games

There are four responses to the interesting development of game theory in economics. The British theologian Donald MacKinnon, who was fascinated by politics, lectured and wrote on this topic regularly. It was a characteristic irony of this theologian that he was himself a pacifist, who felt that the integrity of the Christian faith forbade any compromise. He would however have replied that compromise was one thing, and a good games player was another.

The first area to be considered is whether God can be said to be an altruist in Christian theology. This topic has recently been discussed in Colin Grant's book on altruism, and he refers to the philosophical questions raised by God's own self-love. Can this be said to be altruistic? Secondly we move to the attitude which the Bible and Christianity has taken to game playing, especially in the area of power politics, where the proper strategy is of the essence. Thirdly, we look at the parables of Jesus, which refer to such characters as the unjust steward, and others that fail to count the cost of their activities, especially if there is an element of risk involved. Such parables are of course set against the many stories in the Old Testament where David plays games with Saul, Jacob outwits Esau, and where there is an acceptance of the need to outwit the other adversary. Finally we move on to the topic of love, as it is described in the New Testament.

Divine altruism

In his study *Altruism and Christian Ethics*,[196] Colin Grant, who is a Canadian philosopher of religion, asks how far it is possible to represent the Christian God as altruistic. He puts the question like this because he is well aware that the Aristotelian God, or first mover, has influenced much of Christian theology in ways that make God self-sufficient, and therefore disinterested in the fate of the universe which he has created. While this may or may not be game playing, it is certainly a rationality devoid of affection for anything but its own existence, or being. However, this is not the account which contemporary theology gives of the Trinity. M. Douglas Meeks speaks for many theologians, when he writes about traditional theism.[197]

196 Grant, C., *Altruism and Christian Ethics*, CUP, 2001.
197 Meeks, M. D., op. cit.

> God is a perfect individual meditating for ever on his own perfections. This God is a model for the individual who, according to the logic of the market household, lives privately and narcissistically.

In theologians such as Barth the sovereignty of God consists in his ultimate freedom, and not in his self-sufficiency. What preserves the divine sovereignty is the free will of God, and in this freedom God can choose how he will be. It is possible that God can play games, and there are novelists like Thomas Hardy, who have seen God as the 'President of the Immortals' who has a game with Tess in the novel *Tess of the D'Urbervilles*. But the God whom Barth describes is one who chooses to share his life through creation and redemption. How far does this mean that God is altruistic? If the choice of sharing reflects the very nature and character of God, in the depth of God's being, then God has a need to act in this way. Game playing is fundamentally impossible for God, even if he chooses differently. These are deep waters for theology which have produced some of the major topics in recent years. Grant quotes the English Baptist theologian Paul Fiddes, who has written much on this. 'Understanding God's will as desire indicates that there can be no "otherwise" in the love of God for mankind. Because he thirsts and longs for fellowship with his creatures, it makes no sense to say that he need not do so.'[198]

However the possibility of game playing is not removed because of the nature of Christian theology. Over against this is the harsh necessity of existence in what has often been called a 'fallen world', where evil and political expediency predominate. One answer is of course to turn one's back on all this, and to refuse any involvement in politics or economic struggle, if one is a Christian. However this has not been the strategy adopted by every Christian. At the time of Jesus Herod and the religious leaders, who were the high priests, combined both religious and political power. The trial of Jesus shows this all too clearly. We turn to a theologian who was fascinated by the ambiguity of the meeting place of power politics and Christian faith. In the writings of the British theologian Donald MacKinnon this tension is discussed with great skill.

198 Fiddes, P., *The Creative Suffering of God*, OUP, 1989.

MacKinnon lectured on this issue many times. In one lecture he examined the strange role played by the master politician, statesman and religious leader Cardinal Richelieu in the French civil and international wars of the sixteenth century. While this is far removed from the biblical narrative, nevertheless MacKinnon realised that in Richelieu the theologian encountered both a devout Bishop of the church, and a supreme politician, who played the game of political advantage very well. He accepted the autonomy of the state's authority, although this underestimates the subtlety with which he defended his position. MacKinnon writes:[199]

> Yet the statesman must cultivate at personal cost, his own peculiar style of impersonality. For he is a man who must act, whose actions are prescribed by his purposes. Yet those purposes in turn are themselves prescribed in part by the situation with which he has to deal [...] we see in him a man who unquestionably raises for us by his actions a whole number of central questions in respect of the relation of religious faith and power politics.

One could well say that in Richelieu MacKinnon is reflecting on the roles of Herod, the High Priests and Pilate in the New Testament Gospels. He argues that:

> the impersonality of the true statesman makes his ruthlessness less frightening; further the character of his objectivity may be so defined as to leave room for the admission of the mysterious authority of the 'kingdom not from hence'.[200]

If, on the other hand, the enterprise is seen as a crusade, then the possibility of criticism is weakened enormously.

MacKinnon was very aware that the events which made up the life of Jesus belonged to the same time order as the conspiracy of Seianus against Tiberius Caesar. 'Between prophet-prelate and

199 MacKinnon, D. M., *Themes in Theology*, T and T Clark, 1987. The lecture 'Power-politics and Religious Faith' was first given at the London School of Economics in 1979, and then published in *British Journal of International Studies*, April 1980.

200 ibid.

statesman there is a great gulf fixed', but the only way to contrast the two is to look at the game playing actions in the light of eschatology, or the end of history. MacKinnon recognises that it is the tragedy of human existence that such questions will continue to be raised.

In particular MacKinnon argued that the theory of power politics meant that Jesus must be seen as a moral failure, as much as the saviour of the world. Jesus 'abdicated any responsibility that his influence might have conferred on him to arrest the movement of his people towards the final catastrophe of AD 70'. He asks how far it is possible to use the language of tragedy of the Gospels. This is because alongside the redemption of the world there is also the abandonment of his followers to the terrible retribution of the Roman army, when they put down the revolt of the Jewish people in AD 70, and destroyed the Temple.[201]

MacKinnon was deeply aware that Jesus rejected the outburst of popular devotion which would have made him a king. In an interesting comment he pointed out that not only did Jesus reject it, he also rejected it 'without seeming even to consider attempting to manage it'.[202] This entails an acceptance of the inescapable conflict of the claims of love and truth, and therefore Jesus becomes (as argued above) a morally ambiguous figure. Yet this is so because he will not play games, for to do so would be to reject the heart of his mission. Jesus sought to make himself utterly vulnerable. However the strange paradox is that this is the same person, who told parables about servants who were quite unscrupulous. The next section will examine how much such illustrations of game playing figure in the parables of Jesus.

201 MacKinnon, D. M., *The Stripping of the Altars*, Collins, 1969. The article 'Theology and Tragedy' was first published in 1967 in *Religious Studies*.

202 Lampe, G. W. H. and MacKinnon, D. M., *The Resurrection*, Mowbray, 1966.

In the parables Jesus speaks of those who take on a great task but are outwitted in its completion:

> For which of you, desiring to build a tower, does not first sit down and count the cost, whether he has enough to complete it? Otherwise, when he has laid a foundation, and is not able to finish, all who see it begin to mock him, saying 'This man began to build, and was not able to finish'. Or what king, going to encounter another king in war, will not sit down first and take counsel whether he is able with ten thousand to meet him who comes against him with twenty thousand? And if not, while the other is yet a great way off, he sends an embassy and asks terms of peace. So, therefore, whoever of you does not renounce all that he has cannot be my disciple. (Luke 14:28–33)

The harshness of Jesus' words, taken from military strategy, are reinforced by some of his parables. In Luke 18 there is a parable of a judge who feared neither God nor man: in sum, a story of a corrupt judge. Then in the next chapter there is another parable of a hard businessman, who will reap where he did not sow. Jesus is demanding complete commitment, and the necessity of reflection before action. Weighing the costs is certainly part of religious faith. Equally the small group of disciples must be prepared to commit everything in faith before God. The only way of describing how great a commitment this involves is to illustrate it by the pleas of a widow, who is powerless in a patriarchal society. She achieves her end by annoying the corrupt judge into action on her behalf. The point of the story is not to emulate the corruptness of the judge, but to show that the almost foolhardy strategy of the widow is what is expected of the disciples. In Chapter 19, the parable illustrates that as the suffering of Jesus draws near, there can be no safe position. The only road to success is to take the risks of the first two servants. Those who do nothing will fail. Again the illustration is shocking. The safe option fails in the parable because the nobleman is cruel and harsh. His servants who take no risks on his behalf are punished ruthlessly. In a discussion of these parables, Roger White says that there:[203]

203 White, R., 'MacKinnon and the Parables', in Surin, K. (ed.), *Christ, Ethics and Tragedy: Essays in Honour of Donald MacKinnon*, CUP, 1989.

> Is a kind of grim humour at work in many of the parables. [...] Parables such as the 'Unjust judge' are meant to disturb our complacency. We do not understand these parables if we ignore the extent to which their analogies contain a grim truth about the nature of life in this world in its relation to God. We *are* [italics original] in a world where justice and virtue are not naturally triumphant, where the wicked flourish, and the saints' cause founders. For the man in need turning to God for deliverance from his sufferings, praying that the cause of justice and peace should prosper, hungering and thirsting after righteousness, it is very much as if he is confronted in his prayers by an unusually corrupt magistrate who has no particular concern to see that justice prevails. In such parables, Jesus continually presses beyond the conventionally pious, inviting us to explore the full reality of life before God without sheltering behind platitude: inviting us actually to *look* [italics original] at it.

Something of the Christian attitude to game playing now becomes clear. The realism of the game player is certainly to be admired. Players in the Christian faith, if such a term may be allowed, are certainly expected by Jesus to have thought out their strategy if there is uncertainty. In the case of the impending trial of Jesus, the uncertainty is very high. Equally Jesus anticipates that there will be little co-operation in human life, and that self-interest will be paramount. All this is to be expected. But calculation is ruled out, in terms of self-interest for the Christian.

This is especially so in the case of the famous parable of the prodigal son, in Luke 15. The father receives back his son. The son rehearses what excuses he can come up with, but the father behaves as if the son's wrongdoing does not enter into the calculation. Again the parable stresses the acceptance of God, and the need for action. The altruism of the father is completely realistic, and without any calculation as to what game may be played. This is all the more remarkable because Jesus would have known how many of the narratives of the Jewish Scriptures are full of attempts (game playing, in fact) by the characters to outwit one another, and gain a blessing, or to obtain an advantage. All these stories are set aside, and yet the stark realism of human relationships remains paramount in the teaching of Jesus. It is in this world that the followers of Jesus must practise altruism.

The modern concept of benevolence is far from the biblical world. In the Old Testament, even altruism is placed within the confines of the tribal society which was ancient Israel. As we have discussed in previous chapters, there is no recognition of the individual who forms relationships outside of the covenant which God makes with his people. There is of course a Hebrew term for personal love *('ahebh)* which can be extended to include the love of food or even sometimes find itself employed as a curse.

What is of relevance to the question of game theory is the biblical account of love. This dominates the biblical usage, where there is an obligation from one to another. Clearly this concept of obligation, as in the love between friends such as David and Jonathan, (1 Samuel 20:17), or the love between husband and wife, draws on the fidelity which is at the heart of the covenant between God and his people. Israel is called to 'love the Lord' in Deuteronomy 6:5 and this leads on to the keeping of commandments, as we have seen above.

The love of neighbour in Leviticus 19:18 is taken up again by Jesus, in the Jewish tradition of rabbinic teaching, and expressed in the conversation with the scribe in Mark 12:28. Jesus and the scribe both take the term 'love' as having the same meaning in Deuteronomy and Leviticus. Jesus teaches the importance of a complete self-giving, which can be characterised only by the term 'love', as the basis for his disciples' action.

Love in the New Testament epistles acts again as the inner spring and core of fidelity. It binds together individuals so that Ephesians can speak of the love which enables each person to forbear one another, and maintains the unity of the Spirit in the bond of peace. This is strong language, and here as in Colossians 3:14 *shalom*, which is weakly translated wholeness or peace, is maintained by love. John sees the church as the new Israel, bound together in love, which unites all its members. Therefore, in contrast with the individualist understanding even of altruistic behaviour in economic theory, the biblical view emphasises the uniting power of love.

Once again we notice the lack of any individual perspective in the biblical account. Paul sees love as the greatest of the gifts of the

Spirit – and why? The answer of course is straightforward. Love builds up the community in the Spirit, as in 1 Corinthians 13. The ethical implication however is derived much more from the imitation of the life and death of Christ, where God is shown as forgiving the repentant sinner, and seeking the lost. Christians are therefore to forgive as they have been forgiven in Christ, and to respond to cases of need. However the love of enemies which is such a feature of the teaching of Jesus becomes narrowed into a concern with 'the brethren' in the letters of John.

Section Three: Summary and Discussion

The view of human behaviour adopted by economic theory works best when relationships are conducted anonymously, impersonally and at arm's length. It does not work so well when emotions are involved and relationships of competition or of co-operation are conducted face to face. Nevertheless some interesting results do emerge from analysis of 'games' in which the 'players' seek their own advantage by anticipating how others will respond to the 'moves' that they make.

We all know, of course, that human relationships are not adequately described by the mathematical theory of games. Emotions are involved as well as rational calculation. This is true of economic affairs, just as it is of the rest of life. Paradoxically, it is sometimes the case that one can serve one's own interest best by not seeking it too consistently. It may be that the emotions which we feel and display in our relationships have survival value, or did so at an earlier stage of the evolution of our species – but that is not properly the concern of economic theory.

It would be possible to extend the mathematical treatment of strategies to take account of objectives which are not purely selfish, which are motivated for example by love or by hatred. This would require a very precise formulation – for example, one should distinguish between hatred which seeks the ill fortune of another from rivalry which cares only about relative scores. There is also a difference between the love which simply wants another to be happy, and the love which wants that person to enjoy particular pleasures – and so on.

But, however the aims of the game are specified, the procedures of game theory are essentially manipulative. They treat other people as instruments, or as objectives, even if the attitude towards them is entirely benevolent. Other people are like us in that they think the same way as we do, but that is as far as the empathy goes. Other people are never treated as partners with whom we can share a common experience, or form a common mind. That is why the theory of games, as used by economists, cannot give an adequate account of love.

Jesus told his followers to be 'as wise as serpents', although also 'as harmless as doves'. He told stories in which it paid off to be smart. He said that 'the children of this world are wiser in their generation than the children of light'. Yet, he himself did not attempt to 'outsmart' his human enemies. He let himself be betrayed, condemned and executed.

The Bible tells of the developing relationship between God and his people. It knows just how difficult it can be for trust and faithfulness to be maintained. God is offering a relationship of love, like that of a parent for a child. His people, like spoilt children, respond by trying to manipulate God's feeling for them, making purely ritual sacrifices, but not loving him in return. Hence it is a story of repeated breakdown, repeated reconciliations, followed by yet further betrayals of trust. From a purely rational point of view God ought to adopt a different strategy, either forcing his people into submission or else abandoning them to their fate. But it seems that God's response is not based on calculation. He does not 'play games' at all, because that would be against his nature, which is to love without reserve.

Economic theory cannot comprehend love because of its prior commitment to rational calculation, but also because of its prior commitment to individualism. Love, in Christian belief, and in common human experience, involves a sense of unity that goes beyond mere co-operation, and even beyond mutual trust and good-will. It involves some surrender of autonomy.

In an earlier chapter we said that the people of God, according to the Bible, were united as one body. That unity is maintained by mutual love and by their common identification with the community as a whole. Selfishness, or even just self-awareness, threatens that unity. Pride is therefore the greatest of sins, and love is the fulfilment of the law.

The nearest that we can get to this understanding, whilst maintaining methodological individualism, is to demonstrate the value of trust and mutual commitment. The theory of games can show, rigorously and mathematically, the conditions under which trust can be initiated and maintained. These conditions turn out to be stringent, with the implication that the common advantage of co-operation will often be lost. Christians preaching the benefits of peace and concord will often appear unrealistic.

This is where Christian belief and ethics necessarily come together. Trust may indeed be impossible, and conflict inevitable, in a world of autonomous individuals. Trust, and indeed love, may be possible however between human beings if they each individually place their trust in a loving God.

Chapter Ten

History and the Concept of Equilibrium

Introduction

We have now covered much of the ground of an elementary introduction to economic theory, plus some less elementary assessment of it. In doing so we have engaged with some of the principal assumptions of a modern, liberal, humanist anthropology. In this chapter we take a theme which would not necessarily be given separate treatment in an economics textbook, but which is of some interest to a dialogue with theology. We shall examine notions of time and history in economics and in Christian belief. As has already been indicated in the first chapter, about 'the real world', narrative plays an essential part in the biblical revelation. The same might be said of Marxist economics, but surely not of economic theory in the neo-classical tradition.

The events of human history occur in sequences: the past leads into the present, and the present looks on to the future. Life is not static, but dynamic. The passage of time brings with it changes that may not be reversible. Every branch of knowledge has to give some account of developments over time. This is certainly true both of economic theory and of Christian belief, although they address the issues involved in very different ways. We begin with some very general propositions derived from pure mathematics.

Mathematical statements are of such generality that they can unite fields of enquiry and academic disciplines which at first sight may seem to have little in common. They provide a language for the exchange of ideas across the whole range of human knowledge and speculation. They are neutral in all disputes between ideologies and schools of thought. They are independent of culture, in substance if not in the form of their expression. Some of the same mathematical statements are fundamental to such apparently unrelated subjects as economic theory and Christian belief.

The behaviour of all kinds of dynamic systems can be described by differential or difference equations. These statements relate changes in one or more variables over time to the state of those variables at a point in time. For example the acceleration of a physical body through space depends on its distance from the earth. By solving the appropriate differential equations the motion of the body can be predicted. The same general kind of mathematics can be used to describe demography, business cycles, traffic flow and the expansion of the universe.[204]

One thing which dynamic systems have in common is the need for end-point conditions, or constants of integration. The laws of motion of the planets describe their movements, but they do not, on their own, tell us where a planet will be found at a particular point in time. For that we require an additional bit of information, for example where it was last week or for that matter at a definite date thousands of years ago. Often this extra piece of information about a dynamic system concerns either the beginning or the end of a trajectory. We may know the position from which a shot was fired, or we may know the point at which it was aimed. The laws of physics will tell us how it gets from the one to the other.

Theology does not make use of formal mathematics in this way at all. But it necessarily adopts ideas and models in which similar propositions in logic or in mathematics are implicit. Within the created universe the passage of time necessarily runs in one direction only, even if God himself lives in a timeless eternity. Whilst it may be logically possible to conceive of the universe as infinite in time as well as in space, the Bible in fact attaches great significance both to the beginning of time and to the end. It has a great deal to say about end-points, both initial and terminal.

Nevertheless the disciplines of economics and theology do not stand in the same relationship to history. As we shall see, history is not intrinsic to economic theory, at least in its orthodox, neo-classical

204 Allen, R. G. D., *Mathematical Analysis for Economists*, Macmillan, 1938 and *Mathematical Economics*, Macmillan, 1956.

mould. Arguably, history is of the essence of Christian belief, since its definitive statements take narrative form.

Section One of this chapter begins with the mathematics, and especially the significance of initial and terminal conditions in economic theory. This is followed by a discussion of the concept of equilibrium, as a point of rest to which an economic system will, under certain assumptions, always return. Section Two takes up the theme of time in relation to theology. It starts quite a long way removed from the issues discussed by economists, especially with the issue of 'truth' in relation to a historical narrative like those in the Bible. The two sides to the dialogue come together again as we relate theology to the dynamic processes of cosmology.

Section One: Economic Theory

Looking forward and looking back

We begin with an illustration of how standard economic theory deals, in a formal way, with a dynamic relationship, tracing out optimal paths through time. The model of savings and investment which was originated by Frank Ramsey in the 1920s has proved to be one of the most fertile uses of formal mathematics in the development of economic theory.[205] It provides an excellent example of the derivation of dynamic relationships between economic variables from standard assumptions about rational choice. In its simplest form the problem is presented as that of a planning agency choosing the path for total savings and investment in a national economy with full knowledge of the economic environment, past, present and future.

The objective is to maximise the total well being, or utility, to be derived from consumption in the present and all periods into the

205 See Blanchard, O. J. and Fischer, S., *Lectures on Macroeconomics*, MIT Press, 1989. The original article is Ramsey, F. P., 'A Mathematical Theory of Saving', *Economic Journal*, December 1928.

indefinite future. Utility for all individuals in all time periods is simply added together. The utility of consumption is subject to diminishing returns, so that more utility is derived from an increment to consumption in periods of dearth than in periods of plenty. All other things being equal the planners would therefore keep the level of consumption constant over time. It is also assumed, however, that consumption now is preferred to consumption in the future if all else is the same. One has, of course, to be an unreconstructed utilitarian to take all this literally, but it is instructive nevertheless.

At all points in time the total of consumption and investment must be equal to national income. That is just a matter of accounting. The level of the capital stock grows by the addition of investment in each time period. The level of national income and output depends on the size of the capital stock. Increments of capital are subject to diminishing returns; in other words the larger the capital stock already is, the smaller the addition to output you can get from a given rate of investment. The problem is to find the optimal time path of consumption in the present and all future time periods.

The mathematical solution takes the form of differential equations defining the rate of change of consumption and of the capital stock. Planned consumption may either rise or fall gradually over time depending on such factors as technical progress, population growth and the impatience of consumers. The accounting identity between income, investment and consumption means that the options open in the future depend on the use of resources today, so the whole of the optimum time path must be computed simultaneously. To complete the solution we need two end-point conditions since two time paths have to be computed, one for consumption and one for the capital stock.

One of these conditions is provided by the initial value of the capital stock, which is inherited from the period before the plan begins. That is not a matter of choice, but something which must be taken as given. In that sense the solution looks back to the origin. The level of consumption, however, is a matter of choice even in the initial period. It is part of the plan. To understand how that choice is made we need to look forward to the relationship between income and saving which will hold good in the long term.

As capital accumulates its return diminishes. There must be a point (described in Chapters 5 and 7 above) at which the return on capital is just enough to match the cost of delaying consumption. At that point the stock of capital is in equilibrium. There is no incentive to raise or reduce it. Any sensible plan must lead towards that equilibrium path. It would not be sensible, however, to go straight there if one starts a long way away from it. To do that would involve a transition period in which consumption was either much too high or else much too low; the decreasing marginal utility of consumption suggests, on the contrary, that consumption should be as constant over time as is possible. The optimum plan reconciles these conflicting considerations as best it can.

The equilibrium relationship of capital to output provides the second end-point condition. We know that the optimum time path must converge towards the equilibrium path. In this case, that information is enough to tie down the initial level of consumption. Once that is known the rest is just arithmetic. The levels of consumption and capital can be calculated for successive time periods using the differential equations derived from the optimality conditions. Since we are assuming a world of perfect foresight, the optimal plan will be executed and define the path of the economy in real time.

The plan looks both forward and back. As time goes on the importance of looking back diminishes. The optimal capital stock in the limit of time depends only on the production function and the function that relates utility to consumption. The initial capital stock becomes less and less relevant. This is typical of dynamic adjustment models: in the end all bygones are bygones. The final outcome is not dependent on the path by which it was reached. In that sense there is no history in equilibrium.

Most of the dynamic relationships used to describe economic behaviour are at least partly forward looking. They are defined by terminal conditions, not just by initial conditions. In this they differ fundamentally from the dynamic laws of the physical sciences. Even when a physical system is tending towards a position of rest or equilibrium its motion is determined by the past, not by the expected future. There is no knowledge in the system of where its equilibrium will be. The mathematics of purposeful action is not the same as the mathematics of determinism. This important distinction can be made even in the context of perfect certainty.

Economics and history

In a standard neo-classical general equilibrium model, history takes place 'off-stage'. The economic system reacts to change; it does not initiate it. Markets can absorb the shocks of wars, of revolutions, of changes in technology and social customs. Equilibrium is the state to which the system would tend if it were not subject to such disturbance. If that equilibrium is stable and unique, then it will always be restored irrespective of past history. The theory therefore defines precisely under what conditions equilibrium will have those characteristics.

It needs to be emphasised that the approach to equilibrium in this sense can be very slow indeed. In the long run the size and composition of the capital stock adjusts to the available technologies, to the willingness of the population to save, to the level of participation in the labour force, and so on. But capital may be very durable: machines are now in use which were made say fifty years ago; the housing stock now in use may be much older still. Similarly it takes a generation to work through the effects of changes in education and vocational training. To explain where we are now, even in purely neo-classical economics, requires information as to where we are coming from. Yet all this would be transitory in the absence of further shocks, since the effects of initial conditions ultimately wear away and the effects of terminal conditions predominate. History is only important because new shocks are hitting the system all the time.

The case of multiple equilibria is also very important. A set of non-linear mathematical equations will often have more than one solution. Similarly, there may be more than one set of relative prices which will clear all the markets. If a shock to the system moves the economy from the neighbourhood of one such set to another, then the effects of that shock may be permanent – or at least persist until another shock comes which reverses the process.

Economists, recently, have borrowed from engineering the concept called 'hysteresis'.[206] A spring, for example, will normally be restored to its shape after being subjected to stretching. But if the force is too strong then the stretching will be permanent. In economics, the normal fluctuations of the business cycle will not change the institutions of the labour market, or the motivation of the work force. A long and deep depression, however, could result in de-skilling, demoralisation or emigration. Such changes may prove irreversible. Again we have to recognise that history affects the present. Whether the changes are described as exogenous or endogenous is perhaps little more than a question of convenient terminology. No one seriously doubts that they can happen.

Typically the presentation of neo-classical equilibrium remains timeless. Economic history is then an important field of study in its own right, in which historical and analytical approaches necessarily combine. One can then consider, for example, what were the economic causes of political events, of wars, revolutions and so on. Thus events which are exogenous in the standard model can become endogenous when a wider range of social relationships are being considered. But the kind of explanation which might be given of political events, say the rise of Hitler to power in Germany as a result of the Great Depression, is never really integrated into the consistent model of optimisation under constraints which is the hall-mark of neo-classicism in economic theory.

Recently, a highly quantitative approach to economic history, called cliometrics, has been developed, applying present-day economic theory and statistical methods to such questions as the origins of the industrial revolution, or 'how the West was won'.[207] Some economists have seen regular patterns in economic history, for example the Kondratieff cycle, which they explain using mathematical models of the dynamic interactions between economic variables. But

206 The term is used, for example, in the explanation of the rise in unemployment, see Layard, R., Nickell, S. and Jackman, R., *Unemployment, Macroeconomic Performance and the Labour Market*, OUP, 1991.

207 Crafts, N. F. R., 'Economics and History', in Greenaway, D. et al, op. cit.

this is to use historical data as evidence in an economic investigation. It does not make history itself an economic phenomenon.

Development economics on the other hand has taken a historical process as its subject matter. It is not just about economic growth, the expansion of all sectors of an economy; it also seeks to explain how the structure of an economy changes as it moves from an agricultural base, through greater reliance on manufacturing, towards an emphasis on services and advanced technology. How does trade with more advanced economies help or hinder each stage of development? How can domestic savings be generated to provide the capital needed in an advanced economy? Is free trade the most favourable environment at every point? These are all proper subjects for debate within the world-view of neo-classical economics.

If we are looking for an economic interpretation of history itself, however, we must turn to a quite different kind of economics, the Marxist school still being the leading contender. This tradition of economics has a quite different agenda from that of the present-day neo-classical economists. The followers of Marx do see a grand design in history; the unfolding of a causal sequence which defines the destiny of human society. Economic relationships explain social change, not vice versa. There are deep economic currents which propel political and cultural events. Ideas and ideologies just float on the surface.

There are also opponents of Marx who interpret more recent events of history. Just as the rise of Communism in Russia was hailed by some as the inevitable outcome of historical determinism, so its recent fall is seen as the inevitable consequence of a different destiny. Fukuyama has written about 'The End of History'.[208] This means that the contest between economic systems has now reached its necessary conclusion. The outcome was inevitable, and it is now irreversible, because the free-market system has now demonstrated its inherent superiority. This may or may not be correct as a historical explanation and prediction; it is clearly not a necessary deduction from neo-classical economic theory. Economists of that school have often been profoundly pessimistic, believing that the self-interest of powerful

208 Fukuyama, F., op. cit.

individuals and groups will always threaten the market system which they believe serves best the interests of the majority.

Section Two: Christian Belief

Theology and time

The biblical understanding of history is very different from the economist's view of time and change. Modern economics has developed from the eighteenth-century understanding of the laws of the market, analogous to the unchanging laws of physics. There was an assumption that rational thought was deductive, and therefore unvarying in its findings. The same assumptions governed theology, so that there could be reference in hymnody to 'laws that never shall be broken' or rejoicing in 'reason's ear'. Here Newtonian mathematics and theological deism produced an elegant theory which however replaced the dynamic of Christian theology in history and creation with a series of postulates which were invariant and closed to change. Neo-classical economics interpreted the 'laws of the market' in the same manner, except of course there was an inductive element as well. This could take account of change as societies developed, even if the underlying premises were fixed.

The two challenges for theology are the relationship to history and the ability of theology to be dynamic in its conceptual structure. To give an example, 'Jesus is Lord' may appear to be a dynamic slogan for some Christians, but it remains a concept that often takes no account of ways in which its inner thought can develop, nor does it show much awareness of cultural diversity in its expression. In that sense it is a static concept which remains incapable of original development, although this need not be the case. The next two sections explore whether dynamism and history can become an integral part of theology, and how this might be related to economic theory.

History and hermeneutics

Hermeneutics is the study of the meaning of texts, and their interpretation across centuries of tradition. The two great theologians of the early twentieth century, Karl Barth and Rudolf Bultmann, felt that the question of hermeneutics was inherent in the attitude of Christianity to history. That is to say, if a claim was made that Jesus was crucified but rose from the dead, then this is a historical claim but also one about the meaning of this person for belief in God, since life after death implies certain things for belief in God and the power of God. Their theology in the 1920s was written at the same time as Frank Ramsey's theories on economic savings. It fundamentally changed the nature of their discipline for the rest of the century.[209]

The previous century took history very seriously as a theological issue. After the eighteenth rationalism mentioned earlier, with its appeal to the laws of nature, nineteenth century theology looked for historical accuracy on the person of Jesus. The consciousness of this person in the culture of his day became the most important issue, and careful empirical data were amassed to prove that the picture drawn was accurate. The personality of Jesus was made up of his beliefs, teaching, conduct, the past tradition of Judaism and the reaction of his disciples. Personality was the central feature of the historian's quest, since it was felt that personality could shape experience.

In turn personal experience was greater than any historical events (including death) and so the power of personal religious experience was such that its force could shape individuals, societies and even nations. The implicit belief was that the ideals and values of religious movements and beliefs could shape the empirical reality of economic factors, such as prices, markets, and technological innovation. This was not an argument for an ethical conduct of economic life, but rather a claim that the most important factor in history was the power of intellectual belief. The argument was classically set out decades later in the mid twentieth century by the idealist philosopher and historian, R. G. Collingwood in *The Idea of History*.

209 For an introduction to these debates, see Ford, D. F. (ed.), *The Modern Theologians* (second edition), Blackwell, 1999.

The use of personality by theologians in the nineteenth century was part of this belief in the transcendent power of values and ideas, notably by the group of English, Anglican theologians in the period 1890–1914 called the Lux Mundi school, from a collection of essays entitled *Lux Mundi* published in 1891 in Oxford. (The phrase *Lux Mundi* means 'light of the world' in Latin.) Personality, or as it was sometimes called character, as in the phrase 'the character of Christ', was the benchmark used to judge the ensuing centuries of tradition. The strong assumption made was not only that Christianity was a historical religion because Jesus was a historical reality, but also that the original personality of this person was the purest expression of this faith.

Anglican theologians also wished to defend tradition as the exposition and expression of this character, while liberal, German (and Lutheran) theologians tended to see the ensuing centuries as a falling away of the purity of the message, personality and truth of Jesus. The debate about the relevance of the empirical accuracy of the historical picture of Jesus was the dominant debate in the mid nineteenth century. By the end of the century the debate had shifted to those who saw the personality of Jesus as the 'essence of Christianity', against those who resisted this apparent denigration of the tradition. The issue of the historical reality of the person of Jesus was now a theological issue, but not in terms of the accuracy of the data. Instead there was a clear appeal to the moral power of personality, as a force greater than economic, or any other, social conditions.

It was however the intervention of Barth and Bultmann, in the German dialectical theology school of the 1920s which changed the debate forever. Even in the 1890s the focus on the personality of Jesus was beginning to be challenged by Weiss, and later by Schweitzer. They felt that the accurate historical picture of Jesus was not that of an idealist exemplar of peace and reconciliation, but rather that of a person who believed in the imminent end of history, time and the world as we knew it. This expectation was both nearer to the views of first century Judaism, which held strong beliefs about heavenly battles (apocalyptic) and the end of history (eschatology), and to other Near Eastern societies.

This view also relegated the debate between those who defended the value of tradition against those who saw in the person of Jesus the essence of Christianity to the margins. If Jesus did not expect there to be any further history beyond the present 'end-times' then tradition and the moral power of personality over the course of future history were both redundant. If history had no reality to Jesus then its existence posed a problem. The response of Weiss and Schweitzer was to see this portrait of a prophetic figure in first century Judaism as historically accurate, but needing to be entirely reinterpreted for our own day. They however disagreed on how this was to be done. The hermeneutical question, on the meaning of the ancient texts of Christianity, was unresolved by 1914, while other theologians such as the Lux Mundi School and the German liberals resisted the portrait drawn by Schweitzer.[210]

Barth believed that dialectical theology held the key to resolving this impasse. The biblical texts were not primarily accounts of history, but contained both God's yes and no to any situation. The prophetic figure passes the judgement of God on the history of first century Judaism, and of all subsequent time. However it also affirms human beings as the gracious partners of God chosen by him before all time to be the beneficiaries of his covenant in history and creation. That choice can only be responded to by human beings in repentance and trust. God's choice is made by him in his mercy and sovereign power. Therefore scripture is primarily about the saving message that God has acted decisively in the person of Jesus Christ in history. This is the 'kerygma' or message with saving power.

The theology of Karl Barth sees that the crucial issue is how this deposit of faith is to grow and increase in the subsequent time that has passed since the first announcement of the message in the first century in Palestine. However the message is not to be seen as a deposit that grows with interest compounded, like the stock of capital in economic theory. Instead the message is repeated endlessly as 'the Word' which comes to each individual in their own history and challenges them to accept the good news of the Gospel. This is the action of God in

210 Sykes, S. W., *The Identity of Christianity*, SPCK, 1984. Part Two is a good guide to the debate in the nineteenth and early twentieth century.

electing human beings to be his partners which he ratified irrevocably in the actions of Jesus of Nazareth. The person of Jesus in this action is as the Incarnate Word of God in history.

All theology responds within the parameters of this Word, and is a response to this Word. There can be a dialogue with any secular discipline, for no claims are made about the superiority of religion to any other factor in history. Indeed Barth is sceptical of religion, seeing it as the attempt of human beings to justify their own culture before the dialectical judgement of God. Instead all that matters is that theology has its own integrity, since the Word is to be distinguished from all human words, even the words of the biblical text. The biblical text witnesses to the Word, but is not itself that Word. The Word has integrity all of its own that resists the attempts of any discipline, such as economics, as to how it shall be responded to. However within this integrity theology can and should enter into dialogue with other disciplines, such as economics. The autonomy of the subject matter of theology is not compromised by dialogue, given the integrity of its own way of working.[211]

'Post-critical' interpretations of biblical narrative

The question is whether the accounts of the acts of God found in scripture are therefore to be seen as historical on this understanding of theology. The traditional acts of God included creation, the fall, the history of the people of Israel, and the Incarnation of Christ. This then led into the further history of the life, death and resurrection of Christ, followed again by the Ascension, the gift of the Spirit at Pentecost and the mission to the world by the Church. Eventually this would end with the end of history, the Last Judgement and the vision of Christ ruling all of time and space which is set out in the final book in scripture, the Revelation of St John. Such a historical account was

211 Barth, K., *Church Dogmatics*, T & T Clark, Edinburgh, 1936-69. For a guide to his thought, see Berkouwer, G. C., *The Triumph of Grace in the Theology of Karl Barth*, Eerdmans, 1956 and Sykes, S. W. (ed.), *Karl Barth: Studies of His Theological Method*, OUP, 1979.

often seen as a divine plan, in which God foresees the apostasy of his people and gives his Son as the redemption of the world. The costs to God are accepted by him, perhaps in an analogy to the rational calculations loved by economists.

Barth responds to this traditional account of Christian history by pointing out how this model was implicitly abandoned in the nineteenth century in its focus on the historical life of Jesus. Barth denies that this nineteenth century apologetic for Christianity is valid, since historical data, even if reliable, can never replace or substantiate the claims of the Word of God. By attempting to show that Jesus was real in a historical sense, even if it could achieve a consensus amongst its practitioners, theology abandons its task of responding to the judgement and acceptance that is at the heart of (dialectical) theology.

Should the 'plan' of earlier Christian eras be put back in its place therefore? Barth accepts that the Bible can be read this way but says that such a reading normally sees the text of scripture as infallible, or factually correct. It is a literal, or pre-critical reading of scripture. What many non-Christian thinkers have replaced this reading with is a version of scripture as 'critical' and mythological. This denies that there is any correspondence, or fit, between the acts of God and the events of human history – assuming that God is held to exist at all. The discrepancies in the Gospel narratives for this approach rule out historical accuracy. Narrative reportage in scripture cannot be equated with literal facticity. Instead scripture is seen as symbolic, metaphorical and in need of reinterpretation for its poetic meaning today. Such relevance as it had was universal in an emotive and non-cognitive sense.

Barth, and a later American theologian called Hans Frei, attempted a 'post-critical' reading of the biblical narratives which is now dominant in much of Western orthodox, systematic theology today. The results of the nineteenth century historical-critical school are neither accepted nor rejected, but seen as external to the theological task. The dogmas of Creation, Incarnation and Resurrection were beyond the reach of the historical-critical method. Scriptural narratives about these matters were imaginative descriptions, or 'sagas' in the words of Barth himself. They were legendary witnesses, but were neither factual reports nor mythological picture language.

Instead they were means of witnessing to unique, unrepeatable, events which were beyond human description. Nevertheless the imaginative depiction can be judged to be successful if it allowed the kerygma to be set forth to those who might hear it and respond. The referential aspect of the narratives does not matter so much as the overall structure of the narrative. In the structure of the biblical story the account of God as Creator and Redeemer is set forth.[212]

The approach taken by Hans Frei in the 1970s in his work on the biblical narrative develops this viewpoint further. The narratives lay out the shape of the world in which we live and show the character of the God who calls us to respond to his claims. The task of theology is Christian self-description and not a correlation of theology with the universal search for meaning. The reason this is so, claims Frei, is that in the narrative of the Bible story and meaning are closely related, so there are what Frei called 'special hermeneutics' in this narrative. It is not a claim for Christian theology per se, but rather a plea that some accounts of history unite story and meaning in a unique manner. No doubt some other religious, or literary, sagas do the same. If this is the case then one cannot employ a universal hermeneutic as normative when reading scripture. The truth claims which are made depend on the particularity of a story and its use within a community.[213]

This means, of course, that Frei accepted that the Christian story would function in different ways inside different Christian communities, from fundamentalist Protestant to traditional Orthodox. Frei wrote:[214]

> There is no single road to Christianity, either as a matter of universal principle or in practice. I am convinced that the passionate and systematic preoccupation with the apologetic task of showing how faith is meaningful and /or possible is largely out of place and self- defeating [...] except as an ad hoc and highly various exercise. In this arena an ounce of living is usually worth a pound of talk, and especially of writing.

212 Ford, D. F., *Barth and God's Story: Biblical Narrative and the Theological Method of Karl Barth in the Church Dogmatics*, Peter Lang, 1981.

213 Frei H., *The Eclipse of the Biblical Narrative*, Yale University Press, 1974 and *The Identity of Jesus Christ*, Fortress Press, 1975.

214 ibid.

Frei denied that the experience of a modern person was therefore the correct starting point for understanding biblical hermeneutics. For modernity, truth was found when history was reported accurately, or general truths were revealed about human existence. Frei preferred to start with the biblical world, and then see how the claims of scripture fitted into contemporary society. Such connections would be unsystematic, but nonetheless real.

The worldview of the Bible is narrative shaped, and being a Christian involves taking on these narratives into one's own story. This raises profound questions about relativism and the logic of belief, but Frei did not wish to say that there was a special kind of truth for Christians. Rather he wished to take his stand on the fact that there was a pattern to the biblical story which was lost when it was turned into non-narrative form. Then it loses its true meaning and its integrity is violated.

Others took a different line from Barth in the 1920s. Two main alternatives to the issue of history were developed, and are still present today. One remained committed to the nineteenth-century historical-critical method, but was prepared to consider the person of Jesus as a figure of his own day, with his expectations about the end of history and his Jewish culture. Nevertheless in and through this person God acts in a decisive way, even though the saving message or kerygma has to be expressed in the language of our own day. Much contemporary biblical study has concentrated on the message of Jesus the Jew, while accepting that some of this message is not timeless.

The alternative, and more far reaching approach, is that associated with Rudolf Bultmann in the 1920s, who wrote until his death fifty years later. Bultmann simply discarded much of the message of the New Testament as expressing the beliefs of either the first century Judaism of Jesus or of the dualist Gnostic world. The latter had a particular influence on the writing of Paul. Instead Bultmann replaced the centrality of personality in nineteenth century theology with that of existentialism. The Christian faith was an existential message which called its followers to a decision about the truth of existence in the face of the threat of meaningless and death. Although Bultmann was a rare combination of a gifted biblical historian and a systematic theologian who had read deeply in the existentialist philosophy of his contemporaries, especially Heidegger, in the end Bultmann felt that the historical facts of the life of Jesus mattered little. Beyond his existence, and his commitment to the Kingdom of God as the central reality of all existence, the historical details were secondary. Bultmann therefore felt that much of the New Testament was mythological, and in need of demythologising. By doing this the true message of Christianity could be revealed.[215]

In his acceptance of the value of dialectical theology, and therefore of the divine judgement alongside God's call to new life, Bultmann shared much in common with Barth. However Barth rejected Bultmann's espousal of existentialism and even more disagreed with Bultmann's attitude to the biblical narrative. Both agreed that the narrative was not to be seen as historical in a literal and factual way, and also agreed that history could never support the truth claims of Christianity except in so far as it could be shown that a person called Jesus of Nazareth actually existed. This however proved nothing about the reality of God's redemption through this person. Nevertheless there was a total opposition between Barth, and his later followers such as Frei, and Bultmann and those who succeeded him on the question of whether the narrative of scripture has intrinsic significance, or whether it is simply culturally specific to its own day and to be reinterpreted.

The question of history is one of the most intractable issues in modern theology. There are those who have attempted in 'a new search for the historical Jesus' since the 1950s to sketch again the history of this Jewish prophetic figure, so that his life and message might stand out more clearly from the culture of his day. Secondly, there are those who accept that much of what Jesus said was of his time, but hold in faith that in this person God acted decisively. They therefore stand by the need for demythologising much of scripture and the Christian tradition. Thirdly, there are those post-liberals who take the Bible on its own terms. This does not commit them to seeing every account within it as historically accurate, but it does lead them to accept the structure of the narrative as intrinsically valuable.

215 Bultmann, R., *Jesus and the Word*, SCM, 1958 (first published 1926).

Within the modern Western university all three positions are held. In church life the issues are seen less clearly, but here again the challenge of history and of modernity presses hard. However in recent times a pre-critical fundamentalism (which rejects as irrelevant the debates in theology since 1700) has begun to take root in many evangelical churches in the West. This would accept as literally, and therefore historically, true the narratives in scripture.[216]

Rethinking cosmology and dynamic relationships

Time and space function in cosmological thought as attributes of the existence of the universe. This is so from a Christian or secular perspective. However what is more problematic is the move from cosmological speculation to the belief that creation and history has a 'plan', since the hermeneutics of one particular narrative in scripture is now being taken as appropriate for Christian reflection on scientific debate. The point at issue is essentially hermeneutical, since the narrative of creation and redemption in the Bible may be read by a mathematician in terms of initial conditions, equilibrium and future trajectories. (The Fall defines the starting point, but the cosmos also looks forward to the equilibrium condition that will be reached at the end of history. The mythology of the Fall in the narrative is not however designed to be read in such an analytic manner.)

Theologians who have interpreted the findings of theoretical physics have done so by discussing the nature of space and time, rather than by referring back to the narrative set out in Genesis. Equally any discussion of evil, sin and redemption will see this as an extended reflection on psychology, anthropology and other cognate disciplines, rather than an attempt to see the biblical narratives as autonomous subject matter in their own right. This means that the worldview of the biblical narrative, even with its extensive cosmology and history of salvation, cannot be put alongside the discipline of mathematical dynamics without the mediation of contemporary debates in theology on the meaning of history. Nevertheless, the

216 Placher, W. C., op. cit.

commitment to a dynamic theology is found deeply in all parts of modern theology. The issue for theology is that its dynamic nature has to wrestle with the problem of history and narrative, in a way that other disciplines, economics for example, do not.[217]

Theology is concerned with the dynamics of a relationship with God, focussing on those concepts which make that relationship dynamic. Dan Hardy has concentrated on the concept of praise. There is a proper 'economy' of praise between God and creation, (the word being used in a different sense from that of economics!) which focuses these relationships in a manner determined by the nature of God. This relationship is not like an explosion, which forces itself outward in every direction with uniform thrust. Such a momentum is eventually lost and the expansion becomes a uniform presence. Instead there is a perfection in God's own nature which seeks a fuller and fuller perfection. Hardy writes:[218]

> Thus, the economy which is in God is that of an inner distinction in God, which posits a direction for his expanding perfection, and it can be characterised as praise, one which establishes the character of God as praise.

Hardy describes this as the essence of the inner life of God, or the life of the spirit. This 'economy' of the spirit of God's own life opens up what can be described metaphorically as 'space' for us to realise our true potential in our lives. Praise is made up of attention and determination, and includes the process of knowing something (or somebody) and valuing this. If what is known has a particular excellence, then there will be a direction to this praise which intensifies the attention given to the object before one. However if the excellence is greater than our attention can envisage, then praise will overflow this knowledge. The intensification of praise is thus appropriate to its object and yet inadequate to it at the same time. This leads into a dynamic of the fullest integration of the capacities of the person who praises the object. This praise is a special form of the God-human relationship, although it can exist as well in purely human

217 Peacocke, A. R., *Theology for a Scientific Age*, SCM, 1993, and Torrance, T. F., *The Ground and Grammar of Theology*, Christian Journals, 1980.

218 Hardy, D. W. and Ford, D. F., op. cit.

relationships. Nevertheless once again we see the distinctiveness of the nature of theology.

Barth and Hardy (and many other theologians) see the relationship of God and humanity as being like a dynamic system, with the end-point condition as being the resolution of human brokenness. The way in which that is achieved is enormously variable in theology, from the acceptance of mystery to the hope of social reconciliation. Perhaps the greatest difference between theology and economics is not the question of how history and dynamism is treated, but the very fact as to whether hermeneutics intervenes at all. For economics, there is a closed system of economic theory which dispenses with history and concentrates instead on mathematical modelling in a dynamic manner. For theology, however, the issue is that its discipline serves as an interpretation of history, while not being tied to an empirical definition of historical facts in a straight-forward way.

At this point some unsympathetic observers of modern theology may give up in despair, referring to 'weasel-words' which equivocate in their meaning. However the theologian does not have to accept this lying down. The power of the biblical narrative is such that it can enter into dialogue with other secular disciplines, neither seeking to replace them nor to ignore them. The power of the narrative lies in its dynamic character which has been developed by contemporary theologians as a closed system in a manner analogous to economic theory. The future-oriented nature of both systems of thought is clear, and opens up room for further debate.

Section Three: Summary and Discussion

One of the foundations of modern science is the differential calculus. It can be used to describe any system in motion by specifying laws of change together with the initial conditions. Alternatively terminal conditions can be set, implying some sort of planning or design.

The mathematical relationships used by scientists and engineers show how the past determines or influences the present. Once the laws of motion are known, and also the initial conditions, the time path can be calculated step by step. The behaviour of intelligent systems in real time can be calculated in the same way, as they react to observations. But the plans which are made by intelligent systems, including human beings, follow a different kind of logic. They work back from a terminal condition, using the same laws of motion to determine what the initial step in the plan must be. In an unpredictable, stochastic environment the plan has to be continuously recomputed, as new information becomes available. Thus their actual behaviour in real time depends on their latest expectations for the future and on the whole sequence of actions they now expect to be taking. There is nothing uniquely human about this mathematical description of behaviour: it could apply to a dog chasing a rabbit or a computer flying an aeroplane.

The laws of nature are the same at all times and in all places. The way that they are expressed may reflect the society by which they are discovered, but the underlying reality does not vary at all. The 'laws' of economics and the behaviour it describes are sometimes supposed to be timeless and context-free as well. In principle they should be applicable to any culture in which people are free to engage in consumption, production and exchange. This is just the sort of claim that post-modernists would instinctively reject.

Pre-moderns and post-moderns alike delight in telling stories. They do not necessarily have to be of general application. Anything can happen in a story; there are no fixed rules to govern the narrative. The hearers are free to make their own interpretation. But interesting stories do have elements of continuity as well as change. They do not just describe events, but also indicate why they happened. Stories must have a beginning and an end.

In the Bible the continuity depends on the changelessness of God, even as his purposes unfold. The story begins with the creation and the Fall, continues right through the events of both the Old Testament and the New Testament, looking forward to the end of time and judgement day. Christian belief is expressed in this tale.

Economists do not find stories so congenial. Their preferred language is mathematical like that of the natural sciences. Instead of narratives, they construct models. There is no reason why a similar approach should not be applied to the expression of Christian belief. A model of salvation would be forward-looking, like the models that economists use to describe the plans of economic agents. It would express the purposes of events as well as their prior causes. It would, in other words, be teleological unlike the models used in the natural sciences. The prospect of the future endpoint would have an influence today.

Such a model might begin with the Fall. That is an initial condition, starting the dynamic system off from a point well away from its goal. The path would then involve an interaction between God and his people, governed first by the old covenant and then by the new. The coming of the kingdom would be like a terminal condition, not fully realised until the very end of time, but anticipated in the behaviour of the agents throughout.

Using models like this might help to promote mutual understanding between theology and modern science. It could be one way to present Christian belief to a modern (as opposed to a pre-modern or post-modern) audience. That still seems to us to be a very important task. Christian belief is not just story telling. As we concluded in the first chapter, it is also a description of the real world.

It is possible that the mathematical models used by economists could be useful in such a project, not least because they look forward as well as back. In the next chapter we shall explore some examples where models that are already familiar in economic theory might find an application to Christian belief.

Chapter Eleven

Economic Policy as a Parable of the Kingdom

The method adopted in this chapter is rather different from that which we have followed in the rest of the book – and it is more speculative in character. Up to this point we have been concerned chiefly to compare and contrast the views of human motivation and behaviour as seen in economic theory and in Christian belief – what we have referred to as 'anthropology'. Each chapter has taken the form of a dialogue. Now we shall be continuing with a rather different intention. We shall be asking whether economic theory can provide any useful insights to improve our understanding of Christian belief. Can it serve as a present-day parable?

We shall also be looking at a different area of economic theory. Up to now we have been concerned almost exclusively with microeconomics, that is with the behaviour of particular agents, products and markets. Now we switch attention to macroeconomics, which is about how the economy as a whole behaves, about the determination of total output, employment and prices. We shall be concerned mainly with issues of economic policy, what the government or the central bank can and cannot do to make the aggregate economy function well.

The parables of the New Testament often begin with the words 'The kingdom of heaven is like […]' They do not describe the kingdom directly, but they provide models of some aspects of it. They are illustrations of the essential relationships which exist in the kingdom, even though they describe those relationships in a quite different context. Many of the stories refer to economic relationships. There are the stories of the labourers in the vineyard, the unjust steward, the two debtors, the talents and the pearl of great price. It is entirely appropriate therefore for us today to explore the parallels which exist between our present-day understanding of economic behaviour and our faith as Christians.

The kingdom of God is not a place or a country, but a way of describing how God rules over this world and the whole of creation. The Gospels refer to his kingship, now and in the future. They are about the relationship between a king and his subjects, or as we would now say, between government and people. Kingship is not meant to be taken quite literally, because God is much more than a king. The use of economic policymaking as a parable is to be understood in a similar way. God is not described adequately as a central banker or a finance minister, any more than he was adequately described as a landowner or a ruler. For us, it is possible however that a contemporary illustration may be particularly vivid or enlightening.

This chapter takes five topics from the theory of economic policy.[219] The first is stabilisation policy and how it is dependent on confidence – or faith. The second is the debate about rules versus discretion which is set alongside the Christian doctrine of divine providence. The third is about time inconsistency and the need for commitment which suggests reflections on the nature of God's justice and his mercy. Then there is a section on economic reforms and changes of regime which finds parallels with the central Christian doctrine of redemption. The fifth and last topic is the policy problem of international debt, and how that might relate to the forgiveness of sins.

Stabilisation and economic health

Business, or trade cycles, are an almost universal feature of modern economies. Periods of relatively rapid growth in total output alternate with periods of slow growth or recession. The length of a complete cycle from peak to peak, or trough to trough, is typically between three and ten years. There are many reasons why an economy pushed away from equilibrium might not immediately move back. Suppose that the cycle begins with an external shock, for example an increase

219 Britton, A., *Monetary Regimes of the Twentieth Century*, CUP, 2001.

in the price of imported oil, reducing real incomes and hence the demand for domestic production. The initial effect on activity will be multiplied by the loss of purchasing power of those who become unemployed. This will then be compounded by a fall in fixed investment as existing factories stand idle, and also in inventory investment as stocks of unsold goods accumulate. At this stage business confidence will decline and banks will call in their loans, adding to the dangers of recession by precipitating bankruptcies and company failures.

Then gradually, in a normal cycle, the equilibrating forces should begin to act. The rate of inflation should slow down and prices may even fall; interest rates will normally come down. Most importantly, confidence will begin to recover. Firms and consumers will expect, on the basis of past experience, that the recession will not last for ever. Cautiously at first, they will base their spending plans on a more optimistic view of the future. Output can then rise, followed by employment, typically with a short lag.

Would the economy work better if it stayed closer to its equilibrium path? Would it be better if the business cycles could somehow be ironed out? No one likes recessions, but a case could be made that fluctuations are necessary to the process of 'creative destruction' by which new technology replaces old and the economy progresses. The boom phase makes it possible for some new firms to invest and grow, whilst a slump kills off some old ones. An economic Darwinian could argue that natural selection works best in an environment of disturbance.

Whether one judges business cycles themselves to be symptoms of illness or of health, there is no doubt that an economy stuck for many years at the bottom of a cycle is very sick indeed. That was the situation that confronted economists in the 1930s. The expected recovery was postponed again and again; instead the depression intensified. It had to be asked whether the economy would ever recover at all by means of its own corrective mechanisms. It was suggested that the system had been weakened by the aftermath of the First World War, by the increase in the power of trades unions or by the growth of giant firms. It was described as a complex and fragile system, even by its supporters. Was it really self-stabilising at all?

Business lost all confidence in the future, even the economists began to question the efficacy of the 'invisible hand'. Meanwhile the unemployed continued to suffer, and the social order itself was in danger of destruction.

Keynes, in his *General Theory of Employment, Interest and Money,* presented both an explanation of persistent depression and a means of preserving the free market system. He claimed that the macroeconomy could settle in a position of equilibrium, from which there would be no movement, but in which full employment would not, in general, be attained. Investment would not recover until firms regained their 'animal spirits'; the savings that were made would just accumulate as idle money balances. The depression could go on for ever, or at least for so long that the market system itself would not survive. The alternative did not have to be state planning; the market could still allocate scarce resources to their most productive uses, but the government had to ensure that aggregate demand was maintained at an adequate level.

The remedies proposed by Keynes and his followers were not widely adopted in the inter-war period. Some stimulus to demand came as a number of countries allowed their interest rates to fall and started up some public works programmes specifically to create jobs for the unemployed. Governments tried to restore confidence, asserting that the economy was basically sound, but their words did not carry conviction. Full employment was not in fact restored until the beginning of the Second World War.

After the war, full employment was maintained in many countries for several decades. Governments accepted that this was now part of their responsibility, and they adopted the theoretical framework of the 'General Theory'. They did not in fact need to do much to stimulate aggregate demand. Indeed they were more often required to rein it back. The question was asked, 'Why have we had full employment since the war?' One of the most persuasive answers was that full employment was maintained because it was expected that it would be. Confidence was supported by a government commitment which people trusted. No actual evidence was required that governments were able and willing to keep their promises. It was a matter of faith. In a market economy one needs to have faith in the rational behaviour of other economic agents. In a managed economy one has to trust the 'authorities'.

From the 1970s, governments have no longer been able to maintain full employment by stabilising aggregate demand. Their attempts to follow the Keynesian prescriptions have been defeated by the increase in inflation. Again, it is on expectations that we must focus attention. If everyone expects an increase in demand to produce inflation, then there is little doubt that it will. As soon as the expansionary measures are announced firms will begin to mark up their prices, unions to press for wage rises; no one wants to be left behind. Many economists themselves, since this period, have lost faith in the teaching of Keynes, saying that there is a relatively high 'natural rate of unemployment' which cannot be shifted by the management of demand. They have ceased to be prophets of stabilisation policy, becoming prophets of the market instead.

Faith and social sickness

It seems a big step from these debates amongst economists to the concerns that Christians often express about the health of the economy and of society. Can it be seriously suggested that Christians, as such, have anything to contribute to the explanation of the business cycle, the level of unemployment or the rate of change of prices? This question was much debated during and after the Great Depression. The response of William Temple is worth quoting at some length:[220]

> If Christianity is true at all it is a truth of universal application; all things should be done in the Christian spirit and in accordance with Christian principles. 'Then', say some, 'produce your Christian solution of unemployment'. But there neither is nor could be such a thing [...] 'In that case', says the reformer – or, quite equally, the upholder of the status quo – 'keep off the turf. By your own confession you are out of place here.' But this time the Church must say 'No; I cannot tell you what is the remedy; but I can tell you that a society of which unemployment (in peace time) is a chronic feature is a diseased society, and that if you are not doing all you can to find and administer the remedy, you

220 Temple, W., op. cit.

> are guilty before God.' Sometimes the Church can go further than this and point to features in the social structure itself which are bound to be sources of social evil because they contradict the principles of the Gospel.

The references in the quotation to 'a diseased society' and to 'social evil' suggest what a Christian contribution to a debate about the state of the economy might be like. But that is not our main concern here. We want to make the less familiar point that the conclusions of economists about the behaviour of the variables that interest them may have something to contribute to our understanding of Christian belief. Economics may, as we have suggested, offer a parable.

Using the language of economic theory itself, it can be argued that the various malfunctions of a market economy are due to a lack of trust or faith. This suggests a point at which contact could be made between economic theory and Christian belief. The starting point could be the understanding of sickness itself. In the New Testament sickness is cured by the power of faith. In Mark 5, to take just two examples, Jesus says to the father of a child who appears to be dead, 'Do not be afraid; only believe' and he also says to a woman who has been cured of a haemorrhage, 'Your faith has healed you'. Without faith there can be no healing: in Mark 6, Jesus could do no miracles in his home town, or hardly any, and 'he was amazed at their lack of faith'.

In these passages there is, of course, no question but that healing is a gift from God, a manifestation of his power. Yet, apparently, it is faith which makes healing possible. The patients have to believe that Jesus has the ability to drive out the devils which have made them ill. He is in the same position as a finance minister who is trying to convince the public that he will restore the health of the economy. He can only do it if they believe that he can.

The accounts of healing in the New Testament can themselves be read as if they were parables about salvation. In order to be saved, one must have faith. Jesus said to a man who was paralysed, 'Your sins are forgiven' (Mark 2). But forgiveness depends on repentance which also requires faith. That is the message for individuals, and the same Gospel applies to communities as well. Perhaps that is where the economic parable is most helpful. A government cannot manage the economy successfully unless it can inspire confidence. Likewise God cannot lead his people unless they put their trust in him.

Rules versus discretion

The proper methods and scope of government intervention in a market economy have been a matter of perennial debate. This is a question about political theory as well as economics. At one extreme are those who see almost no role at all for economic policy as a continuous activity of government, although they would probably emphasise the need for government to provide a proper framework of law within which the market can operate efficiently. At the other extreme are those who see the market as so unreliable, or so unjust, that they prefer to rely on government to supervise all sectors very closely and intervene continuously in the public interest.

Theory suggests, and experience generally confirms, that centralised economic planning is an inefficient use of information. Individual consumers and producers know best their own needs and their capabilities. In a market system that information gets embodied in the set of market prices. It would be very difficult to collect all that information together, process it and communicate it back as a series of instructions to individual economic agents. Moreover the process would depend on the planning authorities being given powers of inquisition which might be incompatible with rights of free choice and of privacy.

Central economic planning by government has few defenders today. It is worth remembering therefore how different things seemed fifty or more years ago. In the great depression the market system was seen as having failed, whilst Soviet Russia and Nazi Germany were succeeding magnificently. Governments could not just stand aside as industry and employment collapsed. It is also worth recalling how all the belligerent nations ran their economies during the Second World War. The information needed to set priorities for the use of resources had to be provided from the top down. The price system was virtually suspended. In any case it would have been thought morally unacceptable for some to profit and others to suffer economic hardship on account of the war effort. This way of thinking about the economy had a profound effect on policy long after the war was over.

In 1944 Hayek published his book, *The Road to Serfdom,*[221] in which he identified the threat to individual liberty implicit in the role being assumed by governments in economic affairs. He argued passionately for the 'rule of law'. By this he meant that governments should set the rules by which the market system was run, but they should not themselves become participants. He saw active intervention by government in the economy as constituting a form of tyranny. It opened the way to the worst kind of abuse of power, to corruption, favouritism and deceit. However well motivated it was to start with, it would bring to power the bullies and the megalomaniacs.

The appeal of Keynes and his *General Theory*[222] was that it offered a way of reconciling individual freedom with overall stability. He made a sharp distinction between microeconomics and macroeconomics. The government needed to monitor continuously the macroeconomic balance between supply and demand, taking action as needed by adjusting the level of interest rates or the difference between public revenue and expenditure. Control of the economy in aggregate did not require control of individual prices or individual decisions to save or to invest. This was the only way, according to Keynes, that liberal democracy could be saved.

What actually happened after the war was something quite different. Those countries that adopted macroeconomic demand management also adopted intervention at the micro level. They nationalised industries, devised national plans, controlled credit and foreign exchange transactions. It ultimately proved impossible to reconcile full employment and price stability simply by manipulating aggregate demand. Prices and incomes policies were introduced which required detailed intervention in the processes of competition and collective bargaining. Governments got drawn into industrial disputes without having the power to resolve them. By the 1970s the post-war

221 Hayek, F., op. cit.

222 Keynes, J. M., *The General Theory of Employment, Interest and Money*, Macmillan, 1936.

policies of the mixed economy were being replaced by a revival of free-market liberalism.

The role of government policy, both macroeconomic and microeconomic, is now seen mainly in terms of rules rather than discretion. Government actions should be as predictable as possible. The growth of the money supply should be constant, or nearly so. The fiscal deficit should never be large and it should not vary much from year to year. The effect is to take economic policy out of politics. The European central bank is not subject to any political control; it simply follows the rules implied by the treaty that created it. Having set the system in motion, the politicians can leave it to run on its own.

Divine providence

There are clearly some cross-references to be made between these debates about the role of government and the disputes within theology about the relationship of God with his creation. Is the world on 'manual control' or on 'automatic pilot'? Does God intervene on some occasions, but not others? Does God respect individual freedom? Can he nevertheless guide the destiny of nations, or of humanity as a whole?

The economic model suggests that we should start with the concepts of omniscience and omnipotence. The case for the free market depends in part on the ignorance and powerlessness of democratic governments. If God knows everything and can do anything, then he is subject to no such limitations. He could behave like a benevolent despot; yet it seems that he chooses not to. The God of the Bible appears rather different. He seems to rely on messengers (angels) who collect information and convey his instructions (ascending and descending). The picture is not one of a central planner with everything under his direct control.

Despite the differences of period and context, this may fit rather well with one view of causation suggested by modern science. The laws of physics and biology, we now believe, leave much to chance. Overall design of the universe would not require detailed involvement in all aspects of its evolution. Perhaps a God of the kind suggested by modern science would have to be a macroeconomist. He would not need to control all the detail, but he would still be in charge of the broad picture.

Clearly, the God of the Bible is not like the God of the deists who made the world and then walked away. The Bible is full of accounts of how God intervenes in the world, responding to events, choosing one course of action rather than another. God interacts with his people all the time. There would seem therefore to be some conflict of roles within divine providence. As in political theory, it is difficult to reconcile being both a player and the referee. There even seems to be evidence in the Bible of God showing favouritism: 'Israel I loved, and Esau I hated'. The righteousness of God in the Bible is not the same as that which is expected of the State in liberal political theory.

Many Christians in modern times would say that God leaves us freedom of choice, perhaps because, rather like the liberal philosopher, he values freedom in its own right. Certainly he wants our worship and service to be voluntary. Without being too fanciful, one can see a parallel with an economic policy which controls the aggregate whilst leaving the individual at liberty. Providence may decide the fate of nations, or of the whole human race, without determining events all the time in the daily lives of ordinary people. The Old Testament prophets saw God's hand in the power politics of their day. Similarly, we may say now that God determined the result of the second world war, or brought down the communist rulers of the Soviet Union, yet we may also want to say that he leaves us free to design our own lives, and make our own mistakes.

Time inconsistency

From the 1960s, theoretical models of macroeconomic demand management became more and more sophisticated. They drew on the existing mathematics of control theory developed by engineers. The most interesting problem seemed to be devising a feedback rule for monetary or fiscal policy which would optimise the performance of the economy over time. The instruments of policy, interest rates or taxes, would respond according to this rule to observations of a few economic indicators. The chosen rule would be the one which minimised the costs, which were calculated by adding together some combination of inflation rates and unemployment over some interval of time. The rules were derived analytically or else by repeated simulations using an estimated mathematical model of the economy.

The problem became even more interesting when expectations were introduced explicitly into the macroeconomic models. Thus the behaviour of wages was made to depend, not just on previous experience of inflation, but also on expectations of future inflation as well. True to the spirit of neo-classical economics, expectations were assumed to be 'rational', that is to say the best guess that could be made using the information available.[223] For most purposes it was assumed that the expectations were actually correct. Any policy rule would therefore be successfully anticipated in the behaviour of the economic agents it sought to control. The nature of the game had changed quite profoundly.

Once expectations are treated explicitly optimisation problems may become time inconsistent. This means that the plan which is chosen at the outset will not in general be the plan which is chosen at a later period. This is the case even if no new information becomes available. The point is that the plan itself will influence expectations and hence behaviour. After the event, when it is too late to have any effect on expectations, a different plan is the best. Before the annual wage round the central bank will want to adopt a very tough line against inflation; after the bargain has been struck it will want to give more weight to other considerations, for example unemployment.

Mathematical economists have rediscovered a very old and well-used wheel. Such dilemmas have been familiar for thousands of years. One answer to them is to tie your own hands. A binding commitment is made; after the plan has been inaugurated no subsequent re-optimisation is permitted. Examples include international treaties, constitutions of government and the laws of the Medes and the Persians.

223 Begg, D., *The Rational Expectations Revolution in Macroeconomics*, Philip Allan, 1982.

The difficulty in making commitments about economic policy is to convince the public that they really will be kept. If they refer to just one action of government then logic suggests that any rational government will go back on its word. That is the essence of time inconsistency. That being so, it is unlikely to be believed in the first place. If, however, the commitment is to repeated actions, then the government will have a good reason for keeping its promises, as it will build up a reputation for reliability. The outcome which can be achieved in this way will often be better than the outcome from re-optimising the setting of policy instruments each period. Thus a central bank with a reputation for toughness will not need to allow unemployment ever to rise very much in order to demonstrate its resolve.

Suppose however that there is a government which really cares only about unemployment, because that is what affects its chances of re-election. Suppose, nevertheless, that it makes a commitment to low inflation, in the hope of impressing the markets. As the time of an election approaches it will be tempted to go back on its commitment so as to improve its chances of re-election. The knowledge that it may do this undermines its credibility from the start. One solution to this problem would be to delegate power to an agent who really did care only about the objectives to which the government was publicly committed. Thus a relatively 'soft' government might hand over the control of monetary policy to a relatively 'tough' central bank.

Justice and mercy

The whole field of criminal justice is pervaded by problems of time inconsistency. If we punish only to deter, then after the event we will regret the need to punish at all. The history of God's relationship with Israel in the Old Testament consists of repeated instances of just this situation. God offers a choice between life and death, saying that life depends on obedience and death will be the consequence of sin. Then Israel, again and again, takes the wrong road. God does punish; but, again and again, he relents. Some at least of the sinful people are restored to his favour and offered the choice again. So history repeats itself.

Why does Israel not choose life all the time? Perhaps the people are just weak or stupid. Or perhaps they are calling God's bluff. If they understand time inconsistency, then, like spoilt children, they will put their God to the test. As the serpent said to Eve, 'You will not surely die'. The recurrent temptation, throughout the Bible is to manipulate God's mercy, as rational calculation suggests that we can.

In the Old Testament judgement is like a repeated game.[224] God has an incentive to build up a reputation for being tough. In the New Testament however, judgement is delayed until the last day. It is a single action with no possibility of appeal. According to the model of time inconsistency used by economists, God cannot make a credible commitment to punish. He may threaten but no one will believe him. However lurid the picture of hell may be painted we will not be frightened by it, because we believe that God really loves us and will relent. Why should he actually punish us when it will be too late for us to mend our ways?

The theory of economic policy suggests one logical possibility. God could hand over the execution of punishment to someone else. Such reasoning may lie behind the belief that the souls of unrepentant sinners belong to the devil. One might imagine that a commitment to delegate punishment in this way would be credible and that human beings would be too frightened to sin. This ignores another important strand of game theory. The results of strategic interactions are seldom known with certainty. People make mistakes or act in ignorance of the facts. If God delegated judgement there would be no guarantee that the deterrent would be effective. As the New Testament makes clear, a quite different strategy is required. In the terminology of economic theory what is required is a change of regime.

224 See Chapter 9 above.

Regime changes

The history of economic policy is punctuated by episodes of discontinuity and fundamental reform. The rules of the game get altered. The institutional and legal setting for policy can be transformed. Political control can change hands. When this happens the behaviour of economic agents changes as well. A relationship which has been observed between say income and saving under one regime will not in general prove robust across the boundary. This does not mean that the underlying parameters which define preferences and production possibilities have changed; they will in general stay the same, but the new regime will change expectations about policy if nothing else, and that will produce a break in the series of observations. It is very difficult therefore to say how the economy will react to fundamental reform.

Examples of regime changes include the currency reforms in Germany and Japan after the war. Then, as often, the change was made in response to a crisis. The shift from fixed to floating exchange rates in the 1970s was also a reform forced on governments by events. There were more gradual reforms in many countries in the 1980s as the institutions of the post-war mixed economy were replaced by those of free-market liberalism. Some of the most dramatic changes have been taking place in Eastern Europe since the fall of communism. New institutions have to be invented, or perhaps imported from the West. But the new institutions do not work well until the new habits of mind that go with them have had time to develop. The disruption in the meantime has been very severe.

Fundamental reform is never without cost. However necessary or desirable change may be there are those who will lose by it and those who will oppose it. The old regime will leave a legacy for which someone will have to take responsibility if the new regime is to succeed. A good example is the unification of the German economy after the fall of the Berlin wall. It was necessary for the government and people of West Germany to act with generosity towards the East before the change of regime could be accomplished. In a currency reform someone may have to give good new money in exchange for old money which is worthless. The most difficult part of a regime change may not be to design a new system, but be to clear up the mess which is left behind by the old one.

Redemption

The central event of the New Testament consists of the death and resurrection of Jesus Christ, by which we are saved. This brings about a fundamental, irreversible and unrepeatable change in the relationship between God and creation. It is called a new covenant. It could equally be called a new regime. The event of salvation in the New Testament does not just reveal new aspects of the nature of God. There is also a real change taking place. The old regime was not an illusion, or a dream. If it were, the introduction of the new regime would not be so difficult to achieve. There would have been no conflict, no need for redemption.

The first requirement is to deal with the legacy of the past, to pay off the old debts; hence the metaphor of redemption. The payment is made by Jesus himself in his death on behalf of us all. That much is clear and unambiguous. A more difficult question is to identify who it is that receives the payment. More than one interpretation is possible.

One way of viewing the transaction, implicit or explicit in various parts of the New Testament and in subsequent Christian doctrine, is that it takes place between God and the devil. The devil is, in effect, bought off. Under the old regime sin had acquired a hold over human life, such that the devil could be described as the prince of this world. He had to be induced to release that hold. We have the related metaphor of Jesus as the good shepherd who stands between the flock and the wolf, laying down his life for the sheep.

A different interpretation of redemption has the payment being made to God in satisfaction for the obligation to him which humankind has not met since the Fall. The death of Jesus is then seen as a sacrifice or gift to God made on our behalf. Another way of looking at it would see Jesus as paying the penalty for our sins. The obligations from the old regime, whatever their form, cannot simply be forgotten. God really is a God of justice as well as a God of mercy. Without recognition of what is his due, the new order cannot come in.

The introduction of the new regime is a one-off unique event. It has to be designed so that the problems of the old regime cannot recur. That is one feature that all reforms, human and divine, must have in common. The process of salvation must not turn into a repeated game of sin, judgement and forgiveness. So long as God and humanity remain opposing players in this game there will be no satisfactory solution for either of them. They will not be able to co-operate on the basis of self interest alone.

The new regime described in the New Testament involves the identification of God with humanity, and of humanity with God. This is not just co-operation, it is an actual merging of identities. This is not a strategic move which is found in the theory of games; it is a complete rewriting of the rules. Economic theory, with its very strong sense of individual identity, cannot easily come to terms with it. Nevertheless it may be the only way in which the problem of reconciling justice with love can be solved.

Debts and forgiveness

The message of the New Testament is that we should deal with one another, as we would expect God to deal with us. We should, in particular, forgive one another as we would hope that God will forgive us. Thus the account of redemption as a change of regime may suggest what kind of new economic relationships would have to be introduced if the nations of the world were to respect the principles of the kingdom of God. It may in particular throw light on the policy problems of international debt.

The origins of the present problem can be traced to the 1970s.[225] At that time rates of interest were often lower than the rate of inflation – in other words real rates of interest were negative, so lenders were in effect paying borrowers to accept a loan. Many of the poorer countries were very keen to borrow at that time, hoping to build up their capacity to replace imports by domestic production and hence become

225 Davis, A. P., *Debt, Financial Fragility and Systemic Risk*, OUP, 1992.

more self-sufficient. The situation changed rather abruptly around 1980 as interest rates rose and the rate of inflation was reduced.

The world economy went into recession, and the demand for primary products fell away sharply. The possibility arose of widespread default by governments in poorer countries. The banks that had lent to them were in serious trouble too. There was nearly a world-banking crisis on the scale of the 1930s which could well have caused another Great Depression. The situation was saved by the intervention of governments, acting mainly through the agency of the IMF. Gradually, as the world economy recovered in the late 1980s, the balance sheets of the big banks began to look healthier. Some of the commercial debts have by now been written down, or transformed into equity holdings. The main problem still outstanding is the official debt, owed by poor countries to rich countries or to the IMF.

One solution would be for the creditor nations to write off the debt. That would be a generous action on their part and highly commendable for that reason. The rich creditor countries owe all that they have to the generosity of God; let them acknowledge that fact by being generous to the poor countries whose debts to them are so small by comparison. One must ask, however, what this would do for the credit worthiness of the poor countries in the future. Is there not some risk that it will look a little like default?

There is another way of dealing with the problem of the debt. The rich countries, whether they are creditors or not, could contribute to a fund in proportion to their national incomes. This fund would then be used to pay off the debts of the poor countries. The fact that the rich countries were willing to do this would actually improve rather than damage the credit ratings of the poor.

This proposal makes quite explicit the sacrificial nature of the gift. The rich countries would be suffering a loss in order to help the poor. They would therefore be a little like Christ who sacrificed himself to free us from sin. The sinner who is redeemed has not defaulted on the debt; on the contrary it has been paid in full. Moreover, in order to be redeemed, the sinner must repent, not questioning that the debt really was a legitimate obligation. Thus, interpretation of the Christian doctrine of redemption could make a difference to the choice between two rather similar proposals for tackling the present problem of poor country debt. The difference is not trivial.[226]

In the Old Testament debt is always viewed as onerous. The debtor is a potential defaulter. The situation of the debtor is like that of a criminal: both suffer as a result of the just demands of the law, and both appeal for mercy. There is no suggestion that these obligations are unreal or unreasonable. The appeal is for generosity, in keeping with the ethics of love and community. We should feel sympathy and compassion, because we identify ourselves with one another.

The institution of the Jubilee in the Old Testament set out conditions for the periodic cancellation of debts. In doing so it defined, but also limited, the obligations of creditors. It was not an appeal for mercy but rather a redefinition of justice. The New Testament teaching about debt remission seems to be different in character. The requirements of the law are not annulled, but they are transcended. The prohibition of usury is irrelevant in the kingdom of God because all loans have been transformed into gifts. Similarly the law of the Jubilee is unnecessary when the regime of strict justice has been replaced by a regime of mercy.

It is clear that in the kingdom of God there are no debts, since each shares freely with all. It defines a new regime, a new covenant, a new relationship between God and his people. The problem of debt arises in the transition, in moving from the old regime to the new. The old regime of debts and punishments was not an illusion; something has to be done to dispose of its legacy. This is especially true of the debts which we owe to God, the debts which we cannot hope to pay.

The New Testament speaks of the death and resurrection of Jesus as an act of redemption or ransom. He pays to set us free, from slavery or captivity. There are many different ways of describing our salvation, but they all seem to involve Jesus, as the Son of God, suffering in our place, taking our burden on himself. If our sins are called debts, then we can rightly say that Jesus pays them for us. He

226 See Chapter 8 above and Selby, P., op. cit.

had to do that before the new regime could be established, because the old regime was neither unreal nor unjust.

Chapter Twelve

Towards a Meeting of Minds?

We began this study by identifying some of the problems that beset any attempt to open a conversation between economic theory and Christian belief. Are they like oil and water, unable to mix at all? Is it possible, on the contrary, to achieve not just a mixture but actually a chemical reaction in which both take part? Having considered in the course of the study much of the agenda of economic theory, contrasted with the treatment of the same subjects in the Bible, we should now be in a better position to see what kind of meeting of minds is possible. It does not come easily.

Theology, economics and the modern world

Part of the difficulty is that economic theory is a product of the modern world, whilst Christian belief dates back to ancient times. We have heightened this contrast by basing our Christian critique of economics as directly as possible on the biblical text. We have not tried to do justice to the vast range of modern Christian writings on the same themes. Christianity is a living religion which changes the expression of its belief as it passes from one culture to another, and as it makes contact with new discoveries or new ideas. It would be quite wrong therefore to present an account of Christian belief as if it were inherently pre-modern in its outlook.

Christians today need to place the modern world within a narrative of faith. The story does not end in the first century, even though the decisive events took place at that time. God is still at work in the world, and faith in him is still the key to interpreting the meaning of history. There are, however, many ways in which Christians can respond to modern times, whether as a blessing or as a temptation. Responding to economic theory is an important part of this task of discernment.

A common Christian response to the main findings of modern science is to accept them, and to incorporate them into a new understanding of God's creation and providence. The evidence in support of those findings is generally so cogent that there can be little real dispute as to their validity. There is not, however, the same compulsion to accept the conclusions of economics. There is not much in economics that can be demonstrated beyond reasonable doubt. This does not mean, at the other extreme, that the whole subject can be dismissed out of hand. It is an impressive body of reasoning, extremely influential in contemporary culture, providing one kind of insight into the way that modern society works.

Many Christians, consciously or unconsciously, accept most of the assumptions and values of the modern society in which we live. Most of us believe in democracy, human rights, religious toleration, equality of opportunity and the benefit of economic growth. None of these are mentioned in the Bible, but we nevertheless welcome them as being appropriate developments related to some biblical teaching, and as compatible with the Gospel message. They are all open to questioning; they may not all be right for all societies, but they do seem right for our own. If we are, to that degree, at home in the modern world, then we shall not find economic theory as foreign to us as it would have been to our predecessors in ancient or medieval times.

If we endorse these modern assumptions and values, we may also respect the social institutions that embody them, in particular the nation state and the market economy. It is, in fact, very difficult to escape from these institutions since we cannot now live without them. This is the air we now breathe. This is not, of course, the kingdom of God, but it may still be one way in which he now provides for his people. Both the state and the market seem essential, although it is a vexed question where the boundary between them should lie.

In moving from the pre-modern to the modern world it is essential that we do not lose sight of God. Implicit in much of what is meant by 'modernism' there is a celebration of human potential that leaves God out of the picture altogether. To be 'humanist' in that sense would be to abandon the core of Christian belief. It would also be to make nonsense of much that Christians have to say in criticism of economic theory. The status of theism in modern philosophy may be controversial, but on one basis or another it has to be maintained. This could be a 'stumbling block' in dialogue between Christian belief and any academic discipline, but if God is somehow written out of the text, then the exchange can be neither fruitful nor sincere.

The modern world is itself changing: the twenty-first century will no doubt be very different from the nineteenth and the twentieth. Neo-classical economic theory, in the form that we have described in this book is coming to look a little out-of-date, as are many of the attempts to modernise theology. It is impossible to foresee what new ideas there will be in the future, or what form 'post-modernism' will take next. There are, however, some recent developments, which we find encouraging. Within economics there is renewed interest in issues of method, especially in the relation of the subject to ethics and epistemology. Within theology there is a renewed concern to avoid intellectual isolation, and to address issues that interest a wider audience. The notion that the two disciplines might have something to say to one another is not as strange as it might have appeared a generation or two ago.

The modern world is all too ready to sideline religion. It is tempting to say that economic theory is serious prose, while Christianity provides the poetic embellishment. Economics, one might suppose is meant to be taken literally, more or less, whilst religion is meant to inspire, to reinforce commitment, but not to inform. Sometimes religion seems no more than social rhetoric, beautiful words to grace a special occasion, but lacking any real meaning. Economics looks like a tough-minded subject, with all those mathematical equations. Religion, by contrast, seems more soft-focus, more like a dream. No doubt many people do resolve the potential conflict in this way, but it does not seem to us a satisfactory escape. Christianity ought to be hard-edged, a proper subject for sustained intellectual effort, resisting wishful thinking. One should also recognise the sentimentality which can surround economics, as shown in many an after-dinner speech by business leaders!

We should also resist the temptation, common in modern times, to confine religion to a limited sphere of life – personal relationships and community celebrations for example. This is, admittedly, how many people actually lead their lives. They behave differently, even think differently, in different contexts. Most of us do, in fact, try to serve both God and mammon. A purely descriptive model of human behaviour might stop here, recognising its incoherence and inner contradictions. There is, however, both for economics and for Christianity, a normative view of human nature which insists that it ought to be consistent and unified, even though in practice it often is not. It is important to both sides in the dialogue to establish where the real differences and similarities are to be found.

Where the differences lie

We might begin with what appears a relatively trivial difference, but one which has appeared in several parts of this study. It could be described in mathematical language, and perhaps arises from the mathematical form in which economics is usually expressed. Economics emphasises continuity, rather than discrete alternatives (although it can treat of both). In the theory of choice most decisions are compromises, a little of this and a little of that. Well-being is measured on a scale with no sharp breaks in it. In production theory all the inputs are divisible and there is a continuous range of technologies to choose from. One is, it seems, never alive or dead, but one enjoys a continuously diminishing expectation of life! This contrasts with the dichotomies of Christian belief. We are made to choose between alternatives. We are either sick or well, either saved or damned. The economist describes a world of scarcity in which resources have to be allocated amongst many different uses; Christianity describes a world of crisis in which all may be lost or won as the result of a single decision.

Economics has borrowed from physics the concept of equilibrium. The market outcome depends on the tastes of all consumers, and the technologies of all producers, but it does not, in the very long run, depend on history. If the equilibrium position is unique and stable (as it is usually assumed to be in a competitive market) then the route by which it is reached is unimportant, 'bygones are bygone'. In orthodox neo-classical economics, as opposed to Marxism, there is no historical narrative. Development, when it occurs, takes place smoothly. Alfred Marshall prefaced his monumental work with the quotation, 'Natura non facit saltum' (Nature does not make a jump). In Christian belief, by contrast, history is of the essence of understanding. The key events are discontinuous, like revolutions or changes of regime. We encounter God in events that are new and unpredictable

More generally we need to recognise that simple, standard, neo-classical economic theory adopts a very simple view of the world, and deliberately so. Often it goes against common sense, that is against the informal self-understanding which our society takes for granted. In our comparisons therefore we sometimes find Christian belief more inherently plausible, more in line with the conventional wisdom. For example, economics adopts the fiction of methodological individualism, whilst Christianity and common sense recognise that groups have identities, preferences and responsibilities of their own.

Again, the simple, standard model of neo-classical economics describes as rational only the formal calculation of the best possible outcome from a particular choice. In Christian belief, as in common sense, (and for that matter in some more sophisticated forms of economic theory) we do not always choose like that: our preferences are ill-defined; our motives are mixed; and the probability of different outcomes is often unknown. The treatment of wealth and power in economic theory misses out much that Christian belief, together with common sense, thinks important – like greed and envy. Sometimes the contrasts that we have identified simply remind us that there is a great deal to human nature which economic theory tends to ignore. But this is not unimportant: Christian belief insists that factors which economic theory tends to leave out, such as the emotions of love and hate, are actually what matters most in any description of human nature and potential.

Another set of differences arise because Christian belief has peculiar things to say about human nature, things which also, in their own way, go against common sense. It is not common sense to forgive debts unconditionally, or to take no thought for the morrow. This was true when Christianity was first preached, and it is still true today. Common sense may recognise the importance of love to human well-being, but it does not go to the extreme of saying that good works without love are worth nothing. Common sense does not often expect self-sacrifice, does not value humility, does not willingly leave itself vulnerable. Yet Christians assert that just these characteristics are essential to the norm of humanity. To be truly human is to fulfil a vocation, not to conform to convention or tradition. Such a strange proposition makes sense only if one believes in the love of God.

In their very different ways, both economic theory and Christian belief say that common sense is misleading, that things are not quite what they seem. But they point to quite different underlying realities. For neo-classical economics what matters most is enlightened self-interest. That is how it explains human behaviour, and also how it envisages that the human lot can be improved. No doubt people have, or claim to have, other motives for their behaviour, but so far as this kind of economics is concerned these are essentially distractions, or possibly illusions. The most urgent task is to improve material well-being, to feed the hungry and to enhance the prosperity of all. This is not, and never has been, an adequate account of the values of modern society; it misses out much that we all know to be essential.

Religion in general, and the Christian religion in particular, introduces another dimension. It also speaks of enlightenment, but it means something quite different. The hidden reality is not human but divine. The secret of happiness is not to satisfy our preferences, but to change them. It is precisely by abandoning what we think is our self interest that we achieve fulfilment. One could see this as a sort of higher-level rationality, but the motive is not simply one of calculated advantage. There is a relationship involved, with one another and with God which requires some surrender of individual autonomy. Christian belief could even be said to point in the opposite direction from economics, to be at the far end of a spectrum that has common sense somewhere in the middle.

Where there are similarities

There is no doubt that the two views of the world are a long way apart, but perhaps they can be brought closer together by identifying a few common enemies. Both of them oppose any process of reductionism. Human beings are not just animals, and not just machines. The view of humanity as seen from the inside is taken seriously as well as the one which a detached observer would report.

There are, in the modern world, many competing views of human nature other than the two we have considered in this study. One of the most powerful ideas today is Darwinism, or natural selection, applied to human behaviour as well as physical characteristics. It carries the prestige of the natural sciences, even though its findings are speculative in the extreme. We have been at pains to distinguish economics, which is about conscious choice, from sociobiology which is about the survival value of instincts that are blind. Economic theory, like Christian belief, draws a line between the behaviour of animals, however intelligent, and human behaviour, even when it looks much the same.

One could also imagine economics and religion finding themselves on the same side of a debate with the followers of Freud. If people are so irrational, so unaware of their own motivation, this would play havoc with the assumptions of mainstream economics. Psychology shows how fragile is that sense of individual identity which is crucial to both positive and normative economics. If human beings are in fact so benighted, then does individualism, and the love of freedom that goes with it, make any sense at all? Christians will also want to take a stand against this kind of psychology, if only to defend themselves against the charge that religion is itself a kind of madness.

A similar point could be made about the influence of Marx. He too regarded our perception of ourselves as false, conditioned by society and our place in it. He too encouraged his followers to approach all creeds with suspicion. Whose interests do they serve? Both economic theory and Christian belief might be dismissed as mere ideologies, defending the social and political regime in power. No doubt Marxism has had a pervasive effect both in economics and in theology over the past hundred years or more, but it is an influence neither can welcome with a whole heart. Marx remains, for mainstream economics, the great heretic, guilty of serious errors. He can also be seen as the founder a kind of secular atheistic religion. It is when his teaching is most attractive to Christians that his influence may seem most dangerous to their faith.

As against some of the great political movements of the twentieth century, economics and Christianity share a love of freedom. They may relate it to different accounts of human destiny, but it means that they can quite often make common cause against an oppressive political power. Economics suggests that people flourish best when they are left to decide their own fate; Christians believe that no human authority should usurp the place of God to direct our lives.

There is constant tension between these two very different ideals, but the interaction between them has, historically, been extraordinarily fruitful. Both have contributed to the way of life characteristic of the most successful societies of the twentieth century. It seems to be easier to reconcile economics and Christian belief in practice than it is in theory. No doubt a good measure of intellectual compromise and shoddy thinking can be involved in bringing them together. Even so, two parents that can produce such a vigorous offspring must surely be regarded as compatible!

Can economics become more Christian?

There are suggestions from time to time that neo-classical economics is itself a kind of religion, and therefore a rival to Christianity. We began our study with some quotations which illustrated that point. There is a tendency for any strongly-held conviction to adopt language similar to that of a religion. But economics is most successful when its pretensions are relatively modest. It is very good at deducing the implications of one kind of rationality. It is good at suggesting solutions to some kinds of social problem. It is not so good as a philosophy of life. Most economists recognise this. To become more Christian might mean to become rather more humble; it would not mean disowning the established method of the subject altogether.

One can imagine a kind of economics which abandoned some of the assumptions about human motivation and behaviour, the ‘anthropology’, which are most at odds with the ‘anthropology’ of common sense as well as of Christian belief. It would have to take more account of aspects of human nature that have often been neglected. It might accept that some kind of group identity is possible, as well as that of individuals. It might give up its exclusive attachment to utilitarian ethics. It might treat relationships as ends as well as means. There are plenty of economists who would dispute these assumptions of neo-classical economics in its standard form. The one non-negotiable commitment of neo-classical economic theory is probably to rationality. That is what differentiates economics from the rest of social science. The definition of rationality might be broadened to bring it closer to the actual experience of decision taking, but the intellectual rigour of the subject should not be lost in the process.

There would still be a wide gap to cross before secular economics of any school could accept the reasonableness of Christian belief as we have found it in the Bible. Christians are meant to believe that economic well-being is of secondary importance. Poverty can be a blessing; the bounty of nature is there to be enjoyed, but it is not to be earned by human effort alone. Each day is to be taken as it comes; nothing is to be stored up for the future. This sounds completely irrational. Presented as it stands it is simply unrealistic. That is the problem with trying to separate Christian attitudes to economics, or more generally Christian anthropology, from theology. One has either to invent a common sense secular kind of economics and pretend that it is Christian, or else put forward something that does not seem to make sense at all.

In the context of belief in God, however, Christian economics makes perfectly good sense. A strategy of self-sacrifice will work, provided that it is underwritten by God. One can give and receive freely, provided that God’s love is known both to the giver and the receiver. It makes sense to pray for your bread each day, if you are willing to accept whatever God provides. A work ethic of service to others, even if it means accepting exploitation, is still consistent with human dignity if God himself is willing to serve us. Many times in this study, we have seen that it is essential to Christian economics that God has a part to play. A secular version of it simply misses the point.

Faith and reason

The contents of this study are, broadly speaking, those of an economics textbook, not those of systematic theology. We have, nevertheless, touched on some issues that are central to Christian belief. Sometimes we have tried to show how ideas familiar in economic theory may throw some new light on theology. The dialogue has not all been one way.

Economics has its core commitment to rationality which we see as its greatest strength. Christians have always used both faith and reason in their search for a deeper understanding of God. Faith is not itself irrational; it can be presented in a way that makes sense to the non-believer. It does not need to speak a private language. Its content must be consistent with reason, even though we may not always be able to see for ourselves that this is so.

Economic theory is one, very significant, product of the modernity with which theology must come to terms. It is at least as relevant as physics or biology. Economics is relatively congenial because it is teleological. It uses a form of mathematics which looks forward as well as back. It describes a world that is neither deterministic nor random. Like theism it believes in design.

We have seen in this study how theories of production can relate to the doctrine of creation; we have also seen how theories of choice can relate to the doctrine of salvation. The concept of a person might be explained using the language of economics rather than that of ancient Greek philosophy. The theory of games and strategies is of use in the development of Christian ethics; it may also be useful to understanding how God's mercy relates to his justice. We have also suggested that the notion of a regime change can be applied to the coming of the kingdom of God. None of this changes in the least the essential content of Christian doctrine, but it may assist its presentation in modern times.

One view of economic theory is that it is really just a branch of applied mathematics. If it is viewed this way then it is easier to see that it could be useful to theology. Mathematical ideas, developed in one context, often find applications of a quite different kind. It is not unreasonable to suppose, therefore, that models developed in the context of economics might be used to assist a better understanding of religious belief.

Select Bibliography

1. Economics and Christianity

Atherton, J., *Christianity and the Market – Christian Social Thought for our Times*, SPCK, 1992.

Atherton, J., (ed.), *Social Christianity – A Reader*, SPCK, 1994.

Brennan, H. G. and Waterman, A. M. C., *Economics and Religion – Are they Distinct?*, Kluwer, 1994.

Collier, J., 'Contemporary Culture and the Role of Economics', in Montefiore, H. (ed.), *The Gospel and Contemporary Culture*, Mowbray, 1992.

Davies, J. (ed.), *God and the Marketplace*, Institute of Economic Affairs, 1993.

Gay, C., *With Liberty and Justice for Whom?*, Eerdmans, 1991.

Gorringe, T., *Capital and the Kingdom*, SPCK, 1994.

Griffiths, B., *Morality and the Market Place*, Hodder and Stoughton, 1980.

Hay, D. A., *Economics Today*, InterVarsity Press, 1989.

Hay, D. A. and Kreider, A. (eds.), *Christianity and the Culture of Economics*, University of Wales Press, 2001.

Meeks, M. D., *God the Economist*, Fortress Press, 1989.

Nelson, R. H., *Reaching for Heaven on Earth*, Rowan and Littlefield, 1991.

Pattison, S., *The Faith of the Managers*, Chapman, 1997.

Preston, R. H., *Religion and the Persistence of Capitalism*, SCM, 1983.

Preston, R. H., *Religion and the Ambiguities of Capitalism*, SCM, 1991.

Sedgwick, P. H., *The Enterprise Culture*, SPCK, 1992.

Sedgwick, P. H., *The Market Economy and Christian Ethics*, CUP, 1999.

Simons, R., *Competing Gospels – Public Theology and Economic Theory*, Dwyer (Australia), 1995.

Starkey, A., *Transforming Economics*, SPCK, 1986.

Van den Berg, A., *God and the Economy*, Eburon, 1998.

Wogaman, J. P., *Economics and Ethics, A Christian Enquiry*, SCM, 1986.

2. Economic Theory (works cited in text)

Ackley, G., *Macroeconomic Theory*, Macmillan, 1961.

Akerlof, G. A., 'Gift Exchange and Efficiency Work Theory', *American Economic Review*, 74:2, 1984.

Allen, R. G. D., *Mathematical Analysis for Economists*, Macmillan, 1938 and *Mathematical Economics*, Macmillan, 1956.

Arrow, K. J., *Social Choice and Individual Value*, Wiley, 1951.

Backhouse, R. E. (ed.), *New Directions in Economic Methodology*, Routledge, 1994.

Becker, G. S., *The Economics of Discrimination*, Univ. of Chicago Press, 1957, 1971.

Becker, G. S., *Human Capital, A Theoretical and Empirical Analysis with special Reference to Education*, Univ. of Chicago Press, 1975.

Becker, G. S., Preface to Tommasi, M and Ierulli, K. (eds.), 1995.

Beckermann, W., 'Economists, Scientists and Environmental Catastrophe', *Oxford Economic Papers*, 24, 1972.

Begg, D., *The Rational Expectations Revolution in Macroeconomics*, Philip Allan, 1982.

Beveridge, W. H., *Full Employment in a Free Society*, Allen and Unwin, 1944.

Blanchard, O. J. and Fischer, S., *Lectures on Macroeconomics*, MIT Press, 1989.

Blaug, M., *The Methodology of Economics*, CUP, 1980.

Brearley, R. and Mayers, S., *Principles of Corporate Finance*, McGraw-Hill, 1996.

Brittan, S., *Capitalism with a Human Face*, Edward Elgar, 1995.

Britton, A., *Macroeconomic Policy in Britain, 1974-87*, CUP, 1991.

Britton, A., *Monetary Regimes of the Twentieth Century*, CUP, 2001.

Chen, Z. and Woolley, T., 'A Cournot-Nash Model of Family Decision Making', *Economic Journal*, October 2001.

Coates, A. W., 'Economics as a Profession' in Greenaway, D. et al., (eds.), 1991.

Coleman, J. S., *Foundations of Social Theory*, Harvard UP, 1990.

Dasgupta, P., *An Inquiry into Wellbeing and Destitution*, OUP, 1993.

Davis, A. P., *Debt, Financial Fragility and Systemic Risk*, OUP, 1992.

Denison, E. F., *Why Growth Rates Differ*, George Allen and Unwin, 1967.

Dow, S., *Macroeconomic Thought – A Methodological Approach*, Blackwell, 1985.

Farina, F., Hahn, F. and Vannucci, S. (eds.), *Ethics, Rationality and Economic Behaviour*, OUP, 1996.

Frank, R. H., *Passions within Reason*, Norton, 1988.

Friedman, M., *Essays in Positive Economics*, Univ. of Chicago Press, 1953.

Fukuyama, F., *The End of History and the Last Man*, Hamish Hamilton, 1992.

Fukuyama, F., *Trust – The Social Virtues and the Creation of Prosperity*, Hamish Hamilton, 1995.

Grossman, M., 'The Economic Approach to Addictive Behavior', in Tommasi, M. and Ierulli, K. (eds.), 1995.

Greenaway, D., Bleaney M. and Stewart, I (eds.), *Companion to Economic Thought*, Routledge, 1991.

Handy, C., *The Future of Work*, Blackwell, 1984.

Harvey, A. C., *The Econometric Analysis of Time Series*, Philip Allan, 1981.

Hausman, D. M. and McPherson, M. S., *Economic Analysis and Moral Philosophy*, CUP, 1996.

Henderson, J. M. and Quandt, R. E., *Microeconomic Theory – A Mathematical Approach*, McGraw-Hill, 1958.

Hirsh, F., *The Social Limits to Growth*, Routledge and Kegan Paul, 1977.

Hirshleifer, D., 'The Blind Leading the Blind – Social Influences, Fads and Informational Cascades', in Tommasi, M. and Ierulli, K. (eds.), 1995.

Iannaccone, L. R., 'Household Production, Human Capital and the Economics of Religion' in Tommasi, M. and Ierulli, K. (eds.), 1995.

Jhally, S., 'Advertising' in Kuper A. and J. (eds.), 1996.

Johnson, C., *Measuring the Economy – A Guide to Understanding Official Statistics*, Penguin, 1988.

Keynes, J. M., *The General Theory of Employment, Interest and Money*, Macmillan, 1936.

Kreps, D. M., *Game Theory and Economic Modelling*, OUP, 1990.

Kuper A. and J. (eds.), *The Social Science Encyclopedia* (second edition), Routledge, 1996.

Layard, R., Nickell, S. and Jackman R., *Unemployment, Macroeconomic Performance and the Labour Market*, OUP, 1991.

Lindbeck, A. and Snower, D., *The Insider-Outsider Theory of Employment and Unemployment*, MIT Press, 1988.

Lovell, C. A. K., 'Production and Cost Functions' in Kuper, A and J. (eds.), 1996.

Maki, U., 'Reorienting the Assumptions Issue', in Backhouse, R. E. (ed.), 1994.

Meadows, D. L. et al, *The Limits to Growth*, Earth Island, 1972.

Mills, P. and Presley, J., *Islamic Finance*, Macmillan, 1999.

Mirrlees, J. A., 'An Exploration in the Theory of Optimal Income Taxation', *Review of Economic Studies*, April 1971.

Oswald, A. J., 'Happiness and Economic Performance', *Economic Journal*, 107(445), 1997.

Oulton, N. and O'Mahony, M., *Productivity and Growth – A Study of British Industry, 1954-86*, CUP, 1994.

Pindyck, R. S. and Rubinfeld, D. L., *Microeconomics*, Prentice Hall, 1995.

Ridley, M., *The Origins of Virtue*, Viking, 1996.

Rifkin, J., *The End of Work – The Decline of the Global Labor Force and the Dawn of the Post-Market Era*, Putnam, 1995.

Rosenberg, A., 'What is the Cognitive Status of Economic Theory?' in Backhouse R. E. (ed.), 1994.

Sargent, T. J., *Macroeconomic Theory*, Academic Press, 1979.

Sen, A., *Choice, Welfare and Measurement*, Blackwell, 1982.

Sen, A., *On Ethics and Economics*, Blackwell, 1987.

Shand, A. H., *Free Market Morality – The Political Economy of the Austrian School*, Routledge, 1990.

Simon, H. A., 'Behavioural Economics', in Kuper, A. and J. (eds.), 1996.

Smith, A, *The Wealth of Nations*, 1828 edition.

Titmuss, R. M., *The Gift Relationship – From Human Blood to Social Policy*, George Allen and Unwin, 1970.

Tommasi, M. and K. Ierulli (eds.), *The New Economics of Human Behavior*, CUP, 1995.

van Raaij, W. F., 'Economics and Psychology', in Greenaway D., Bleaney M. and Stewart, I. (eds.), 1991.
Wood, A., *North–South Trade, Inequality and Unemployment*, OUP, 1994.

3. Theology etc.

Augustine, *On the Work of Monks, Nicene and Post-Nicene Fathers*, Series 1, Volume 3, Eerdmans, 1999.
Baillie, J., *And The Life Everlasting*, OUP, 1934.
Baker, J. A., *The Foolishness of God*, Fontana, 1970.
Barrett, C. K., *Commentary on Romans*, A and C Black, 1962.
Barth, K., *Church Dogmatics*, T & T Clark, Edinburgh, 1936–69.
Berkouwer, G. C., *The Triumph of Grace in the Theology of Karl Barth*, Eerdmans, 1956.
Brown, R. E., Fitzmyer, J. A. and Murphy, R. E. (eds.), *New Jerome Biblical Commentary*, Chapman, 1989.
Brueggemann, W., *The Land*, Fortress Press, 1977.
Bultmann, R., *Jesus and the Word*, SCM, 1958 (first published 1926).
Crosby, M. H., *House of Disciples, Church, Economics and Justice in Matthew*, Orbis, 1988.
Eaton, J., *The Contemplative Face of Old Testament Wisdom*, SPCK, 1989.
Eichrodt, W., *The Theology of the Old Testament*, Volumes 1 and 2, SCM, 1967.
Epsztein, L., *Social Justice in the Ancient Near East*, SCM, 1986.
Esler, P. F. (ed.), *Modelling Early Christianity, Social scientific studies of the New Testament in its context*, Routledge, 1995.
Evans, B. F. and Cusack, G. D. (eds.), *Theology of The Land*, The Liturgical Press, 1987.
Fergusson, D. and Sarot, M., *The Future as God's Gift*, T and T Clark, 2000.
Fiddes, P., *The Creative Suffering of God*, OUP, 1989.
Ford, D. F., *Barth and God's Story: Biblical Narrative and the Theological Method of Karl Barth in the Church Dogmatics*, Peter Lang, 1981.
Ford D. F. (ed.), *The Modern Theologians*, Blackwell (second edition), 1999.
Frei, H., *The Eclipse of the Biblical Narrative*, Yale University Press, 1974
Frei, H., *The Identity of Jesus Christ*, Fortress Press, 1975.
Golka, F., *The Leopard's Spots: Biblical and African Wisdom in Proverbs*, T and T Clark, 1993.
Grant, C., *Altruism and Christian Ethics*, CUP, 2001.
Habel, N.C., *The Land is Mine*, Fortress Press, 1995.
Hardy, D. W., *God's Ways with the World*, T and T Clark, 1996
Hardy, D. W. and Ford, D. F., *Jubilate*, Darton, Longman and Todd, 1982.
Harvey, A. E., *Strenuous Commands: The Ethics of Jesus*, SCM, 1990.
Hengel, M., *Property and Riches in the Early Church*, SCM, 1974.

Hick, J., *Death and Eternal Life*, Collins, 1976.

Horsley, R. A., *Archaeology History and Society in Galilee, The Social Context of Jesus and the Rabbis*, Trinity Press International, 1996.

Humphrey, N., *A History of the Mind*, Chatto and Windus, 1992

Kasper, W., *Jesus The Christ*, Burns and Oates, 1976.

Lampe, G. W. H. and MacKinnon, D. M., *The Resurrection*, Mowbray, 1966.

Lindbeck, G., *The Nature of Doctrine; Religion and Theology in a Postliberal Age*, SPCK, 1984.

Lohfink, G., *Jesus and Community*, SPCK, 1985.

McFadyen, A., *The Call to Personhood*, CUP, 1990.

McFadyen, A., 'Sins of Praise, The Assault on God's Freedom' in Gunton, C. (ed.), *God and Freedom*, T and T Clark, 1995.

McFadyen, A. and Sarot, M. (eds.), *Forgiveness and Truth*, T and T Clark, 2002 article: 'Loosing and Binding, The Liturgical Mediation of Forgiveness'.

MacKinnon, D. M., *The Stripping of the Altars*, Collins, 1969.

MacKinnon, D. M., *Themes in Theology*, T and T Clark, 1987.

Maquarrie, J. and Childress, J. (eds.), *A New Dictionary of Christian Ethics*, articles on 'Slavery' and 'Mosaic Law', SCM, 1986.

Meeks, W., *The First Urban Christians*, Yale University Press, 1983.

Milbank, J., *Theology and Social Theory – Beyond Secular Reason*, Blackwell, 1990.

Moltmann, J., *Man*, SPCK, 1974.

Moltmann, J., *On Human Dignity*, SCM, 1984.

Moltmann, J., *God in Creation*, SCM, 1985.

Oppenheimer, H., *The Hope of Happiness*, SCM, 1983.

Pannenberg, W., *Jesus God and Man*, SCM, 1968.

Pannenberg, W., *Systematic Theology Volume 1*, T and T Clark, 1991.

Pannenberg, W., *Systematic Theology Volume 2*, T and T Clark, 1994.

Peacocke, A. R., *Theology for a Scientific Age*, SCM, 1993.

Placher, W. C., *Unapologetic Theology*, Westminster, 1989.

Riches, J., *Jesus and the Transformation of Judaism*, DLT, 1980.

Roberts, R. H., 'Theology and the Social Sciences', in Ford, D. F. (ed.), *The Modern Theologians* (second edition), Blackwell, 1999.

Rowley, H. H., *The Biblical Doctrine of Election*, Lutterworth, 1950.

Sanders, E. P., *Paul*, OUP, 1991.

Schrage, W., *The Ethics of the New Testament*, T and T Clark, 1996.

Schumacher, C., *God in Work*, Lion, 1999.

Sedgwick, P. H., 'Wealth Creation and the Early Church', *Epworth Review*, 1993.

Selby, P., *Grace and Mortgage*, Darton, Longman and Todd, 1997.

Senior, D. and Stuhlmueller, C., *The Biblical Foundations for Mission*, SCM, 1983.

Surin, K. (ed.), *Christ, Ethics and Tragedy, Essays in Honour of Donald MacKinnon*, CUP, 1989.

Sykes, S. W., *The Identity of Christianity*, SPCK, 1984.

Sykes, S. W. (ed.), *Karl Barth, Studies of His Theological Method*, OUP, 1979.

Torrance, T. F., *The Ground and Grammar of Theology*, Christian Journals, 1980.
Volf, M., *Work in the Spirit: Towards a Theology of Work*, OUP, 1991.
von Rad, G., *Wisdom in Israel*, SCM, 1972.
Whitelam, K., *The Invention of Ancient Israel, The Silencing of Palestinian History*, Routledge, 1996.
Whybray, N., *Wealth and Poverty in the Book of Proverbs*, JSOT Press, Sheffield, 1990.
Williams, R. D., *On Christian Theology*, Blackwell, 2000.
Wyschogorod, M., *The Body of Faith. God in the People of Israel*, Harper, 1983.
Young, F. and Ford, D. F., *Meaning and Truth in 2 Corinthians*, SPCK, 1987.

Religions and Discourse

Edited by James M. M. Francis

Religions and Discourse explores religious language in the major world faiths from various viewpoints, including semiotics, pragmatics and cognitive linguistics, and reflects on how it is situated within wider intellectual and cultural contexts. In particular a key issue is the role of figurative speech. Many fascinating metaphors originate in religion e.g. revelation as a 'garment', apostasy as 'adultery', loving kindness as the 'circumcision of the heart'. Every religion rests its specific orientations upon symbols such as these, to name but a few. The series strives after the interdisciplinary approach that brings together such diverse disciplines as religious studies, theology, sociology, philosophy, linguistics and literature, guided by an international editorial board of scholars representative of the aforementioned disciplines. Though scholarly in its scope, the series also seeks to facilitate discussions pertaining to central religious issues in contemporary contexts.
The series will publish monographs and collected essays of a high scholarly standard.

Volume 1 Ralph Bisschops and James Francis (eds):
Metaphor, Canon and Community
307 pages. 1999.
ISBN 3-906762-40-8 / US-ISBN 0-8204-4234-8

Volume 2 Lieven Boeve and Kurt Feyaerts (eds):
Metaphor and God Talk
291 pages. 1999.
ISBN 3-906762-51-3 / US-ISBN 0-8204-4235-6

Volume 3 Jean-Pierre van Noppen:
Transforming Words
248 pages. 1999.
ISBN 3-906762-52-1 / US-ISBN 0-8204-4236-4

Volume 4 Robert Innes:
Discourses of the Self
236 pages. 1999.
ISBN 3-906762-53-X / US-ISBN 0-8204-4237-2

Volume 5 Noel Heather:
Religious Language and Critical Discourse Analysis
319 pages. 2000.
ISBN 3-906762-54-8 / US-ISBN 0-8204-4238-0

Volume 6 Stuart Sim and David Walker:
Bunyan and Authority
239 pages. 2000.
ISBN 3-906764-44-3 / US-ISBN 0-8204-4634-3

Volume 7 Simon Harrison:
Conceptions of Unity in Recent Ecumenical Discussion
282 pages. 2000.
ISBN 3-906758-51-6 / US-ISBN 0-8204-5073-1

Volume 8 Gill Goulding:
On the Edge of Mystery
256 pages. 2000.
ISBN 3-906758-80-X / US-ISBN 0-8204-5087-1

Volume 9 Kune Biezeveld and Anne-Claire Mulder (eds.):
Towards a Different Transcendence
358 pages. 2001.
ISBN 3-906765-66-0 / US-ISBN 0-8204-5303-X

Volume 10 George Newlands:
John and Donald Baillie: Transatlantic Theology
451 pages. 2002.
ISBN 3-906768-41-4 / US-ISBN 0-8204-5853-8

Volume 11 Kenneth Fleming:
Asian Christian Theologians in Dialogue with Buddhism
388 pages. 2002.
ISBN 3-906768-42-2 / US-ISBN 0-8204-5854-6

Volume 12 N. H. Keeble (ed.):
John Bunyan: Reading Dissenting Writing
277 pages. 2002.
ISBN 3-906768-52-X / US-ISBN 0-8204-5864-3

Volume 13 Robert L. Platzner (ed.):
Gender, Tradition and Renewal
Forthcoming.
ISBN 3-906769-64-X / US-ISBN 0-8204-5901-1

Volume 14 Michael Ipgrave:
Trinity and Inter-Faith Dialogue: Plenitude and Plurality
Forthcoming.
ISBN 3-906769-77-1 / US-ISBN 0-8204-5914-3

Volume 15 Kurt Feyaerts (ed.):
The Bible through Metaphor and Translation:
A Cognitive Semantic Perspective
298 pages. 2003.
ISBN 3-906769-82-8 / US-ISBN 0-8204-5919-4

Volume 16 Andrew Britton and Peter Sedgwick:
Economic Theory and Christian Belief
308 pages. 2003.
ISBN 3-03910-015-7 / US-ISBN 0-8204-6284-5

www.ingramcontent.com/pod-product-compliance
Ingram Content Group UK Ltd.
Pitfield, Milton Keynes, MK11 3LW, UK
UKHW020126290926
15471UKWH00003B/321

9 783039 100156